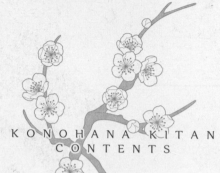

K O N O H A N A   K I T A N
C O N T E N T S

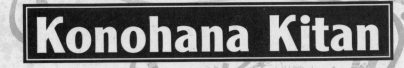

Konohana Kitan

3

Sakuya Amano

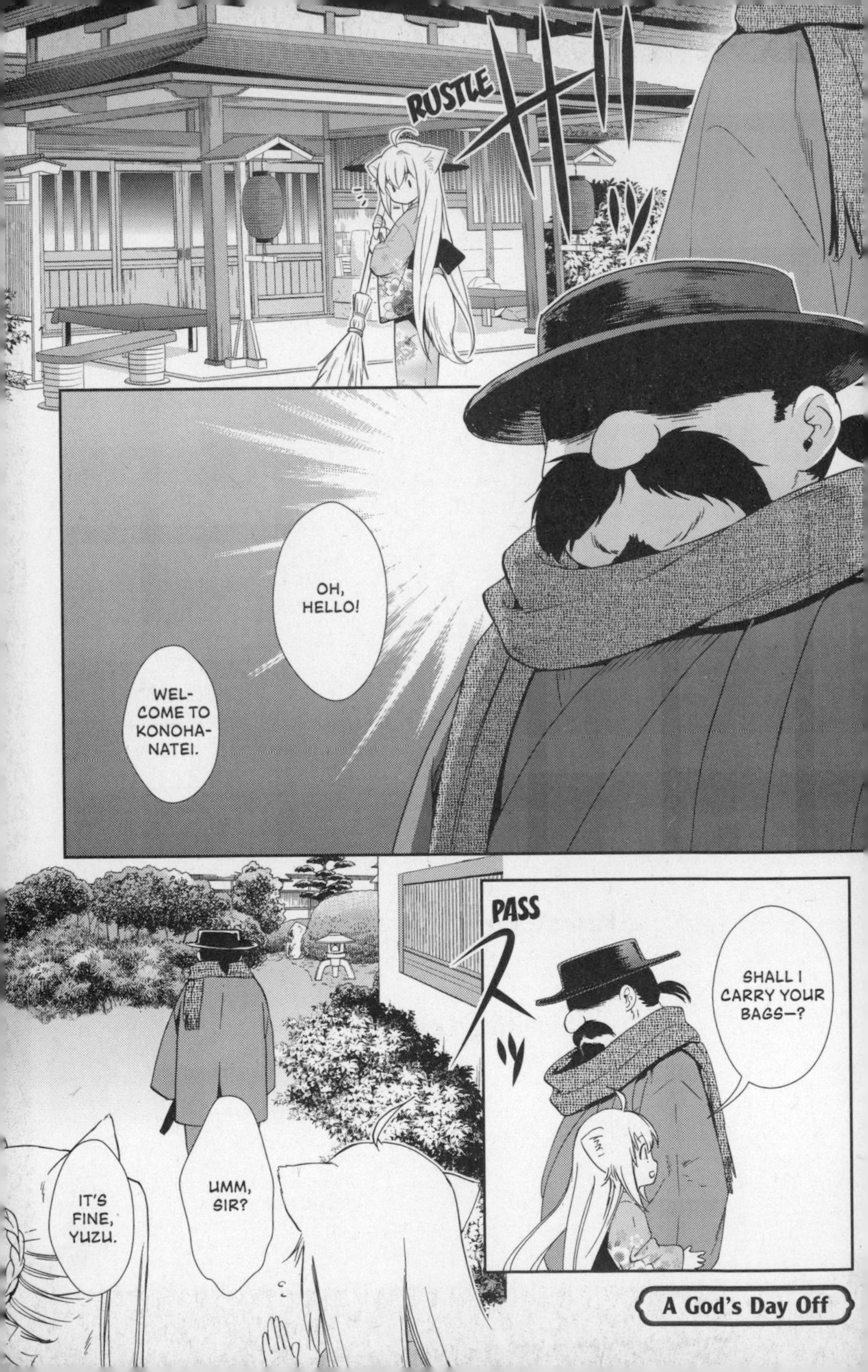
RUSTLE
OH, HELLO!
WEL-COME TO KONOHA-NATEI.
PASS
SHALL I CARRY YOUR BAGS—?
UMM, SIR?
IT'S FINE, YUZU.
A God's Day Off

A God's Day Off

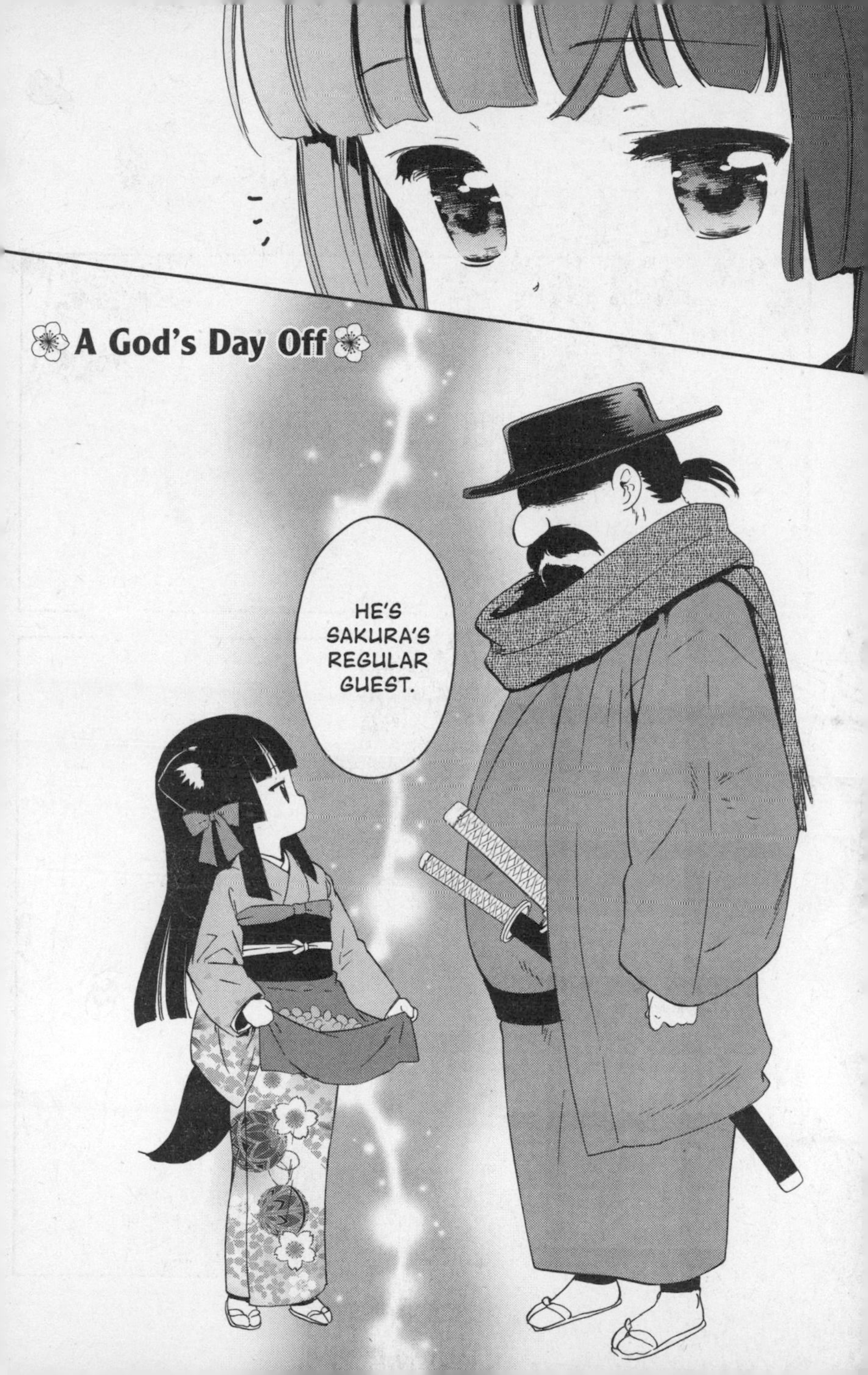
HE'S SAKURA'S REGULAR GUEST.

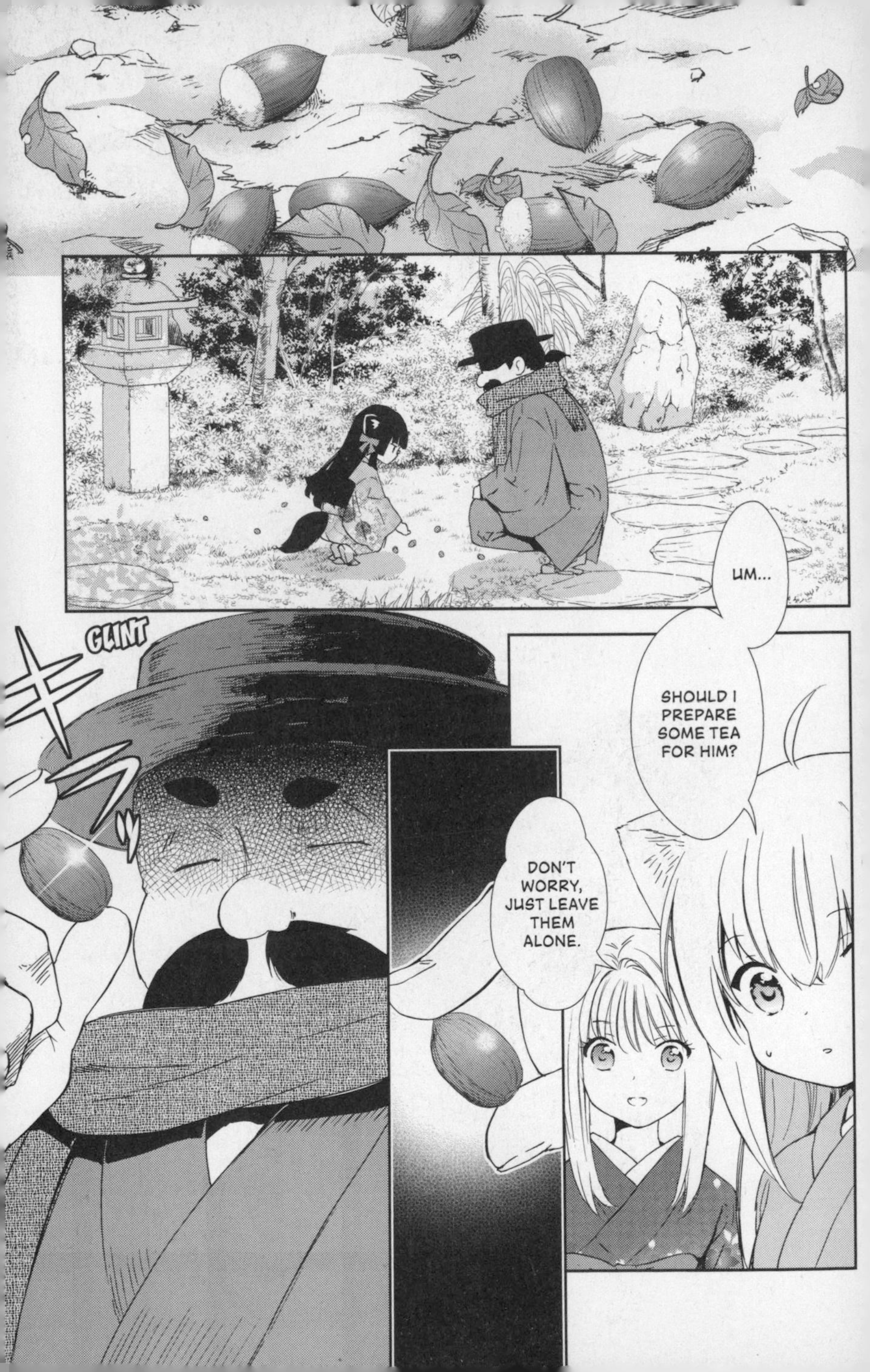

UM...
SHOULD I PREPARE SOME TEA FOR HIM?
DON'T WORRY, JUST LEAVE THEM ALONE.
GLINT

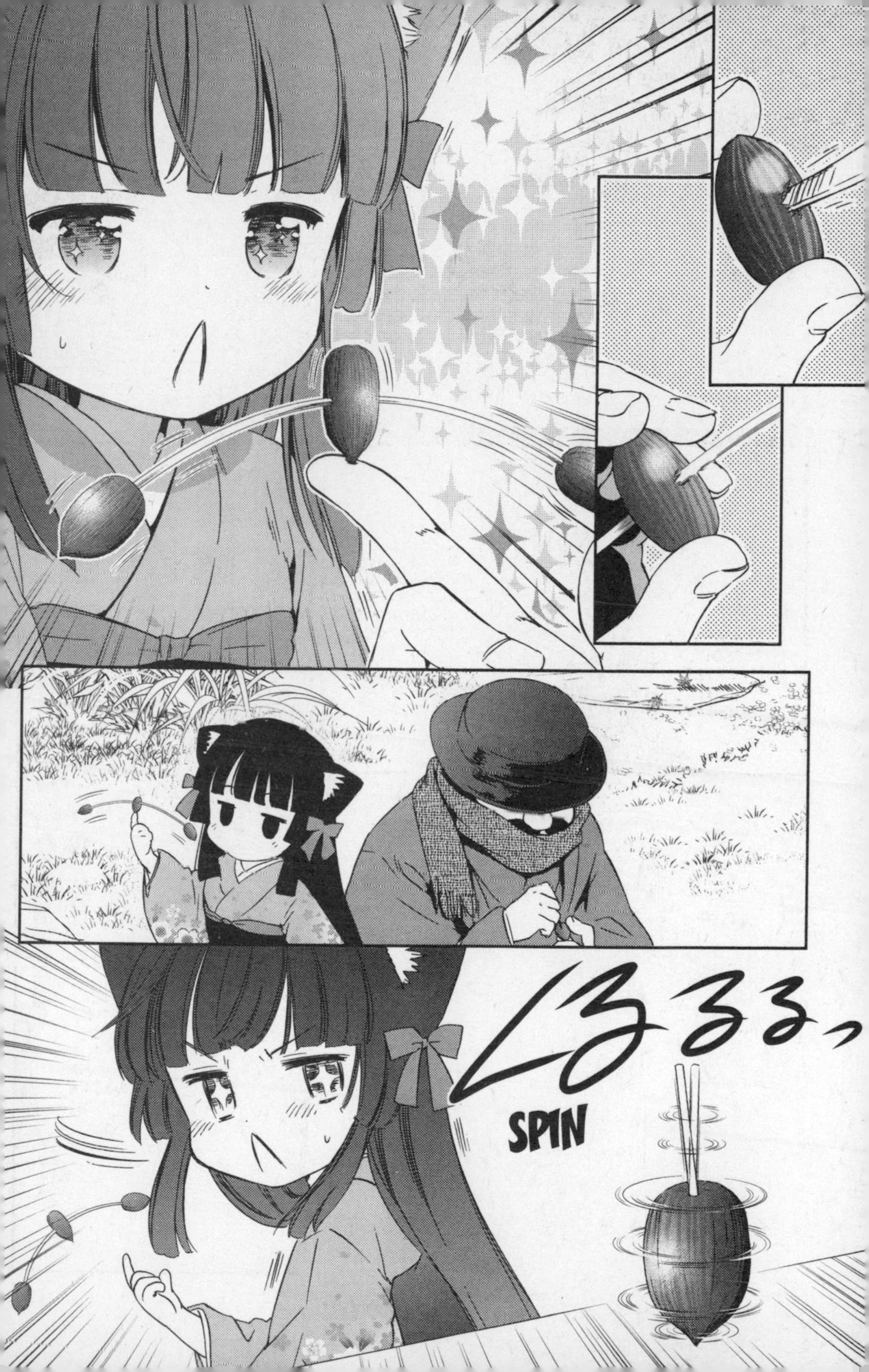
くるるっ
SPIN

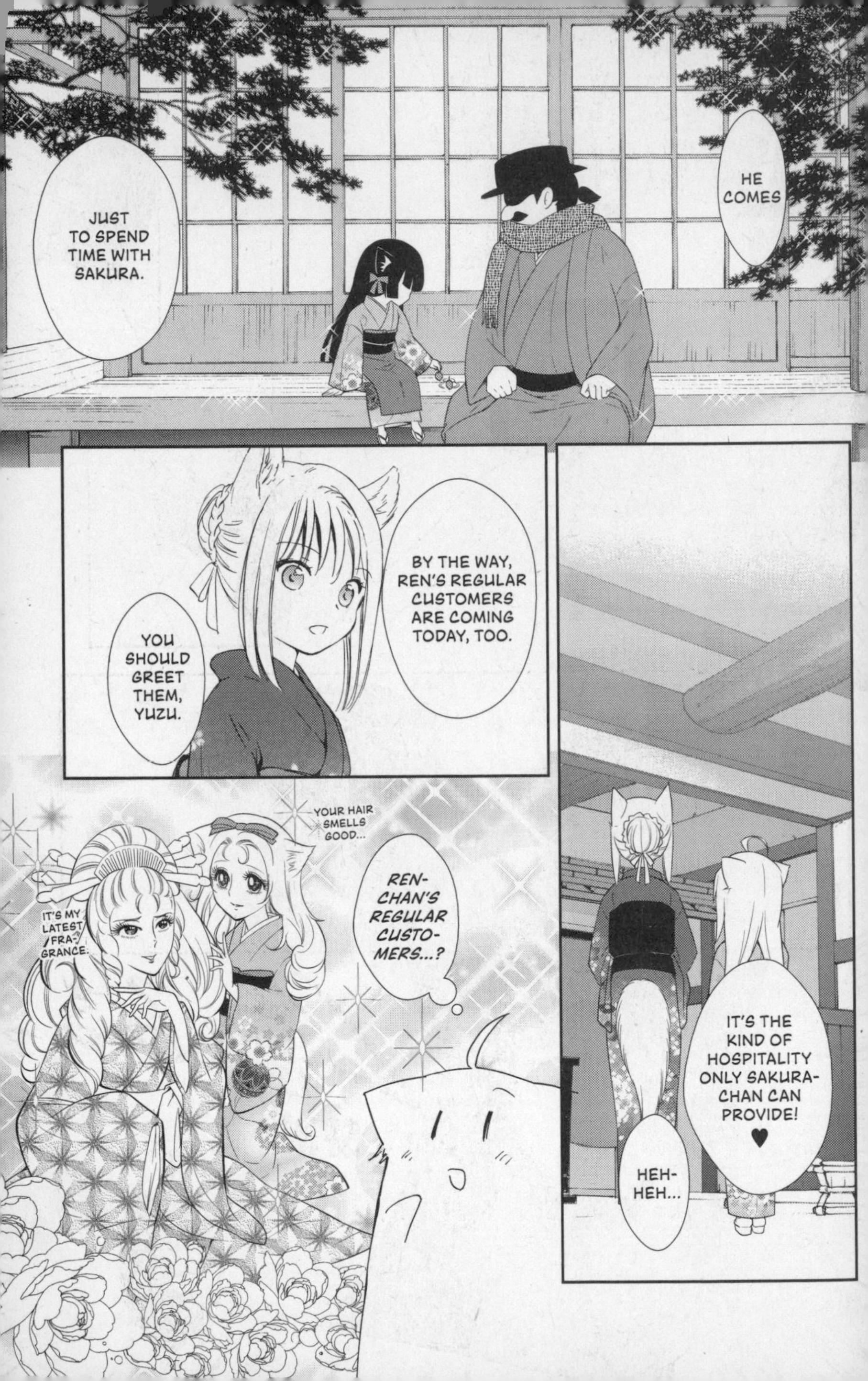
HE COMES
JUST TO SPEND TIME WITH SAKURA.
IT'S THE KIND OF HOSPITALITY ONLY SAKURA-CHAN CAN PROVIDE! ♥
HEH-HEH...
BY THE WAY, REN'S REGULAR CUSTOMERS ARE COMING TODAY, TOO.
YOU SHOULD GREET THEM, YUZU.
YOUR HAIR SMELLS GOOD...
REN-CHAN'S REGULAR CUSTOMERS...?
IT'S MY LATEST FRAGRANCE.

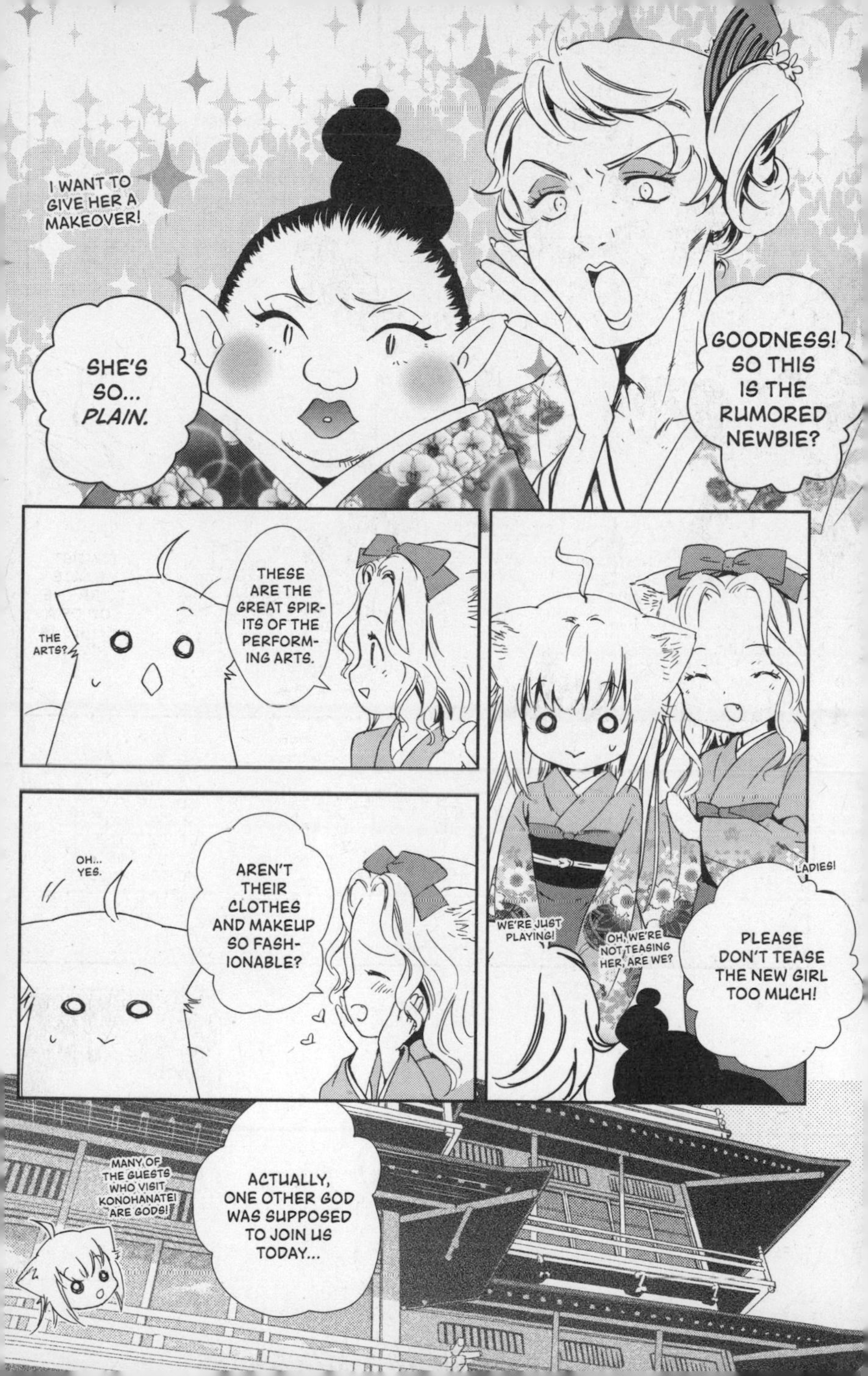
GOODNESS! SO THIS IS THE RUMORED NEWBIE?
SHE'S SO... *PLAIN.*
I WANT TO GIVE HER A MAKEOVER!
LADIES!
PLEASE DON'T TEASE THE NEW GIRL TOO MUCH!
OH, WE'RE NOT TEASING HER, ARE WE?
WE'RE JUST PLAYING!
THESE ARE THE GREAT SPIRITS OF THE PERFORMING ARTS.
THE ARTS?
AREN'T THEIR CLOTHES AND MAKEUP SO FASHIONABLE?
OH... YES.
ACTUALLY, ONE OTHER GOD WAS SUPPOSED TO JOIN US TODAY...
MANY OF THE GUESTS WHO VISIT KONOHANATEI ARE GODS!

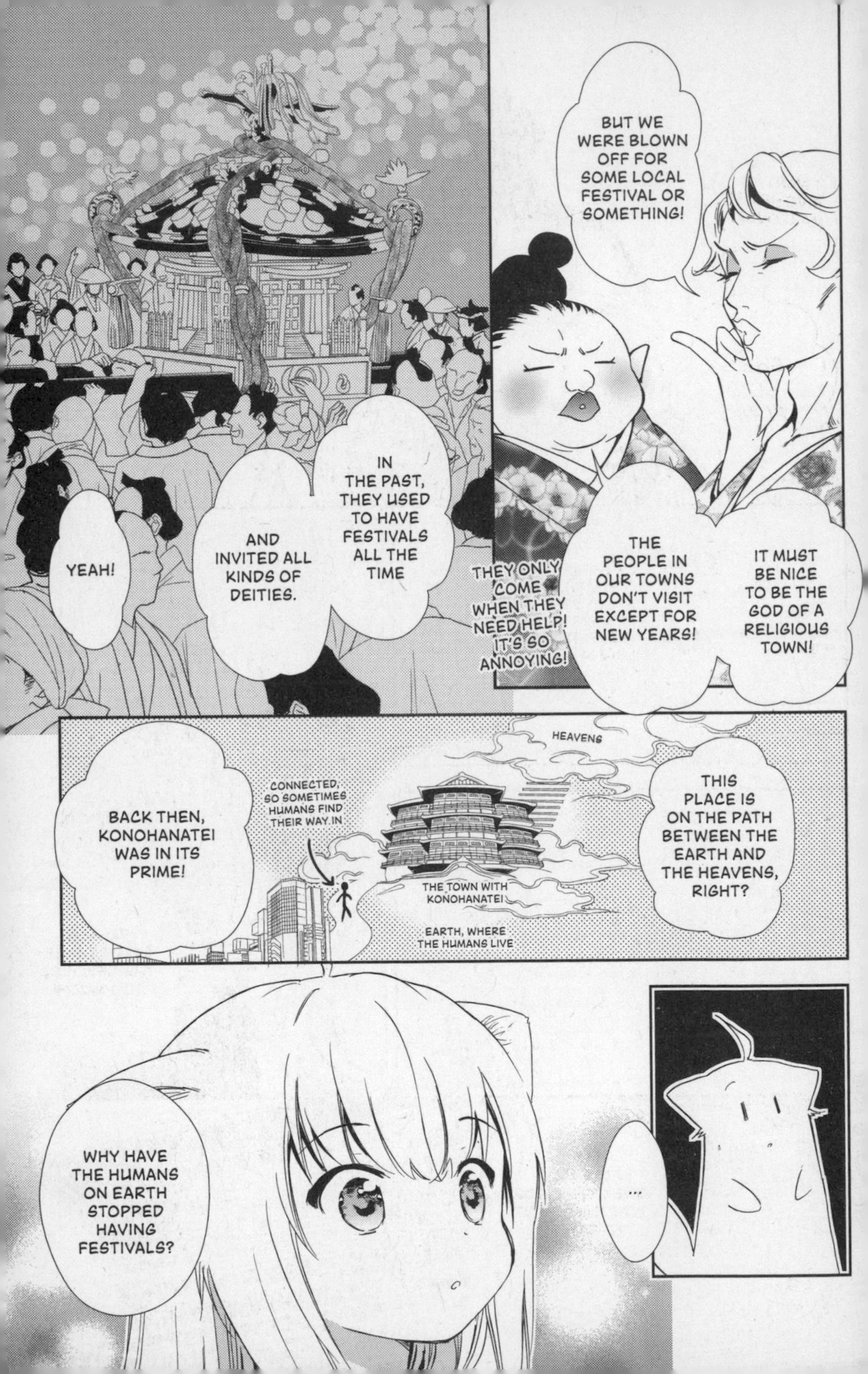
BUT WE WERE BLOWN OFF FOR SOME LOCAL FESTIVAL OR SOMETHING!
IT MUST BE NICE TO BE THE GOD OF A RELIGIOUS TOWN!
THE PEOPLE IN OUR TOWNS DON'T VISIT EXCEPT FOR NEW YEARS!
THEY ONLY COME WHEN THEY NEED HELP! IT'S SO ANNOYING!
IN THE PAST, THEY USED TO HAVE FESTIVALS ALL THE TIME
AND INVITED ALL KINDS OF DEITIES.
YEAH!
THIS PLACE IS ON THE PATH BETWEEN THE EARTH AND THE HEAVENS, RIGHT?
HEAVENS
CONNECTED, SO SOMETIMES HUMANS FIND THEIR WAY IN
THE TOWN WITH KONOHANATEI
EARTH, WHERE THE HUMANS LIVE
BACK THEN, KONOHANATEI WAS IN ITS PRIME!
...
WHY HAVE THE HUMANS ON EARTH STOPPED HAVING FESTIVALS?

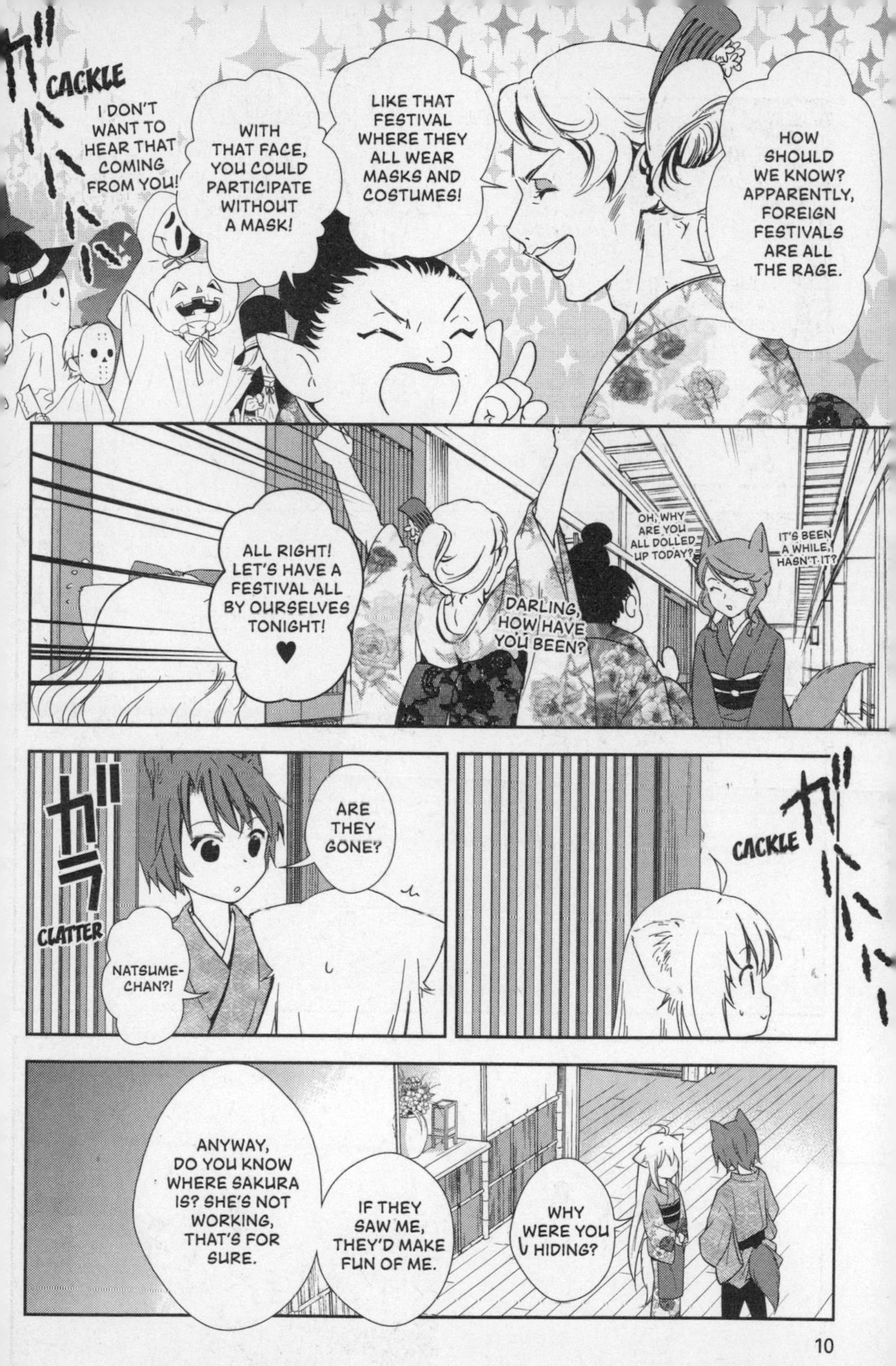
HOW SHOULD WE KNOW? APPARENTLY, FOREIGN FESTIVALS ARE ALL THE RAGE.
LIKE THAT FESTIVAL WHERE THEY ALL WEAR MASKS AND COSTUMES!
WITH THAT FACE, YOU COULD PARTICIPATE WITHOUT A MASK!
I DON'T WANT TO HEAR THAT COMING FROM YOU!
CACKLE
IT'S BEEN A WHILE, HASN'T IT?
OH, WHY ARE YOU ALL DOLLED UP TODAY?
DARLING, HOW HAVE YOU BEEN?
ALL RIGHT! LET'S HAVE A FESTIVAL ALL BY OURSELVES TONIGHT! ♥
CACKLE
ARE THEY GONE?
CLATTER
NATSUME-CHAN?!
WHY WERE YOU HIDING?
IF THEY SAW ME, THEY'D MAKE FUN OF ME.
ANYWAY, DO YOU KNOW WHERE SAKURA IS? SHE'S NOT WORKING, THAT'S FOR SURE.

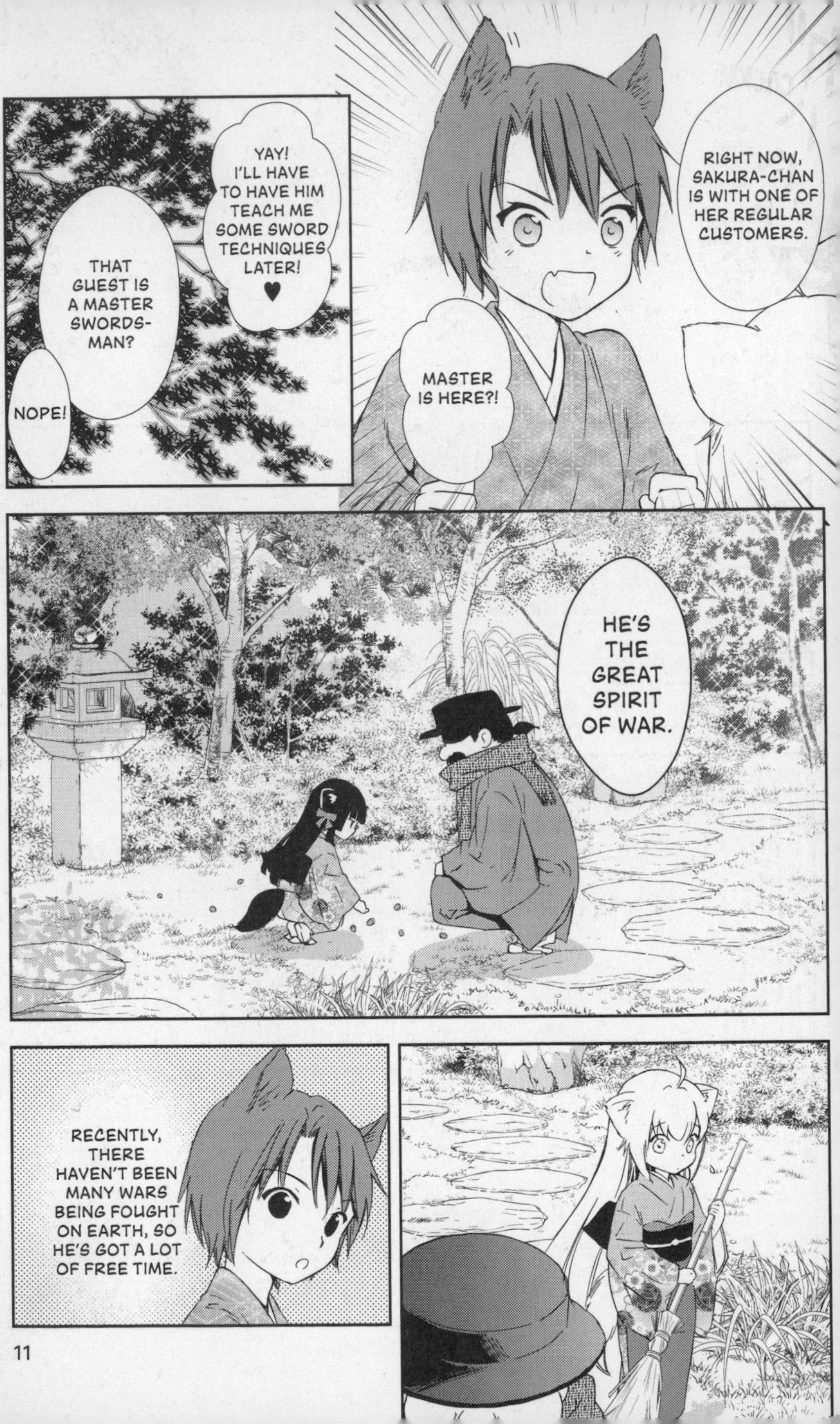
RIGHT NOW, SAKURA-CHAN IS WITH ONE OF HER REGULAR CUSTOMERS.
MASTER IS HERE?!
YAY! I'LL HAVE TO HAVE HIM TEACH ME SOME SWORD TECHNIQUES LATER! ♥
THAT GUEST IS A MASTER SWORDS-MAN?
NOPE!
HE'S THE GREAT SPIRIT OF WAR.
RECENTLY, THERE HAVEN'T BEEN MANY WARS BEING FOUGHT ON EARTH, SO HE'S GOT A LOT OF FREE TIME.

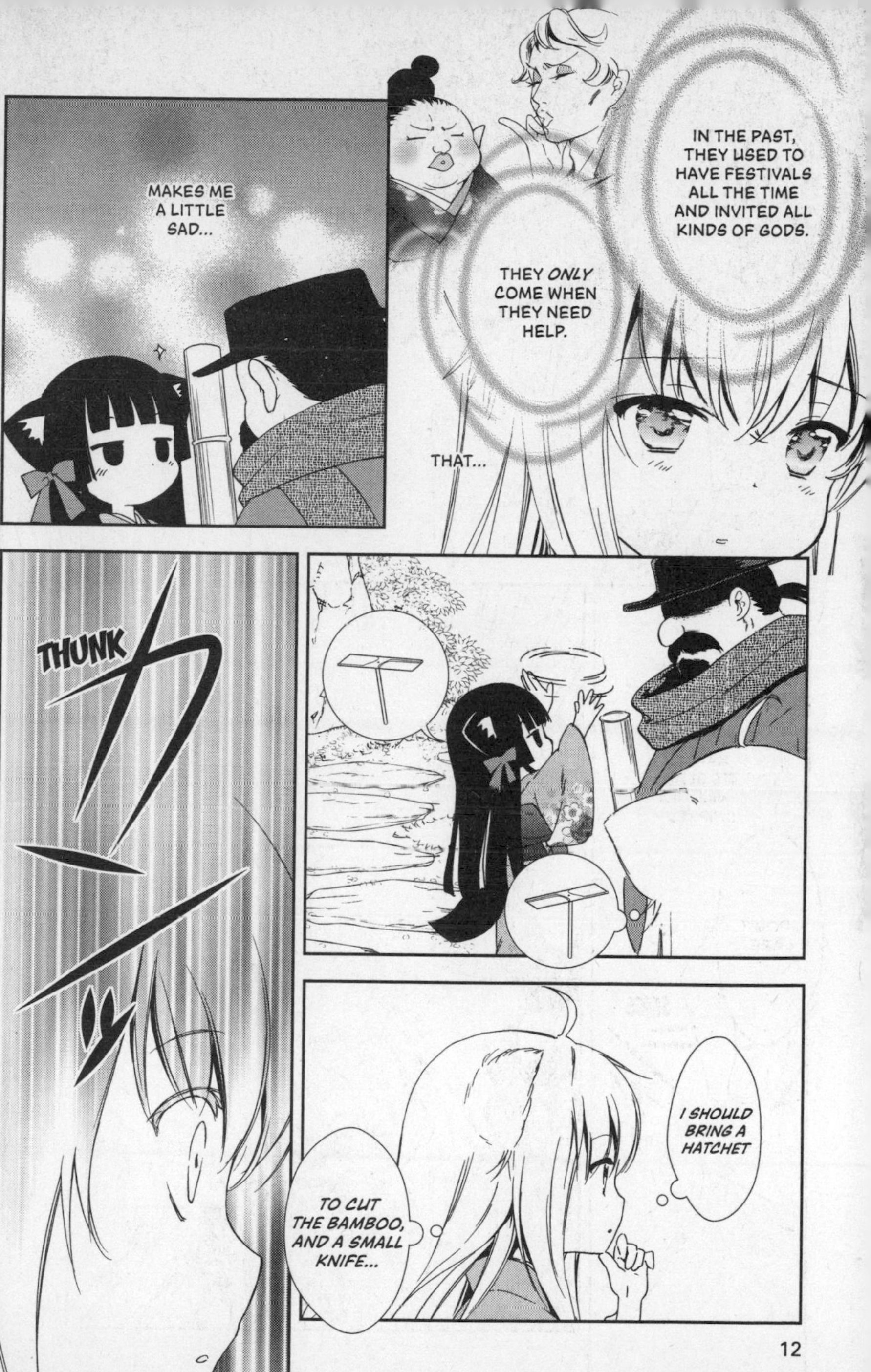
IN THE PAST, THEY USED TO HAVE FESTIVALS ALL THE TIME AND INVITED ALL KINDS OF GODS.
THEY *ONLY* COME WHEN THEY NEED HELP.
THAT...
MAKES ME A LITTLE SAD...
I SHOULD BRING A HATCHET
TO CUT THE BAMBOO, AND A SMALL KNIFE...
THUNK

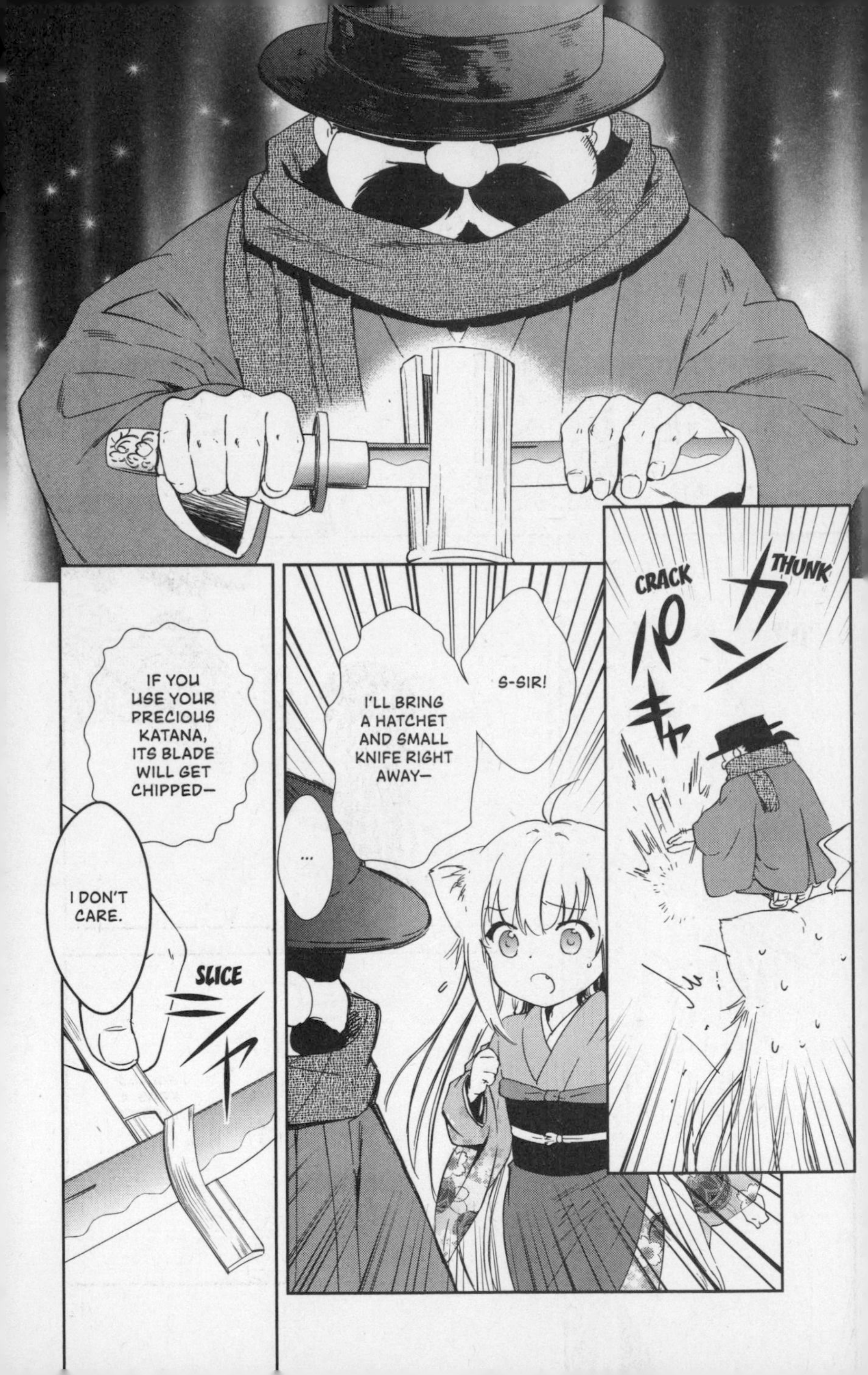
THUNK
CRACK
S-SIR!
I'LL BRING A HATCHET AND SMALL KNIFE RIGHT AWAY—
...
IF YOU USE YOUR PRECIOUS KATANA, ITS BLADE WILL GET CHIPPED—
I DON'T CARE.
SLICE

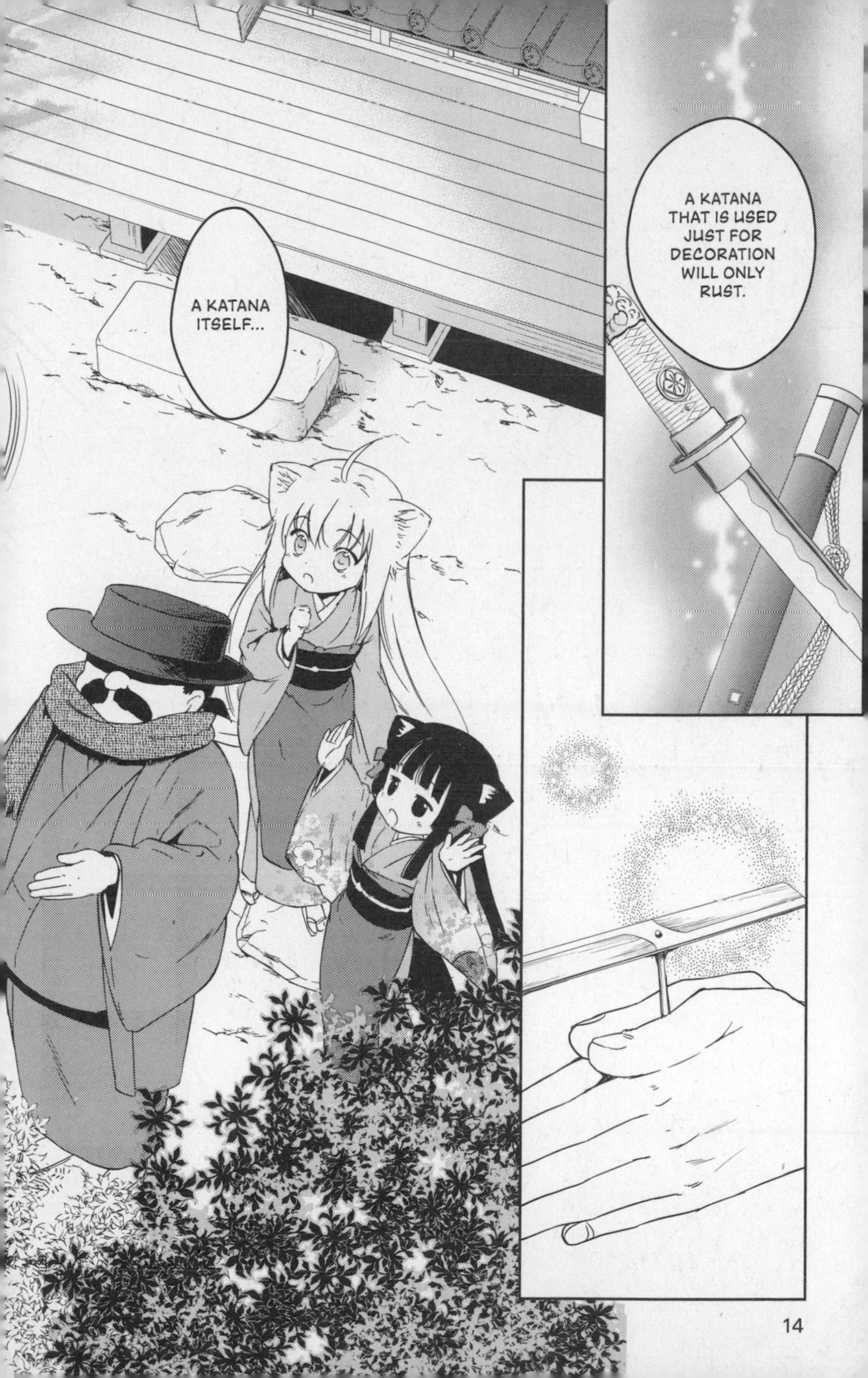
A KATANA THAT IS USED JUST FOR DECORATION WILL ONLY RUST.
A KATANA ITSELF...

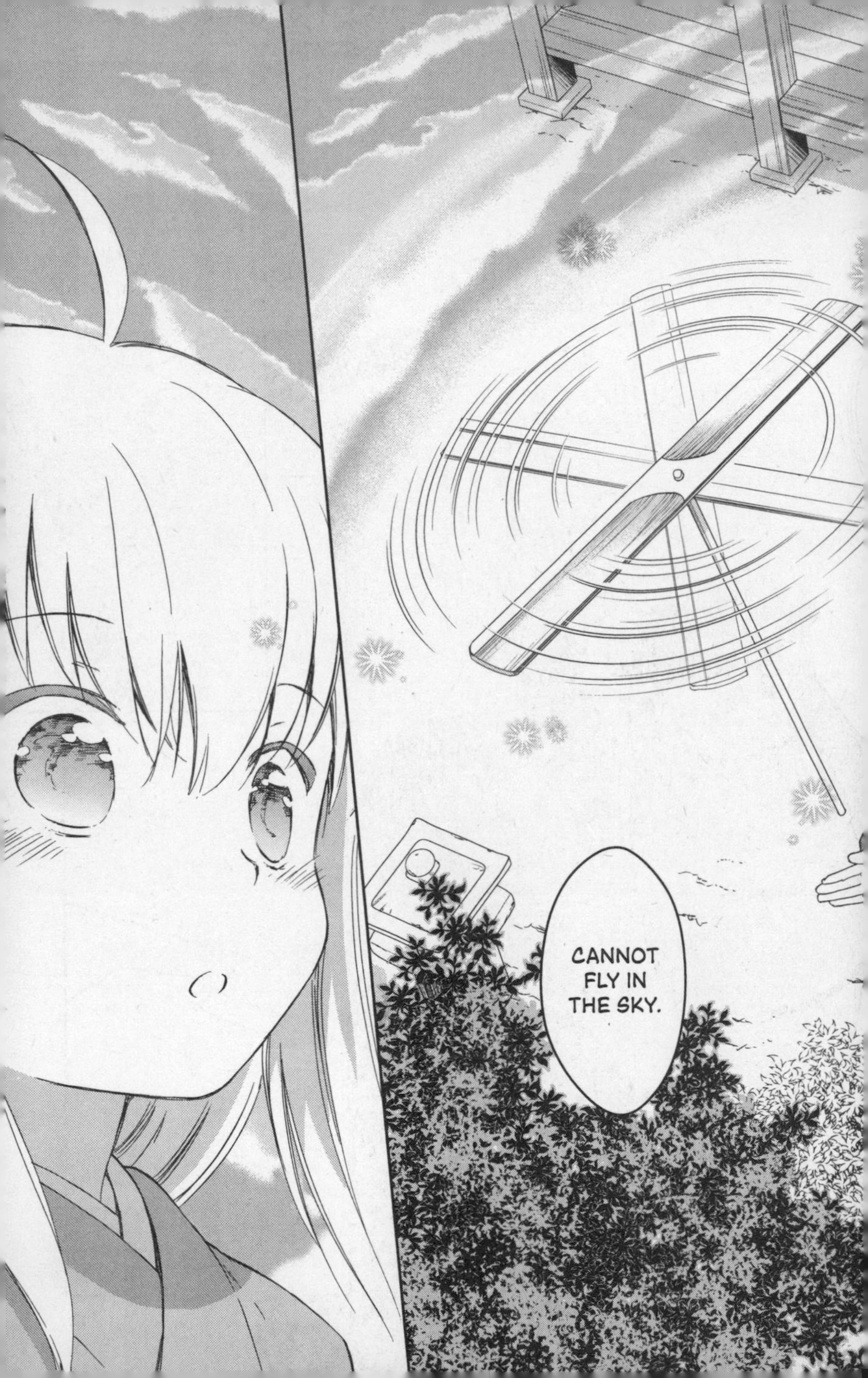
CANNOT FLY IN THE SKY.

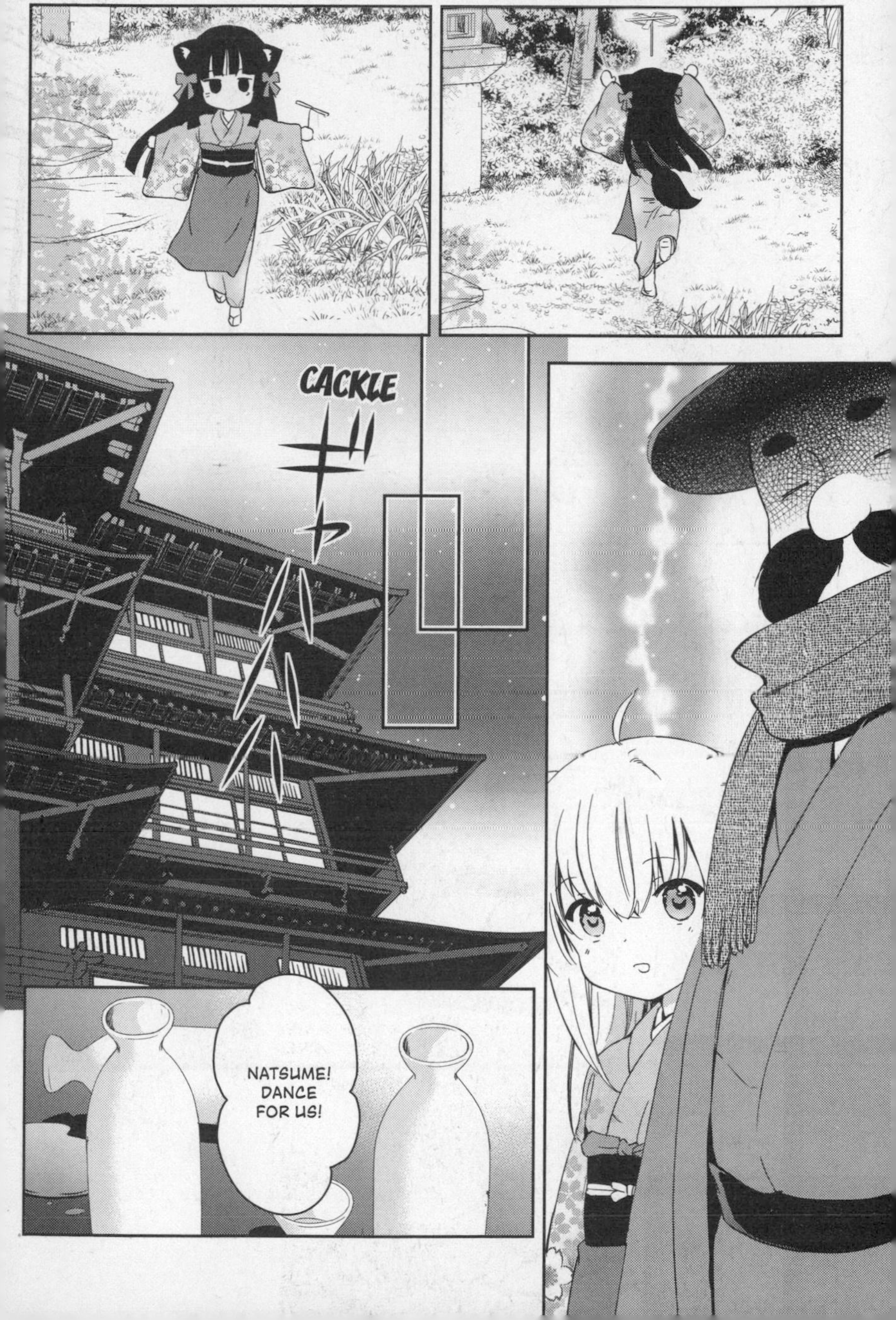
CACKLE
ギャ
NATSUME! DANCE FOR US!

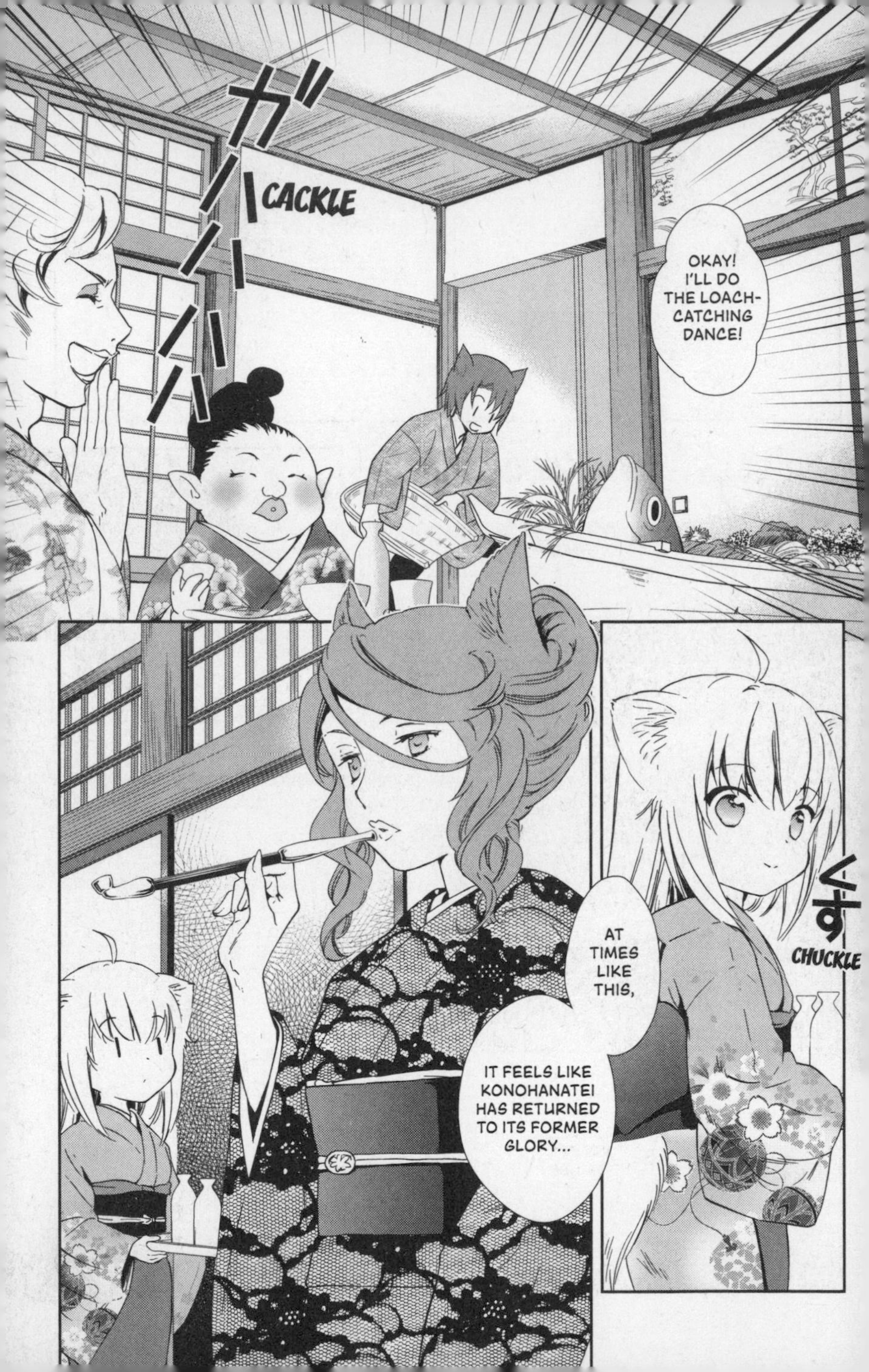
OKAY! I'LL DO THE LOACH-CATCHING DANCE!
ガーハハハ
CACKLE
くす
CHUCKLE
AT TIMES LIKE THIS,
IT FEELS LIKE KONOHANATEI HAS RETURNED TO ITS FORMER GLORY...

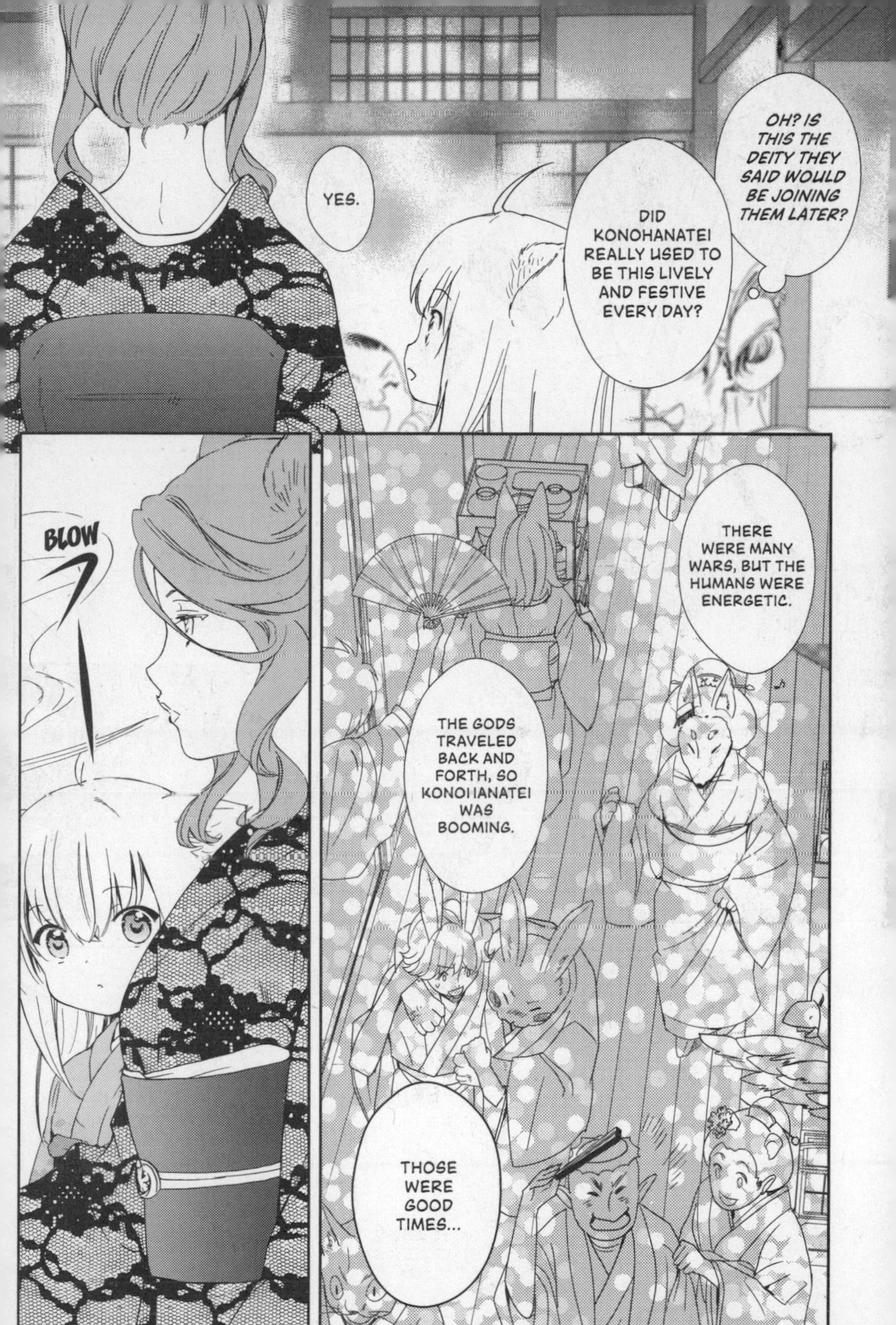
OH? IS THIS THE DEITY THEY SAID WOULD BE JOINING THEM LATER?
DID KONOHANATEI REALLY USED TO BE THIS LIVELY AND FESTIVE EVERY DAY?
YES.
THERE WERE MANY WARS, BUT THE HUMANS WERE ENERGETIC.
THE GODS TRAVELED BACK AND FORTH, SO KONOHANATEI WAS BOOMING.
THOSE WERE GOOD TIMES...
BLOW

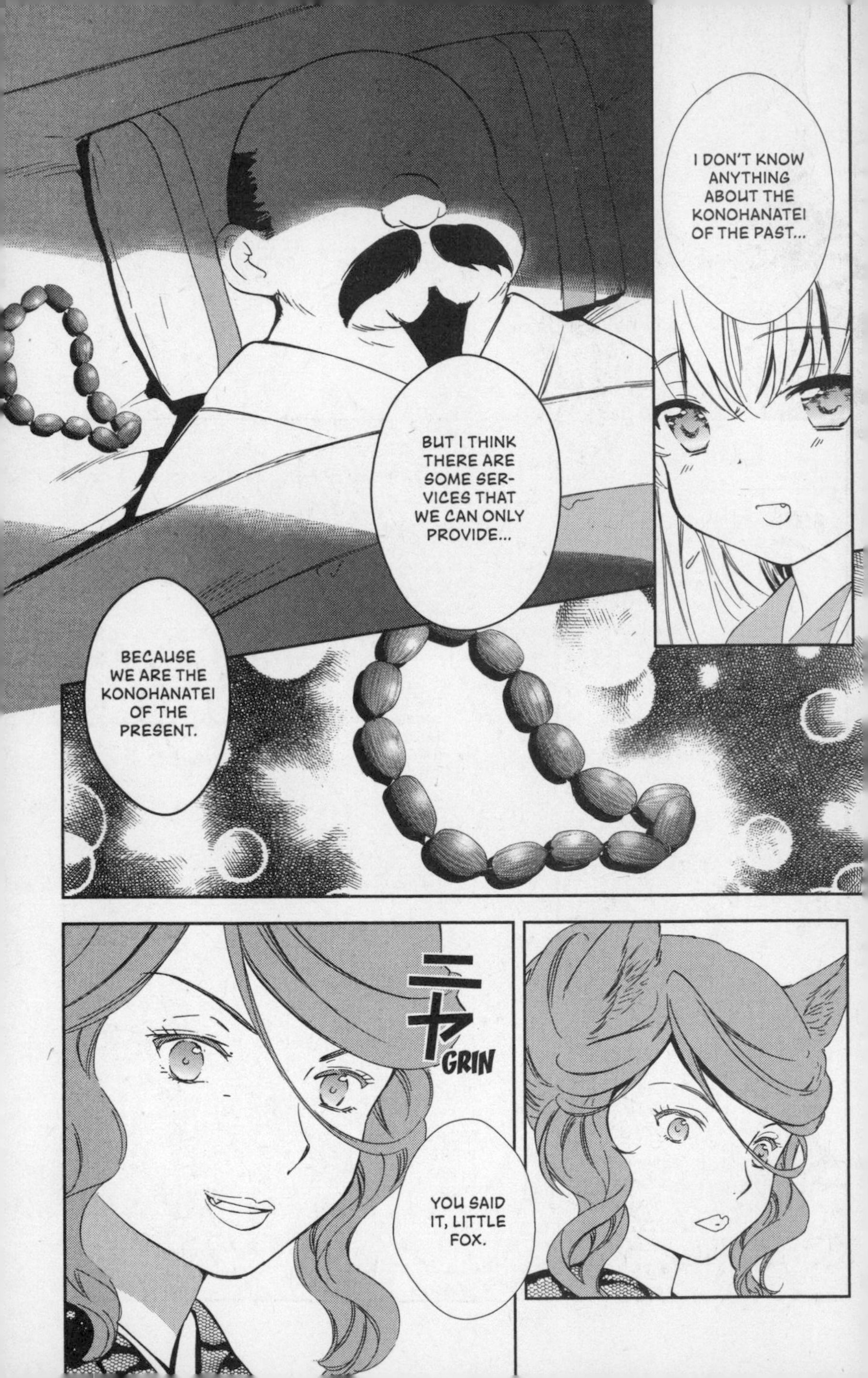
I DON'T KNOW ANYTHING ABOUT THE KONOHANATEI OF THE PAST...
BUT I THINK THERE ARE SOME SER-VICES THAT WE CAN ONLY PROVIDE...
BECAUSE WE ARE THE KONOHANATEI OF THE PRESENT.
ニヤ
GRIN
YOU SAID IT, LITTLE FOX.

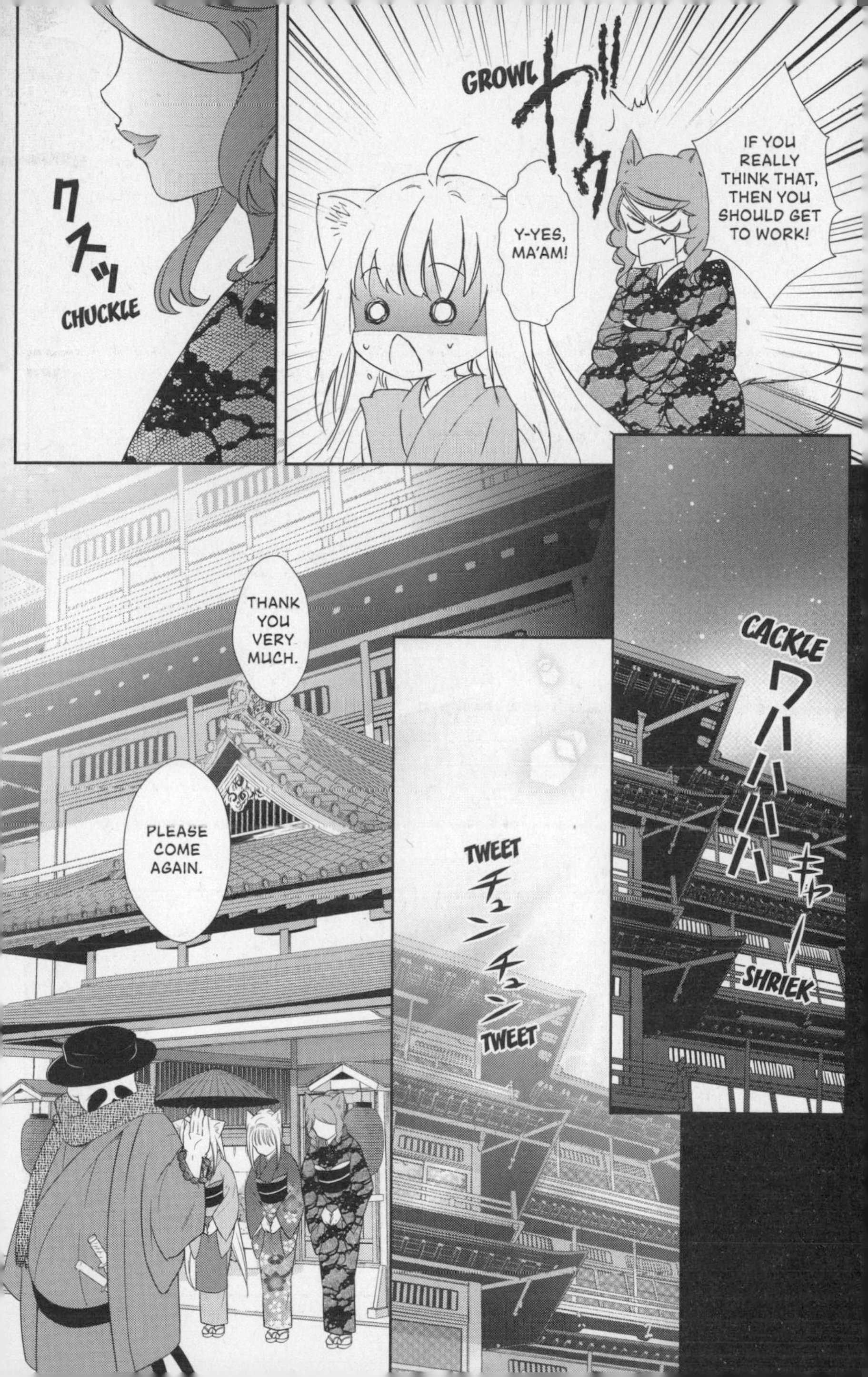
IF YOU REALLY THINK THAT, THEN YOU SHOULD GET TO WORK!
GROWL
Y-YES, MA'AM!
クスッ
CHUCKLE
CACKLE
ワハハハハ
キャー
SHRIEK
TWEET
チュンチュン
TWEET
THANK YOU VERY MUCH.
PLEASE COME AGAIN.

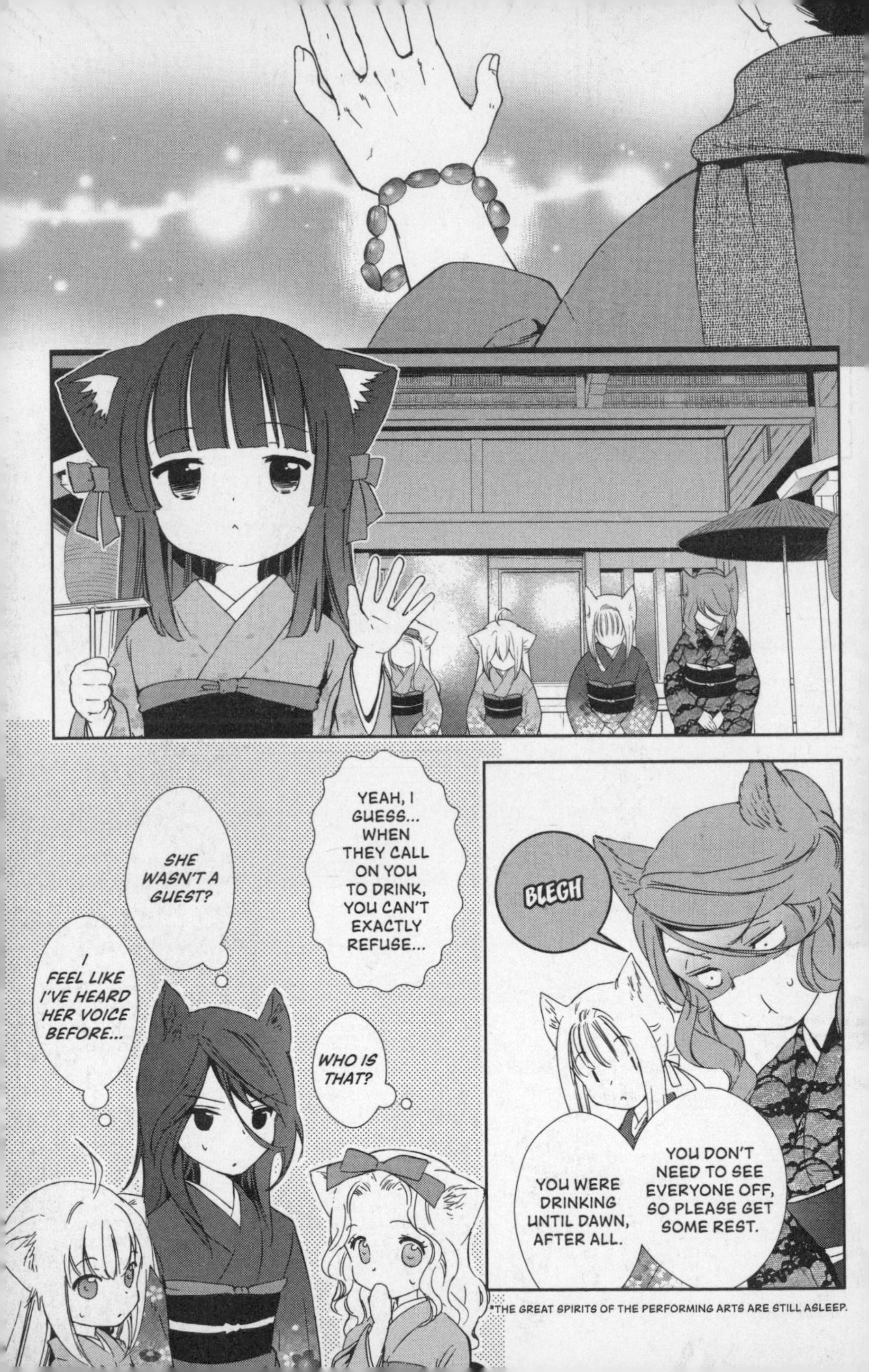
BLEGH
YOU DON'T NEED TO SEE EVERYONE OFF, SO PLEASE GET SOME REST.
YOU WERE DRINKING UNTIL DAWN, AFTER ALL.
YEAH, I GUESS... WHEN THEY CALL ON YOU TO DRINK, YOU CAN'T EXACTLY REFUSE...
SHE WASN'T A GUEST?
WHO IS THAT?
I FEEL LIKE I'VE HEARD HER VOICE BEFORE...

*THE GREAT SPIRITS OF THE PERFORMING ARTS ARE STILL ASLEEP.

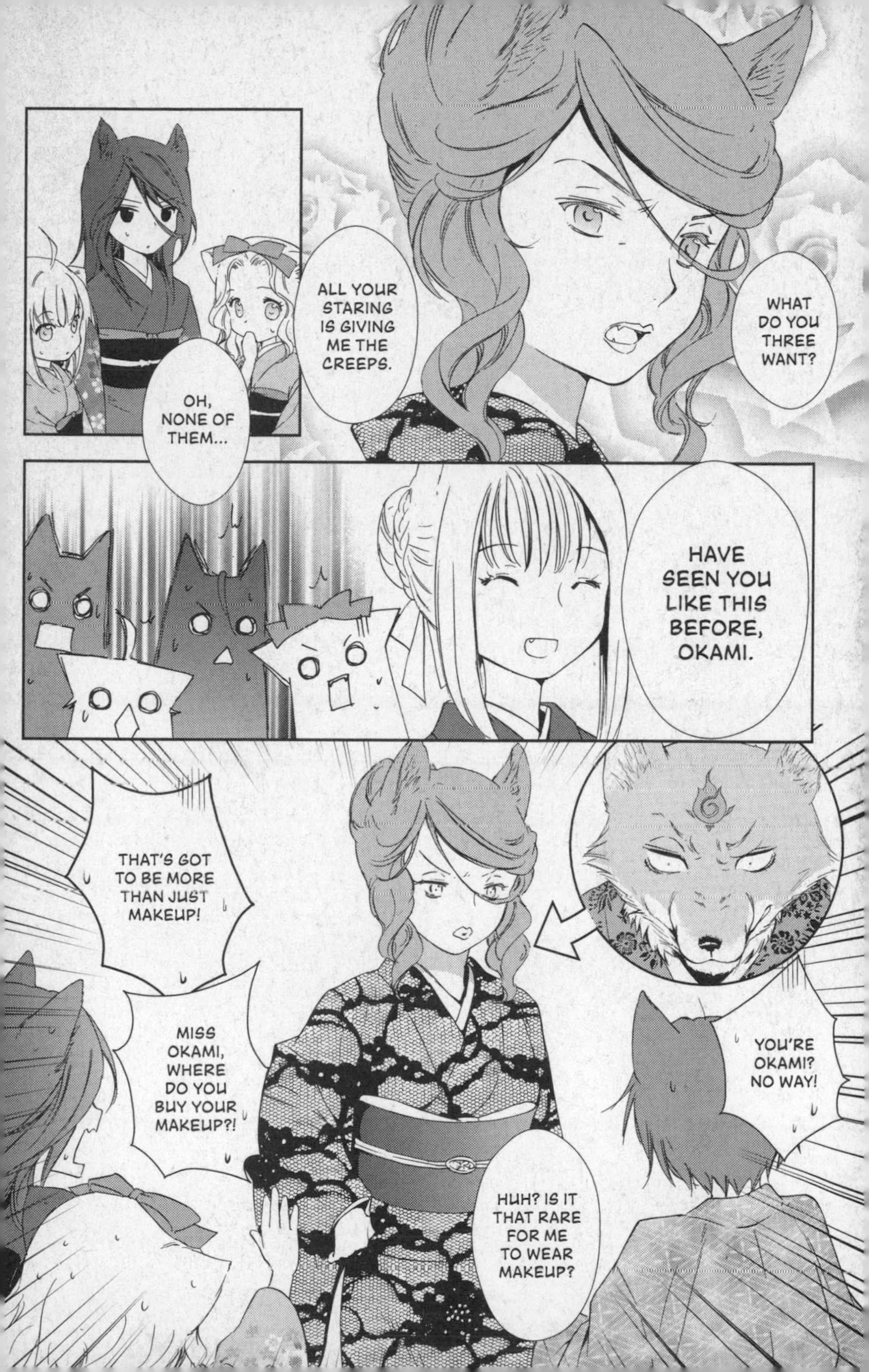
WHAT DO YOU THREE WANT?
ALL YOUR STARING IS GIVING ME THE CREEPS.
OH, NONE OF THEM...
HAVE SEEN YOU LIKE THIS BEFORE, OKAMI.
YOU'RE OKAMI? NO WAY!
THAT'S GOT TO BE MORE THAN JUST MAKEUP!
MISS OKAMI, WHERE DO YOU BUY YOUR MAKEUP?!
HUH? IS IT THAT RARE FOR ME TO WEAR MAKEUP?

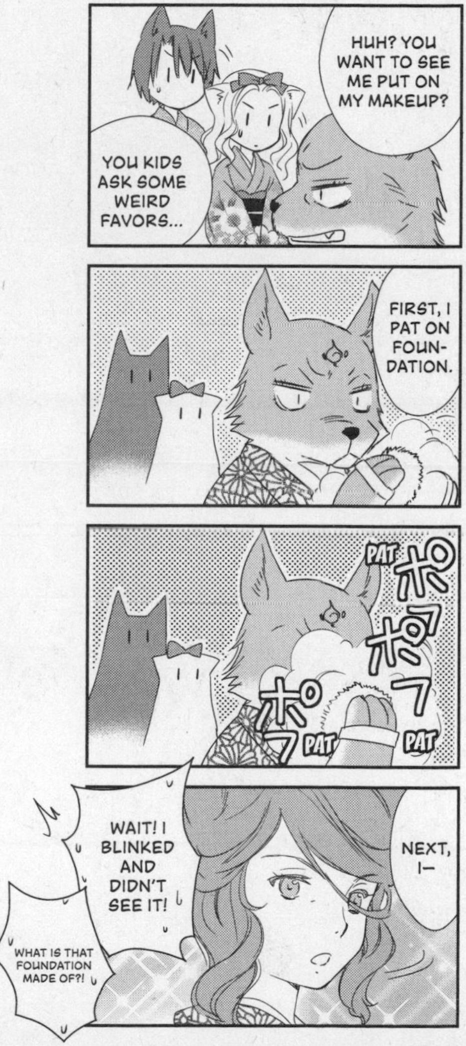
HUH? YOU WANT TO SEE ME PUT ON MY MAKEUP?
YOU KIDS ASK SOME WEIRD FAVORS...
FIRST, I PAT ON FOUN-DATION.
ポフ PAT
ポフ PAT
ポフ PAT
NEXT, I—
WAIT! I BLINKED AND DIDN'T SEE IT!
WHAT IS THAT FOUNDATION MADE OF?!

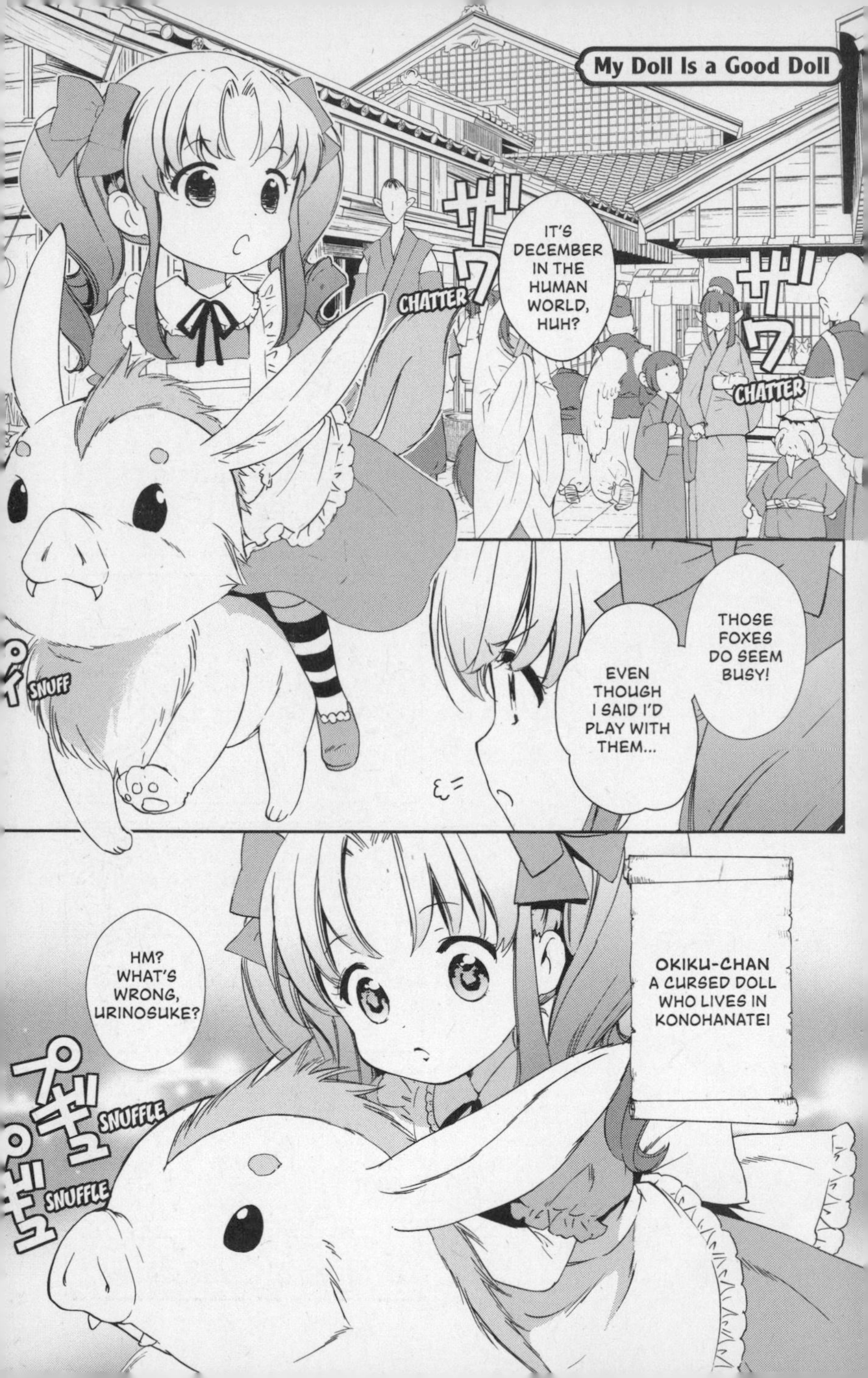
My Doll Is a Good Doll
IT'S DECEMBER IN THE HUMAN WORLD, HUH?
CHATTER
CHATTER
THOSE FOXES DO SEEM BUSY!
EVEN THOUGH I SAID I'D PLAY WITH THEM...
SNUFF
OKIKU-CHAN A CURSED DOLL WHO LIVES IN KONOHANATEI
HM? WHAT'S WRONG, URINOSUKE?
SNUFFLE
SNUFFLE

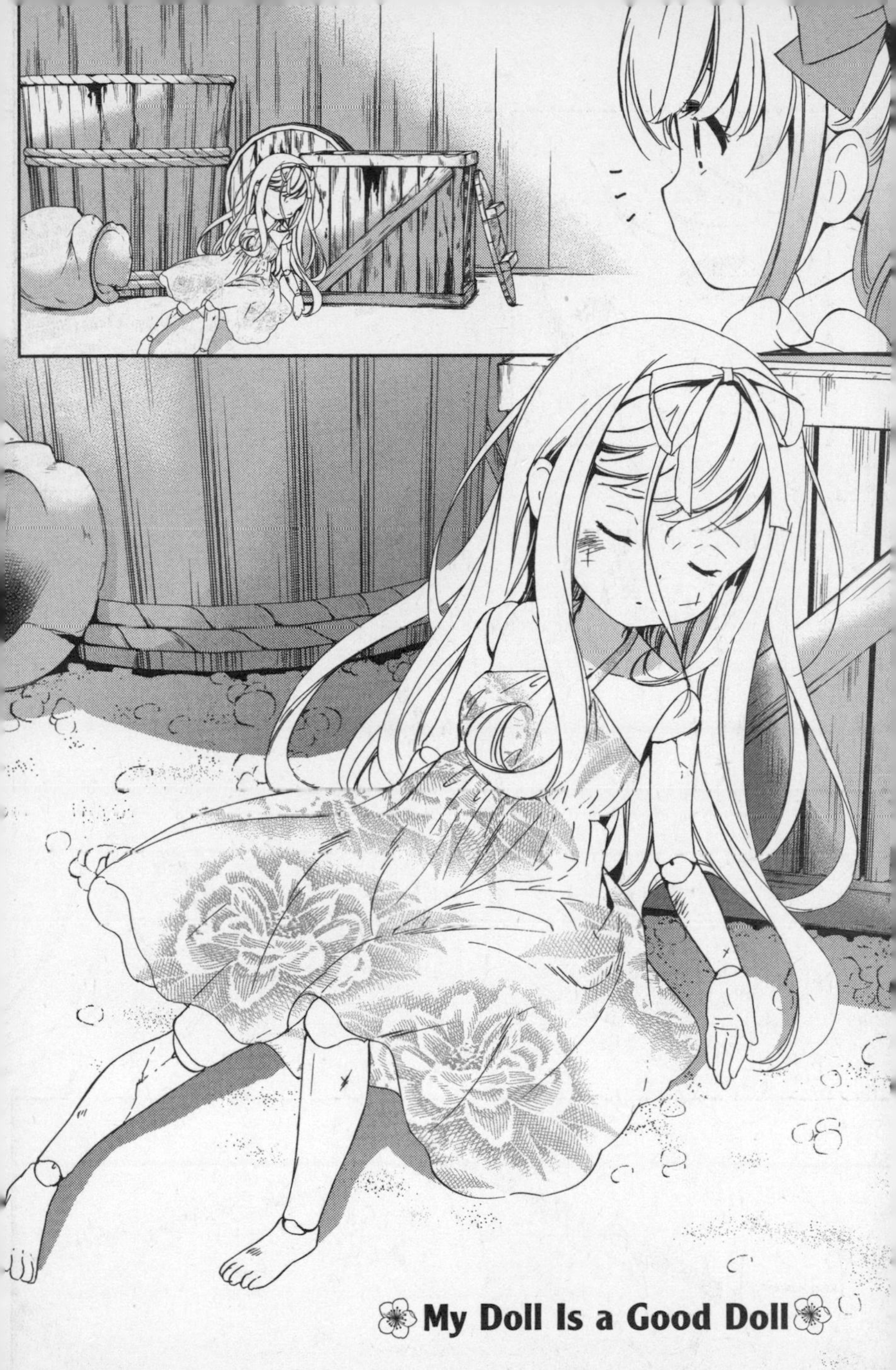

My Doll Is a Good Doll

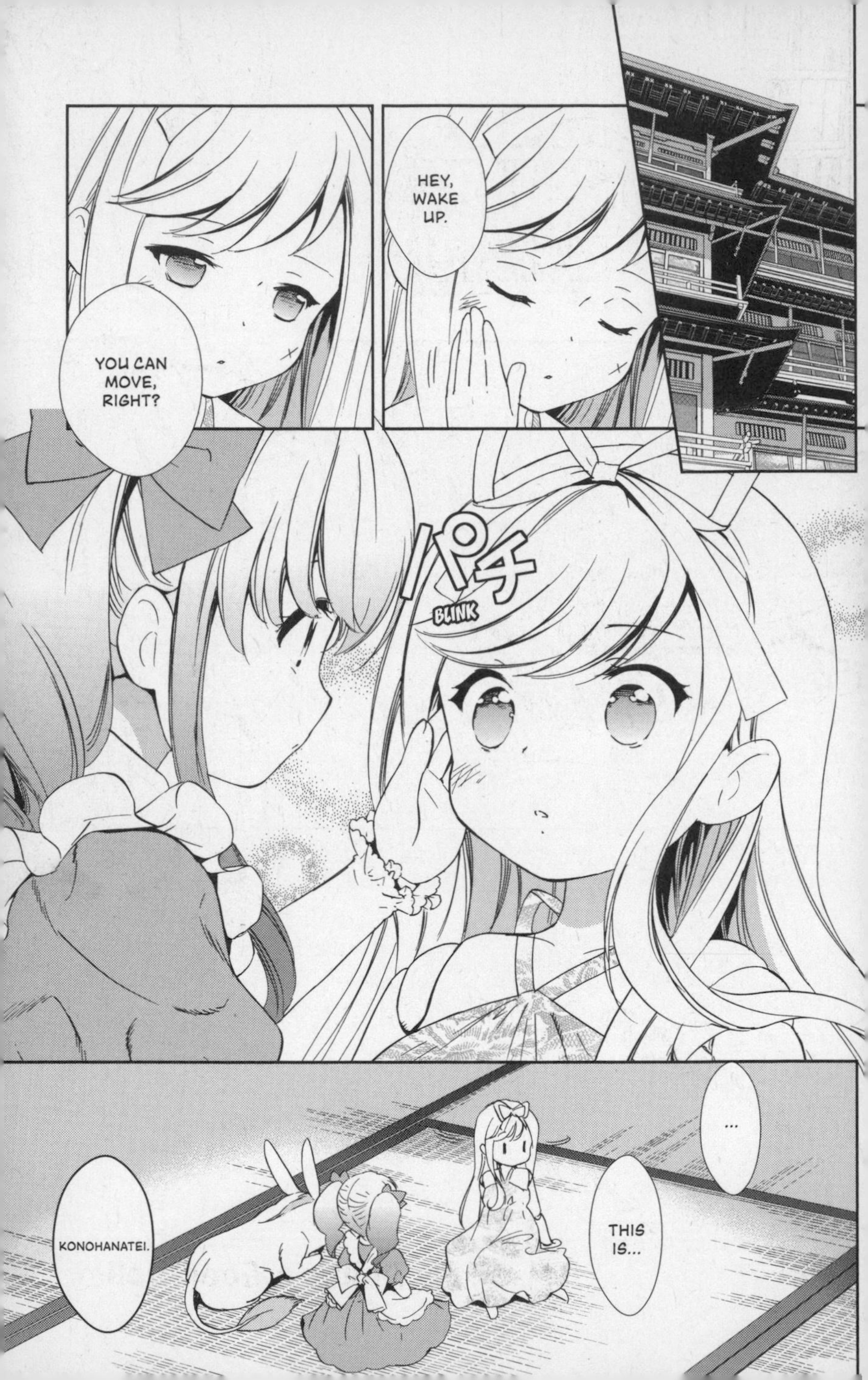
HEY, WAKE UP.
YOU CAN MOVE, RIGHT?
パチ
BLINK
...
THIS IS...
KONOHANATEI.

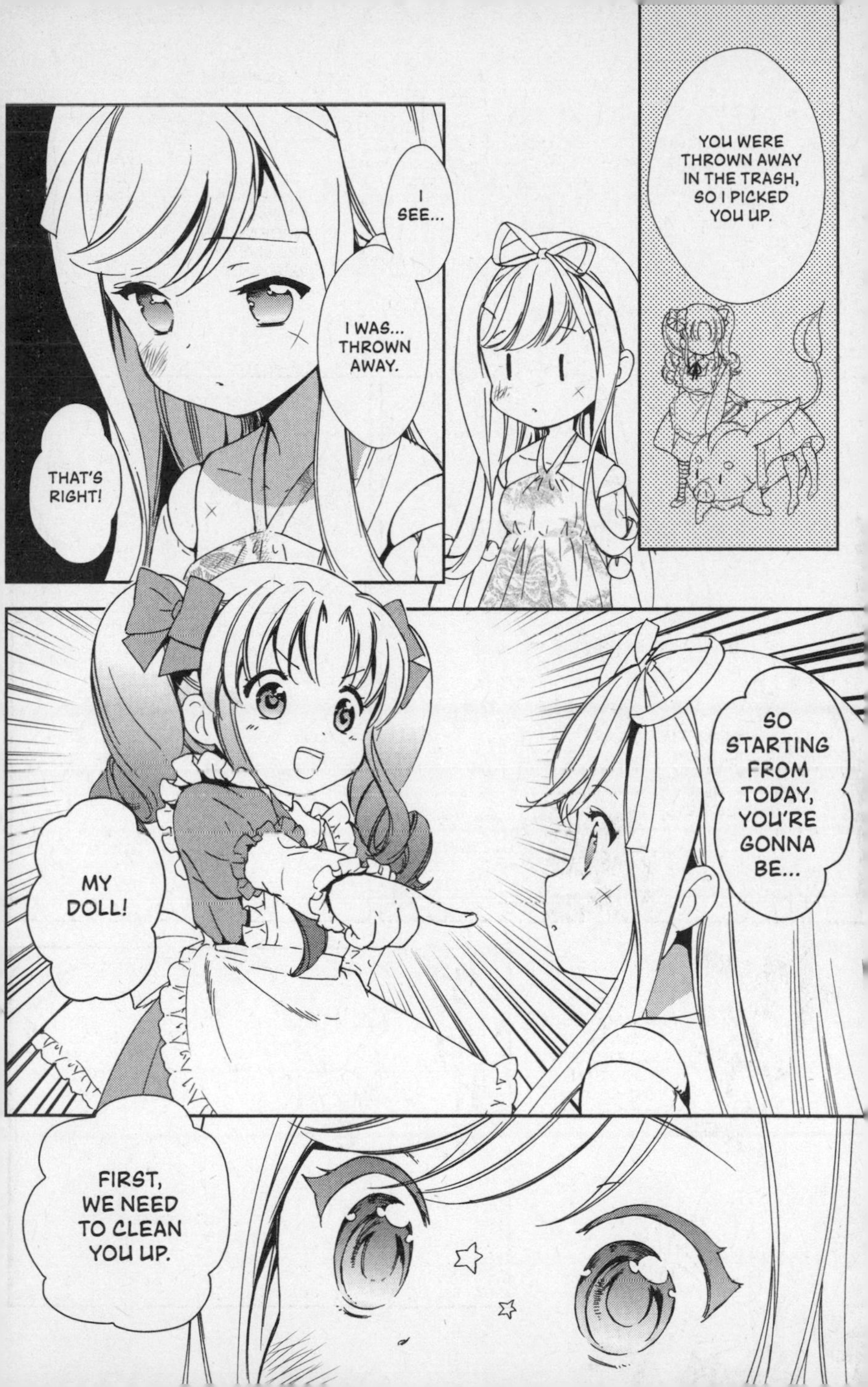
YOU WERE THROWN AWAY IN THE TRASH, SO I PICKED YOU UP.
I SEE...
I WAS... THROWN AWAY.
THAT'S RIGHT!
SO STARTING FROM TODAY, YOU'RE GONNA BE...
MY DOLL!
FIRST, WE NEED TO CLEAN YOU UP.

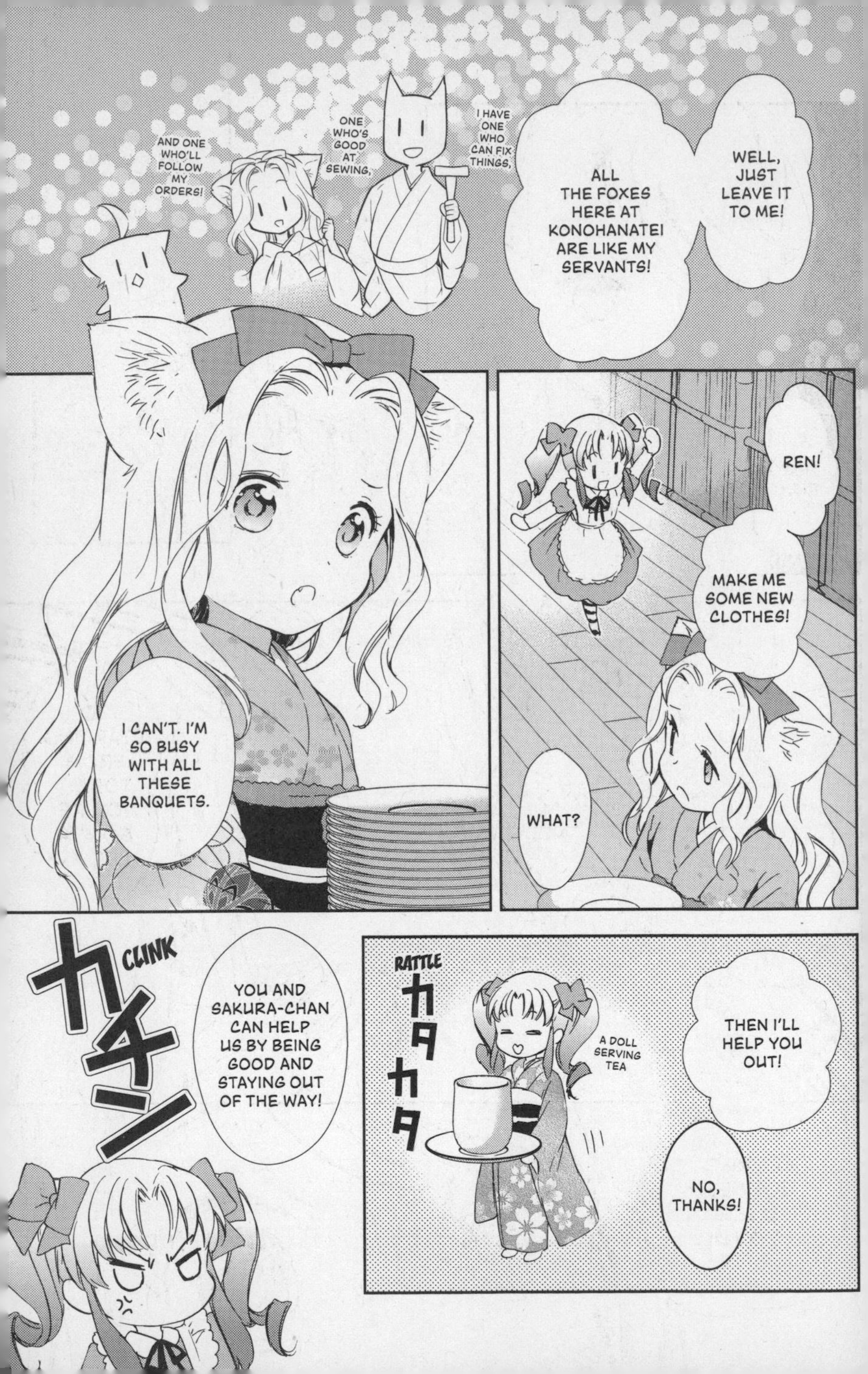
WELL, JUST LEAVE IT TO ME!
ALL THE FOXES HERE AT KONOHANATEI ARE LIKE MY SERVANTS!
I HAVE ONE WHO CAN FIX THINGS,
ONE WHO'S GOOD AT SEWING,
AND ONE WHO'LL FOLLOW MY ORDERS!
REN!
MAKE ME SOME NEW CLOTHES!
WHAT?
I CAN'T. I'M SO BUSY WITH ALL THESE BANQUETS.
THEN I'LL HELP YOU OUT!
NO, THANKS!
A DOLL SERVING TEA
RATTLE
カタカタ
YOU AND SAKURA-CHAN CAN HELP US BY BEING GOOD AND STAYING OUT OF THE WAY!
CLINK
カチン

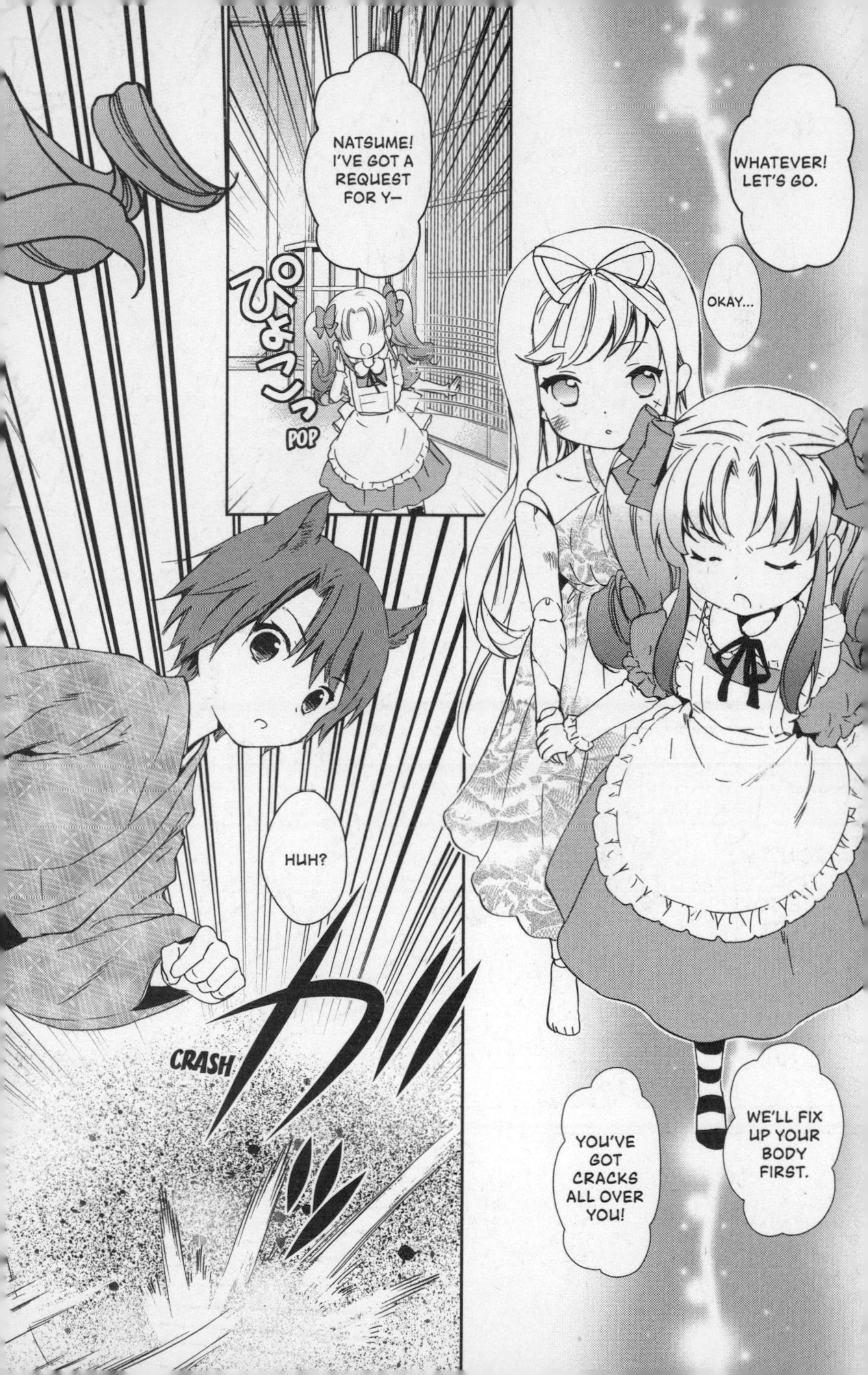
WHATEVER! LET'S GO.
OKAY...
WE'LL FIX UP YOUR BODY FIRST.
YOU'VE GOT CRACKS ALL OVER YOU!
NATSUME! I'VE GOT A REQUEST FOR Y—
POP
HUH?
CRASH

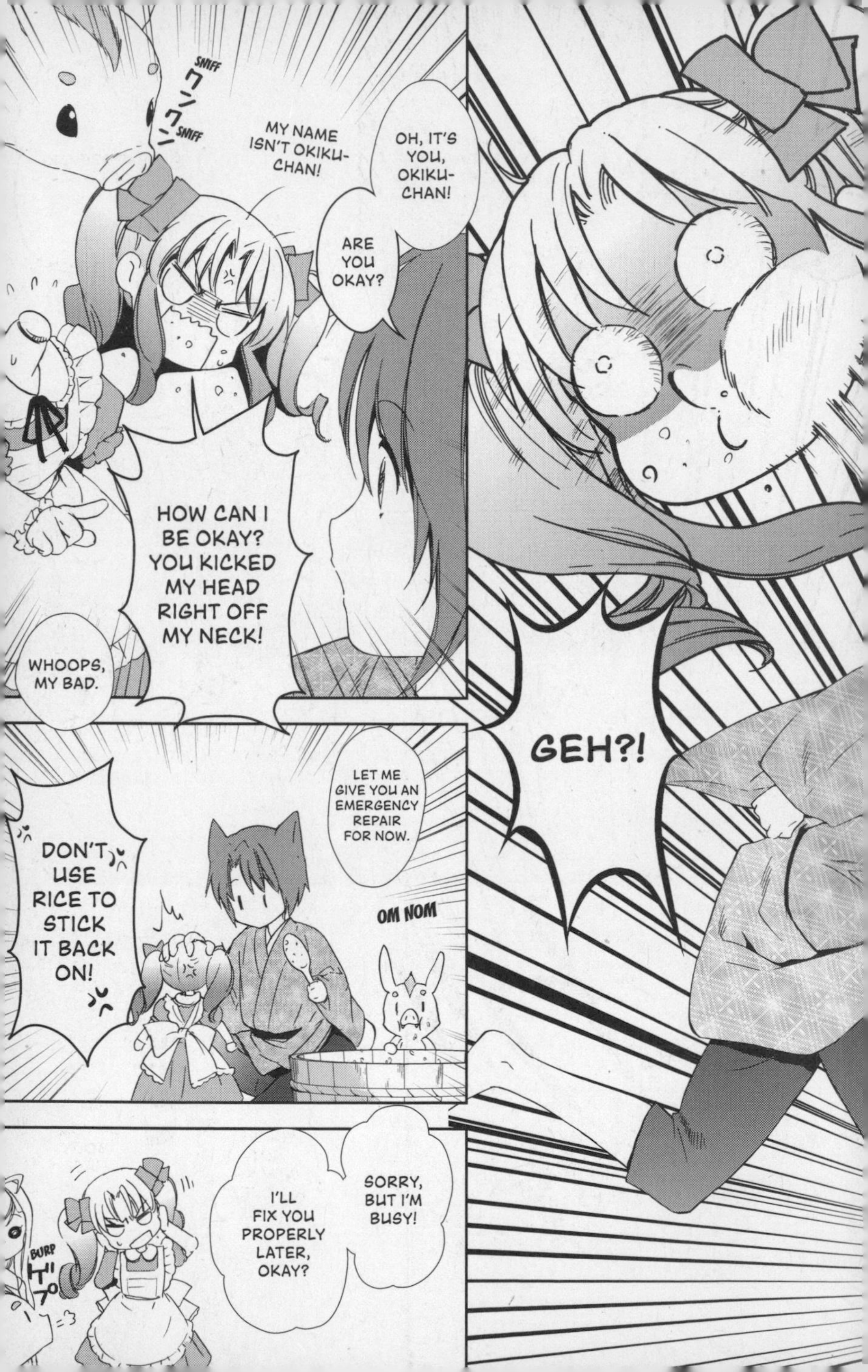
GEH?!
OH, IT'S YOU, OKIKU-CHAN!
MY NAME ISN'T OKIKU-CHAN!
SNIFF
SNIFF
ARE YOU OKAY?
HOW CAN I BE OKAY? YOU KICKED MY HEAD RIGHT OFF MY NECK!
WHOOPS, MY BAD.
LET ME GIVE YOU AN EMERGENCY REPAIR FOR NOW.
OM NOM
DON'T USE RICE TO STICK IT BACK ON!
SORRY, BUT I'M BUSY!
I'LL FIX YOU PROPERLY LATER, OKAY?
BURP

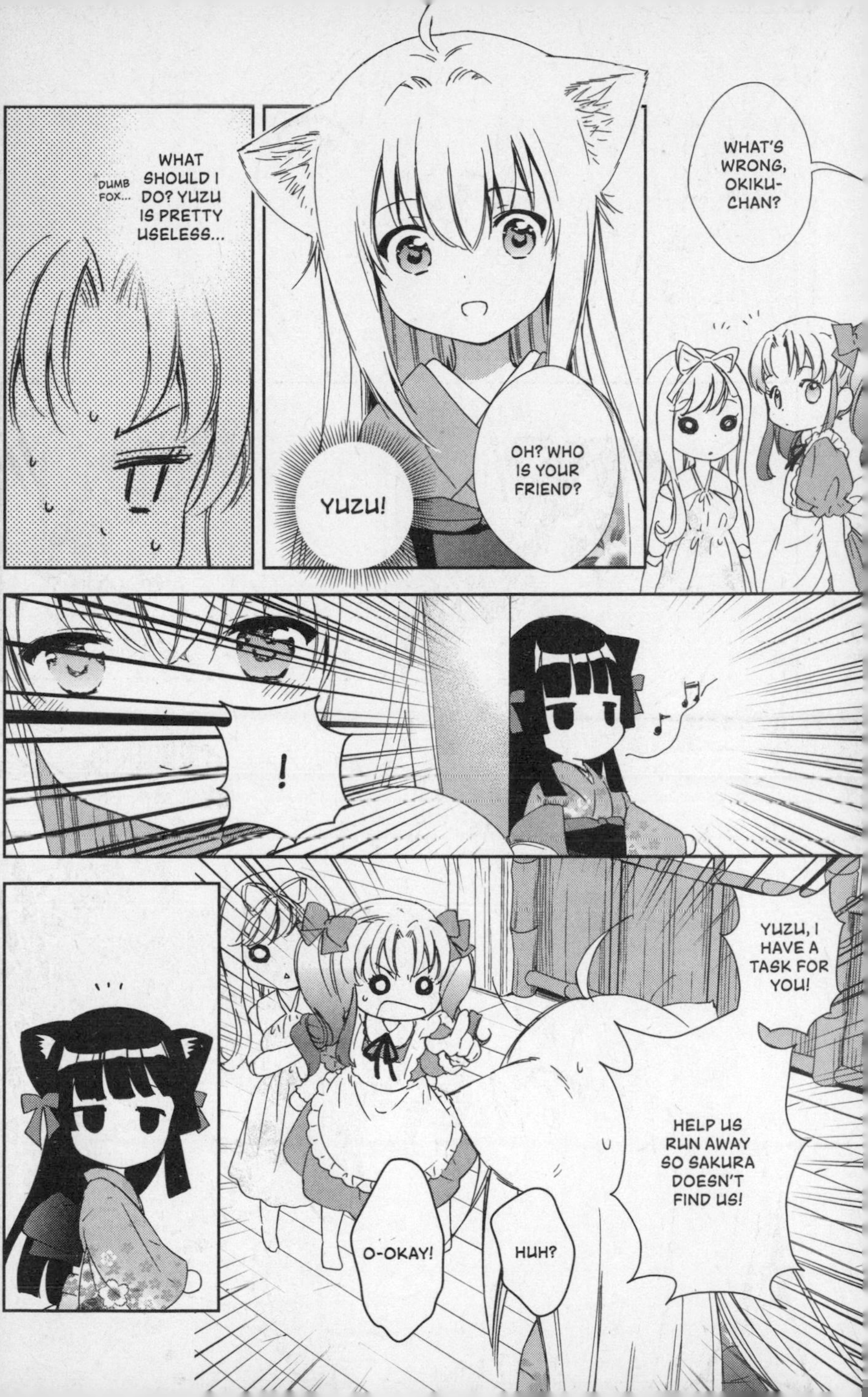
WHAT'S WRONG, OKIKU-CHAN?
OH? WHO IS YOUR FRIEND?
YUZU!
WHAT SHOULD I DO? YUZU IS PRETTY USELESS...
DUMB FOX...
!
YUZU, I HAVE A TASK FOR YOU!
HELP US RUN AWAY SO SAKURA DOESN'T FIND US!
HUH?
O-OKAY!

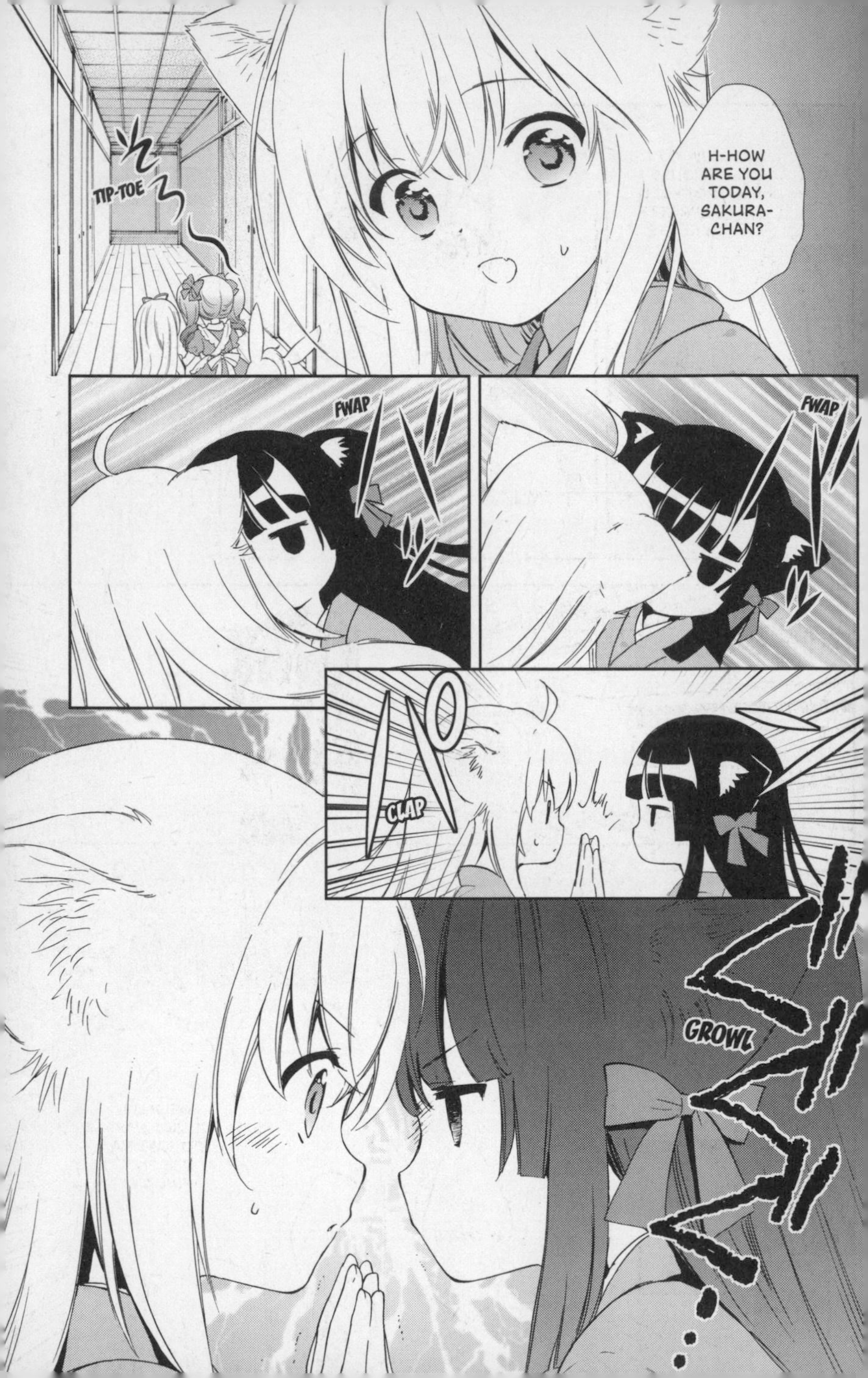
H-HOW ARE YOU TODAY, SAKURA-CHAN?
TIP-TOE
FWAP
FWAP
CLAP
GROWL

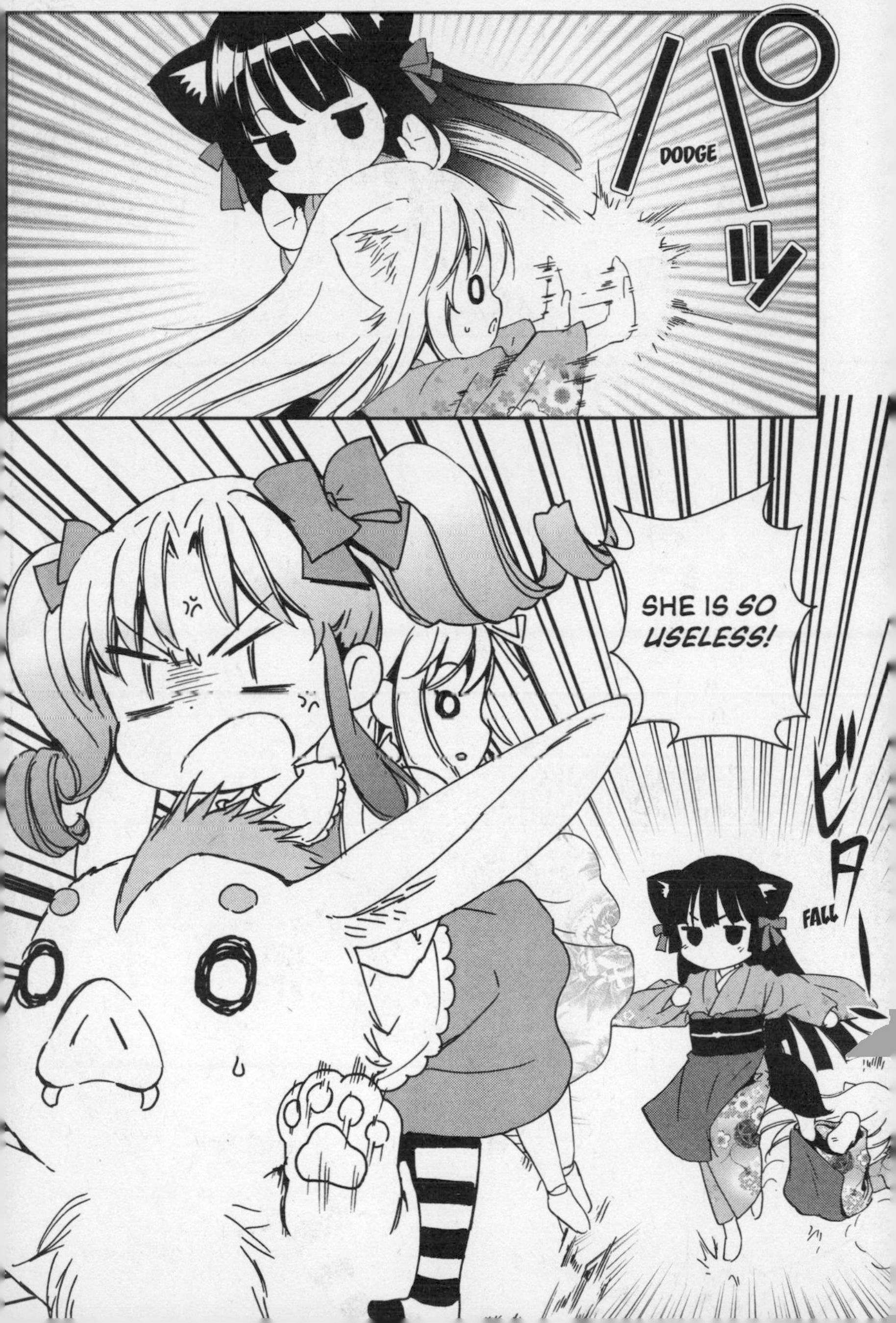
パッ
DODGE
SHE IS SO USELESS!
FALL

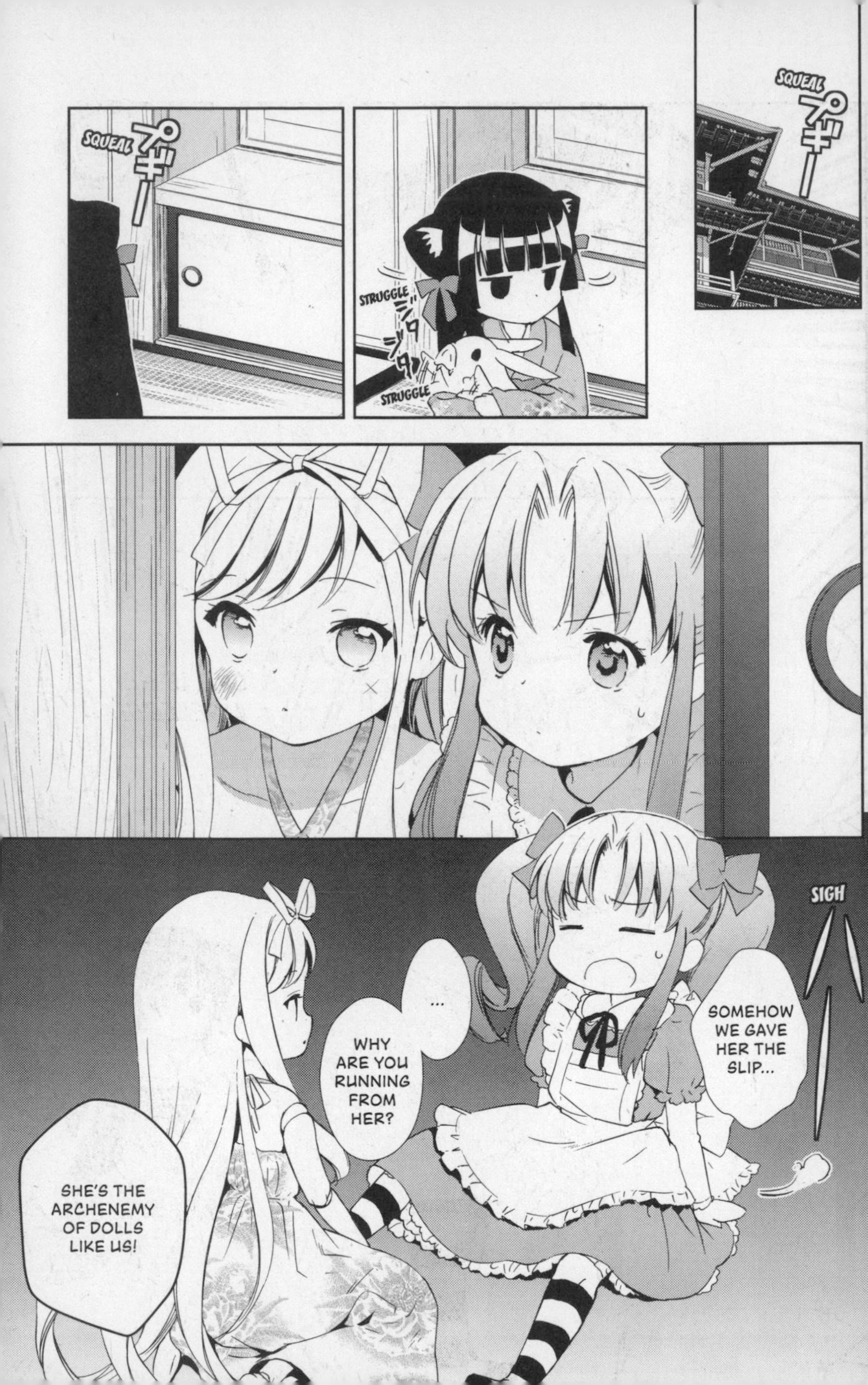
SQUEAL
ピギー
STRUGGLE
ジタジタ
STRUGGLE
SQUEAL
ピギー
SIGH
SOMEHOW WE GAVE HER THE SLIP...
...
WHY ARE YOU RUNNING FROM HER?
SHE'S THE ARCHENEMY OF DOLLS LIKE US!

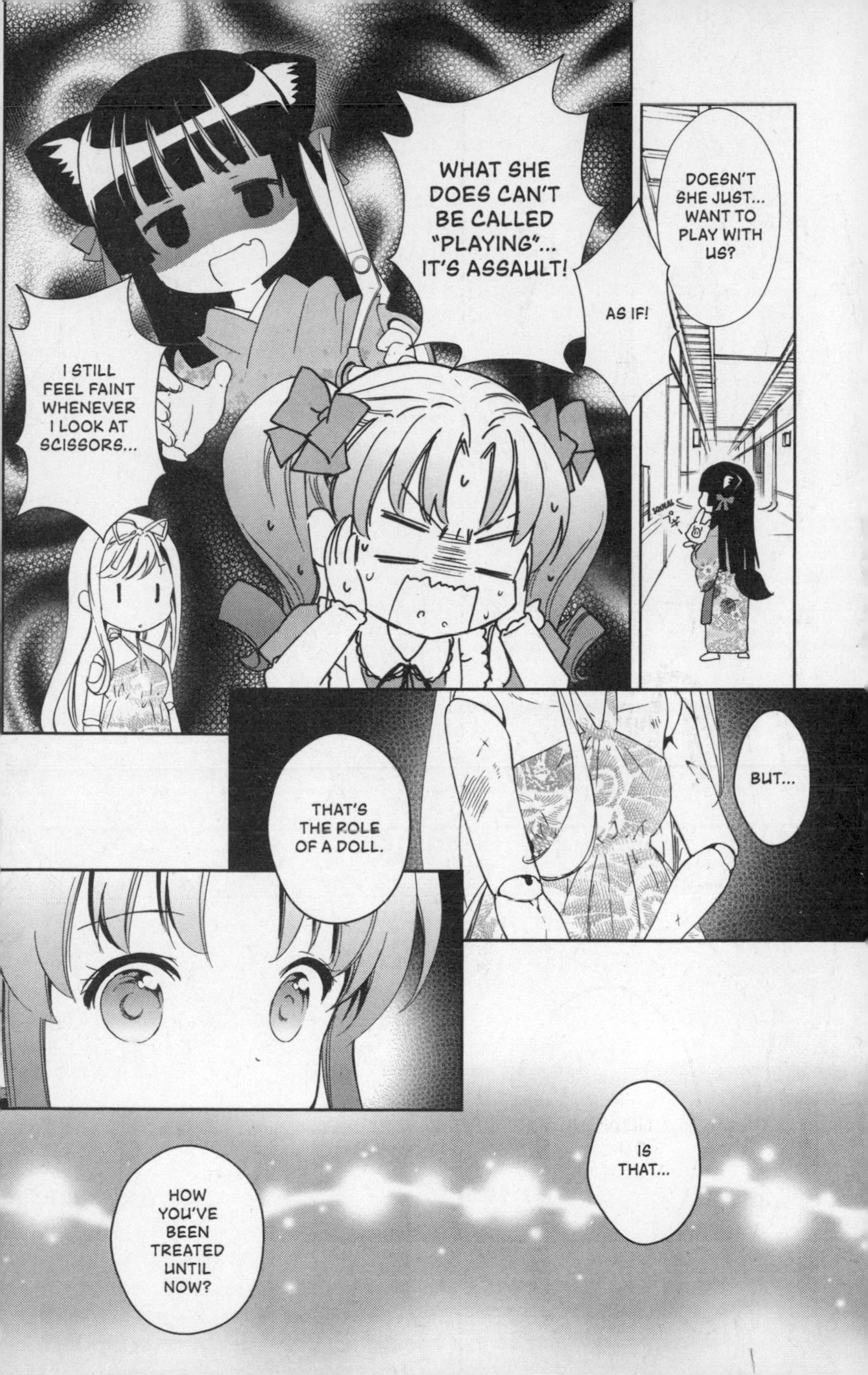
DOESN'T SHE JUST... WANT TO PLAY WITH US?
AS IF!
WHAT SHE DOES CAN'T BE CALLED "PLAYING"... IT'S ASSAULT!
I STILL FEEL FAINT WHENEVER I LOOK AT SCISSORS...
BUT...
THAT'S THE ROLE OF A DOLL.
IS THAT...
HOW YOU'VE BEEN TREATED UNTIL NOW?

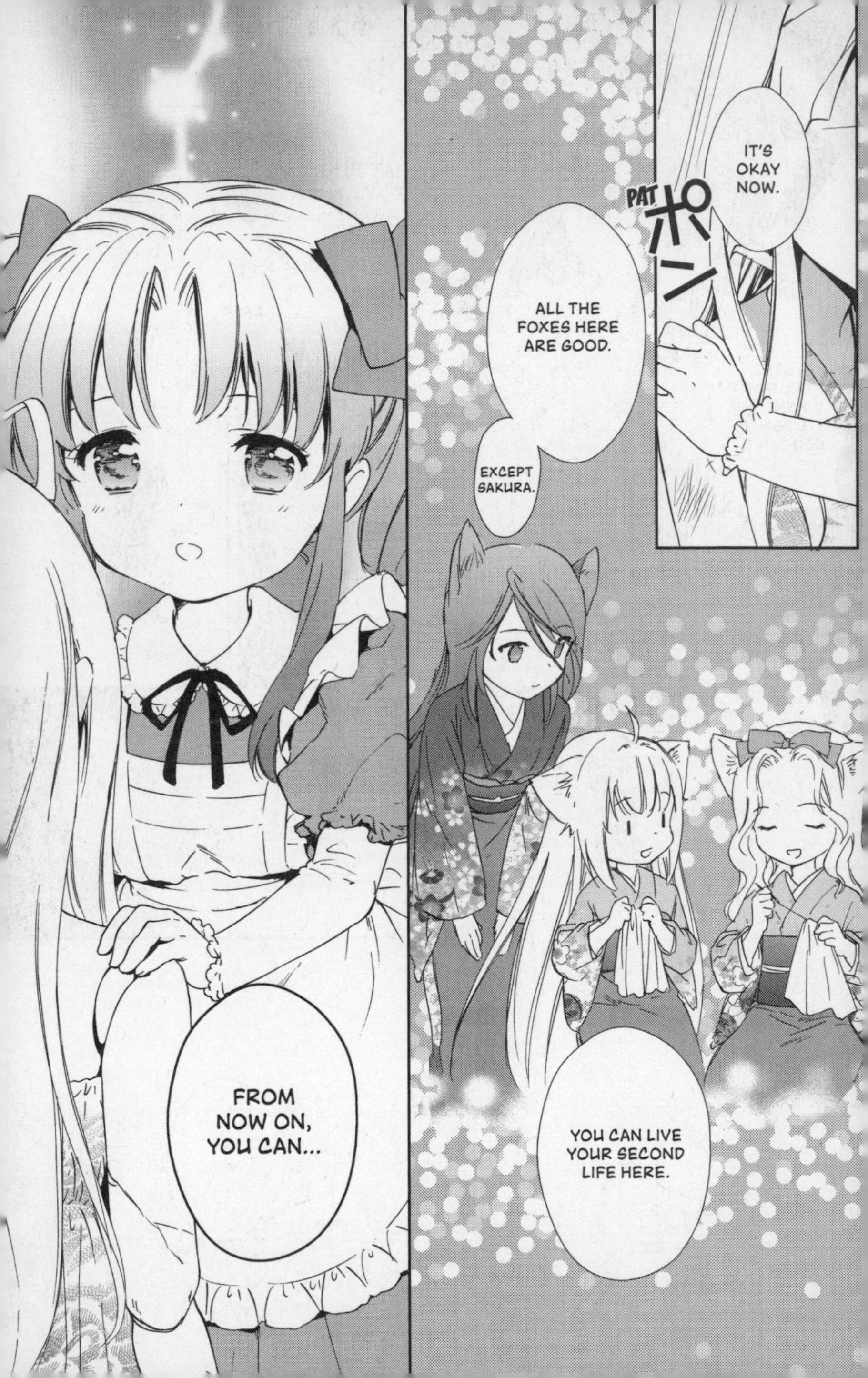
FROM NOW ON, YOU CAN...
IT'S OKAY NOW.
PAT
ALL THE FOXES HERE ARE GOOD.
EXCEPT SAKURA.
YOU CAN LIVE YOUR SECOND LIFE HERE.

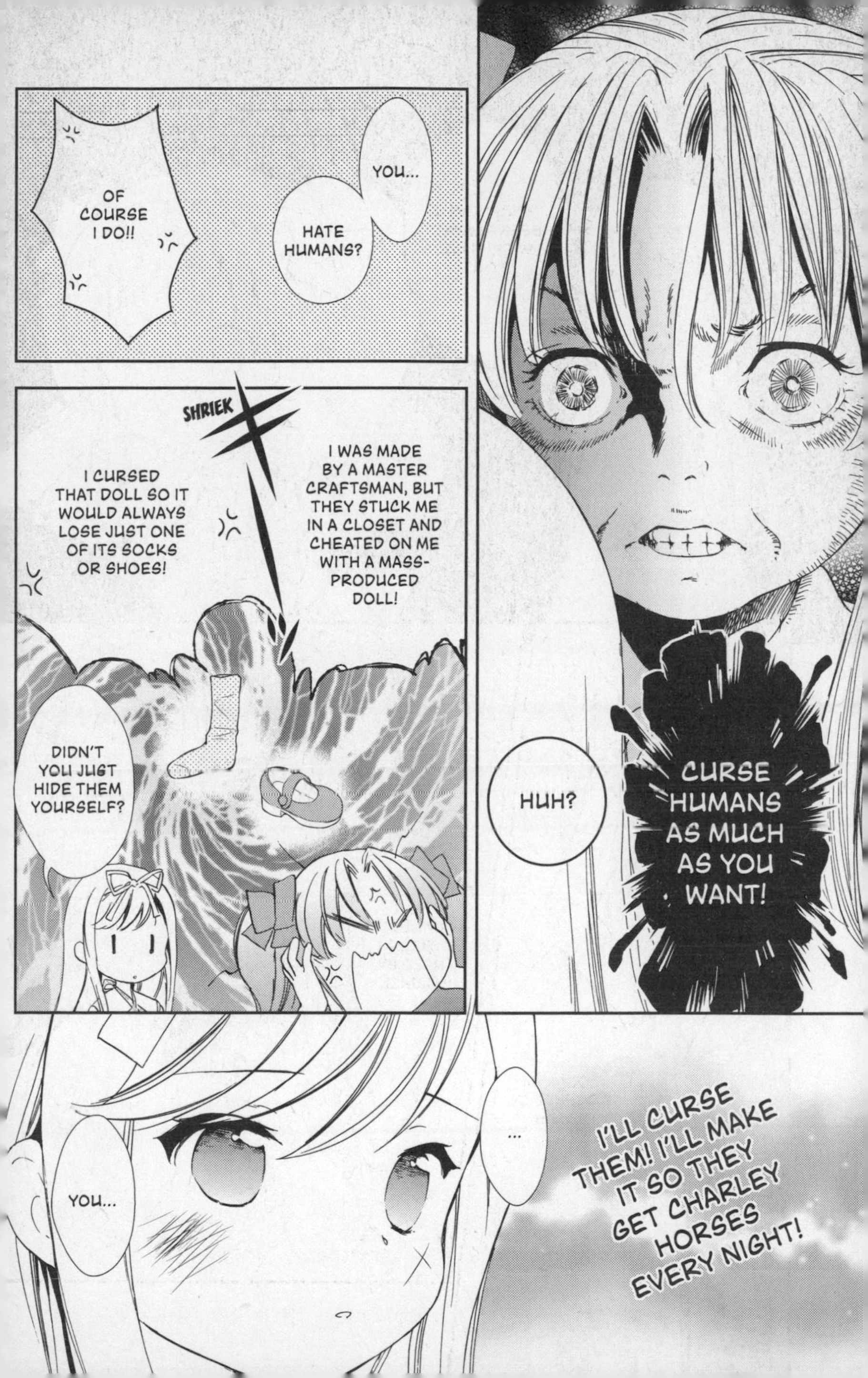
CURSE HUMANS AS MUCH AS YOU WANT!
HUH?
YOU...
HATE HUMANS?
OF COURSE I DO!!
SHRIEK
I WAS MADE BY A MASTER CRAFTSMAN, BUT THEY STUCK ME IN A CLOSET AND CHEATED ON ME WITH A MASS-PRODUCED DOLL!
I CURSED THAT DOLL SO IT WOULD ALWAYS LOSE JUST ONE OF ITS SOCKS OR SHOES!
DIDN'T YOU JUST HIDE THEM YOURSELF?
I'LL CURSE THEM! I'LL MAKE IT SO THEY GET CHARLEY HORSES EVERY NIGHT!
...
YOU...

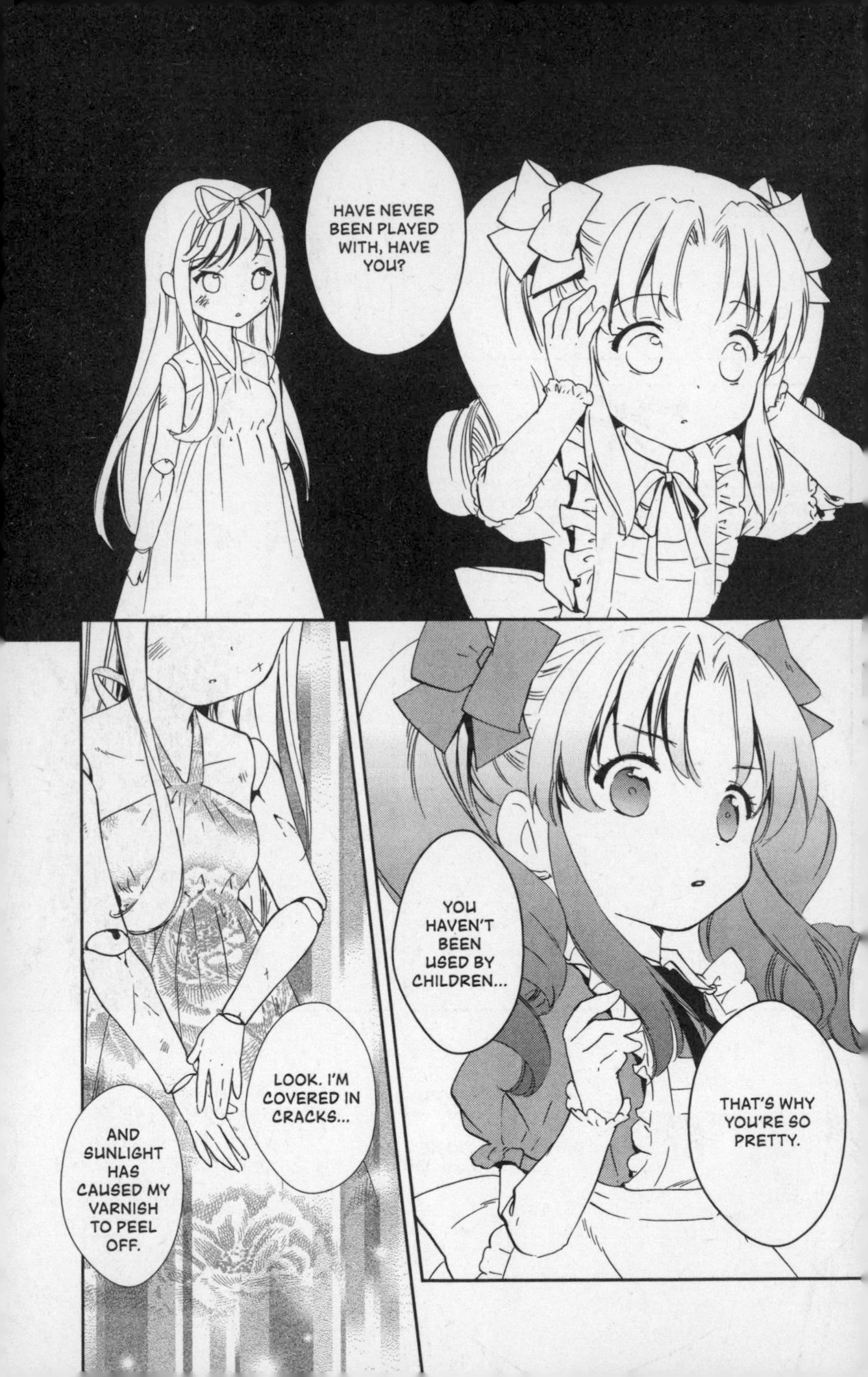
HAVE NEVER BEEN PLAYED WITH, HAVE YOU?
YOU HAVEN'T BEEN USED BY CHILDREN...
THAT'S WHY YOU'RE SO PRETTY.
LOOK. I'M COVERED IN CRACKS...
AND SUNLIGHT HAS CAUSED MY VARNISH TO PEEL OFF.

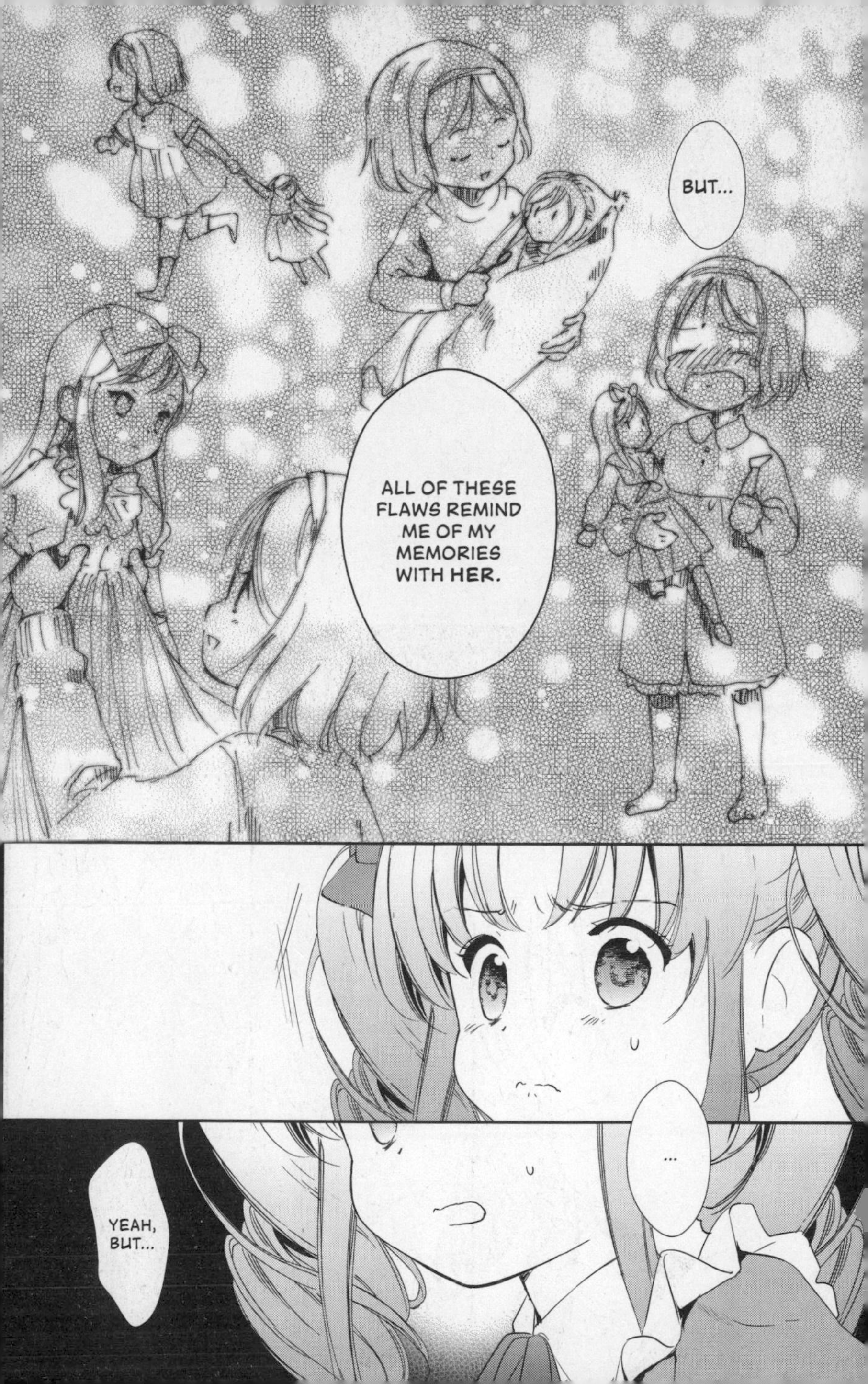
BUT...
ALL OF THESE FLAWS REMIND ME OF MY MEMORIES WITH HER.
...
YEAH, BUT...

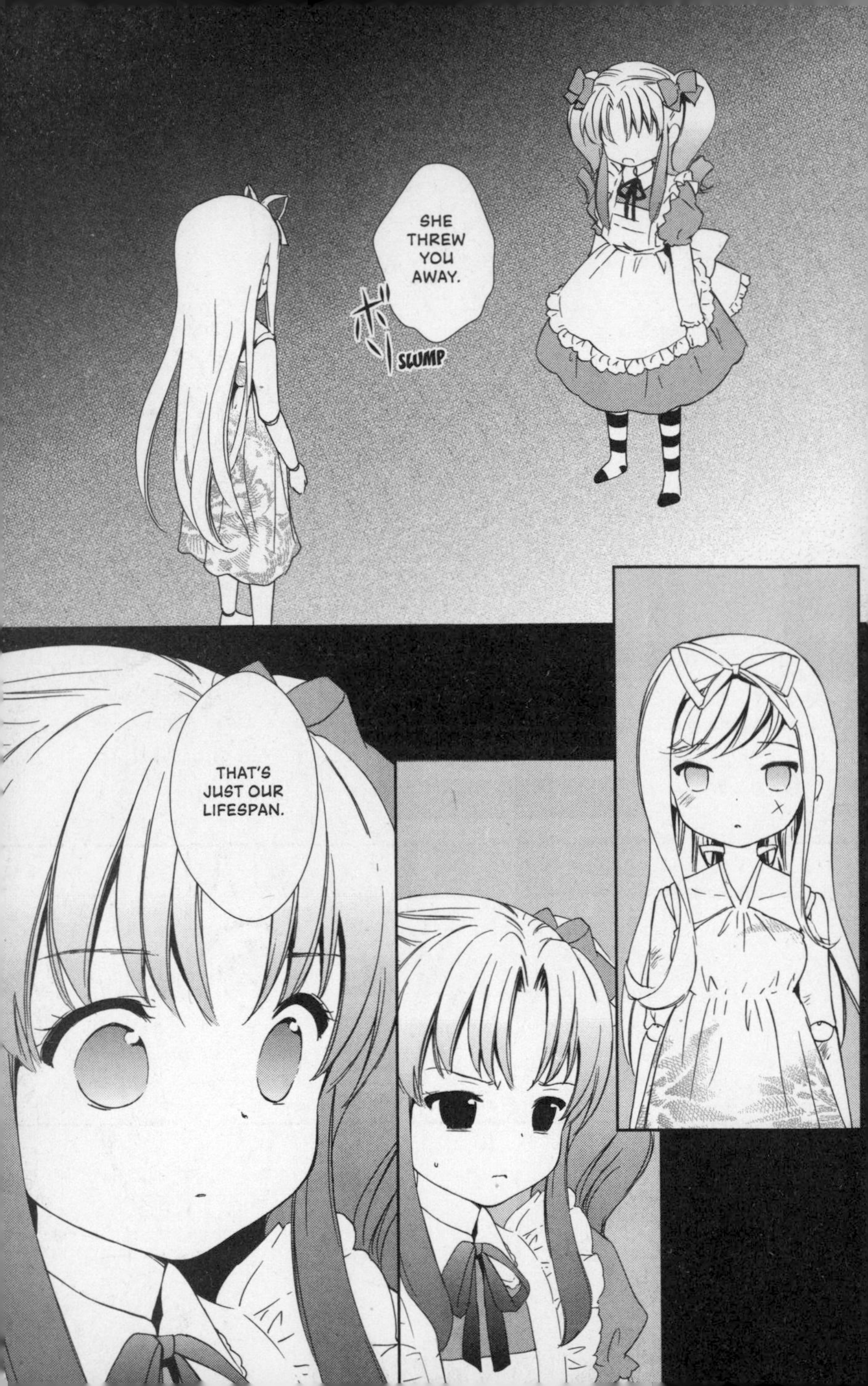
SHE THREW YOU AWAY.
SLUMP
THAT'S JUST OUR LIFESPAN.

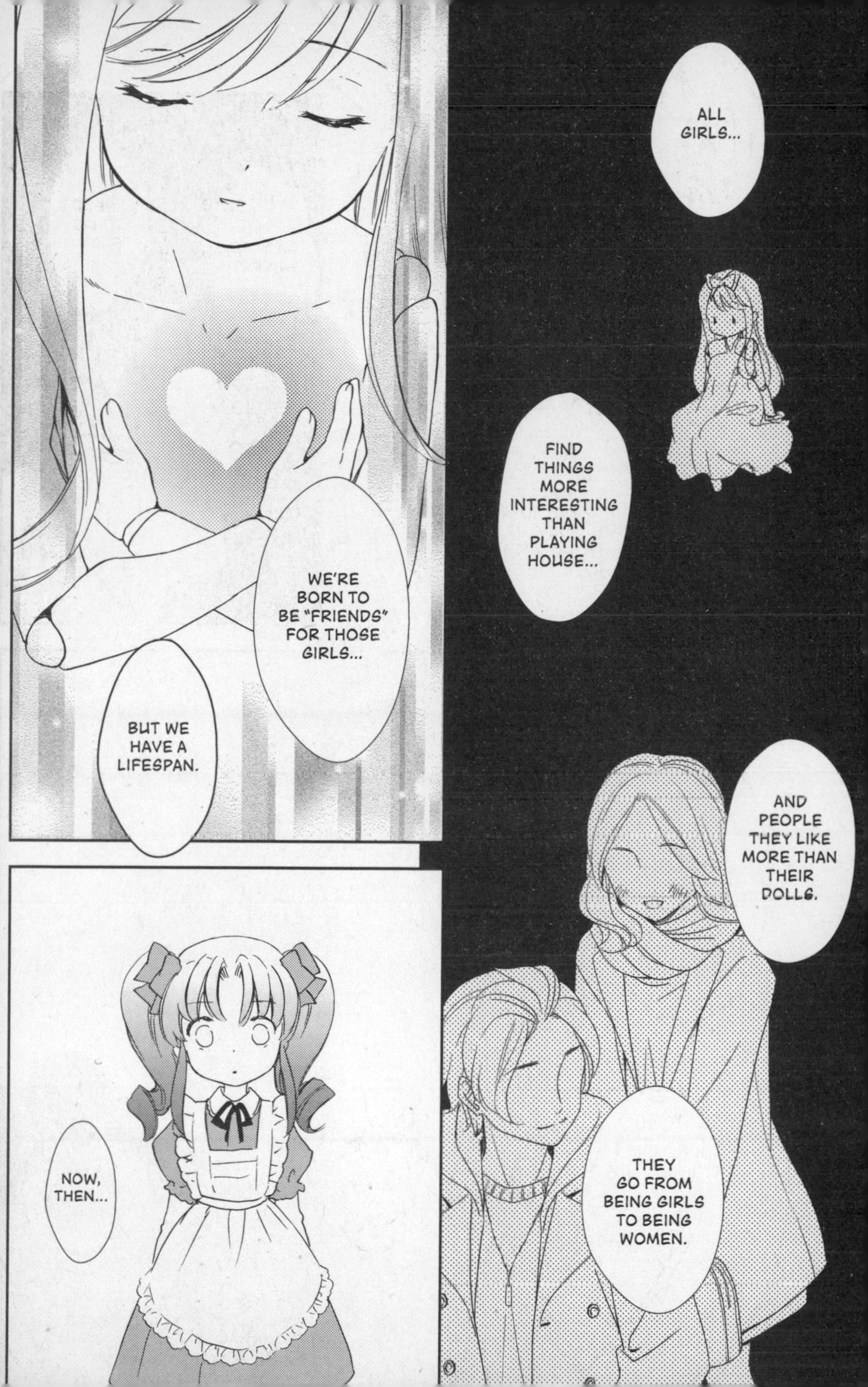
ALL GIRLS...
FIND THINGS MORE INTERESTING THAN PLAYING HOUSE...
AND PEOPLE THEY LIKE MORE THAN THEIR DOLLS.
THEY GO FROM BEING GIRLS TO BEING WOMEN.
WE'RE BORN TO BE "FRIENDS" FOR THOSE GIRLS...
BUT WE HAVE A LIFESPAN.
NOW, THEN...

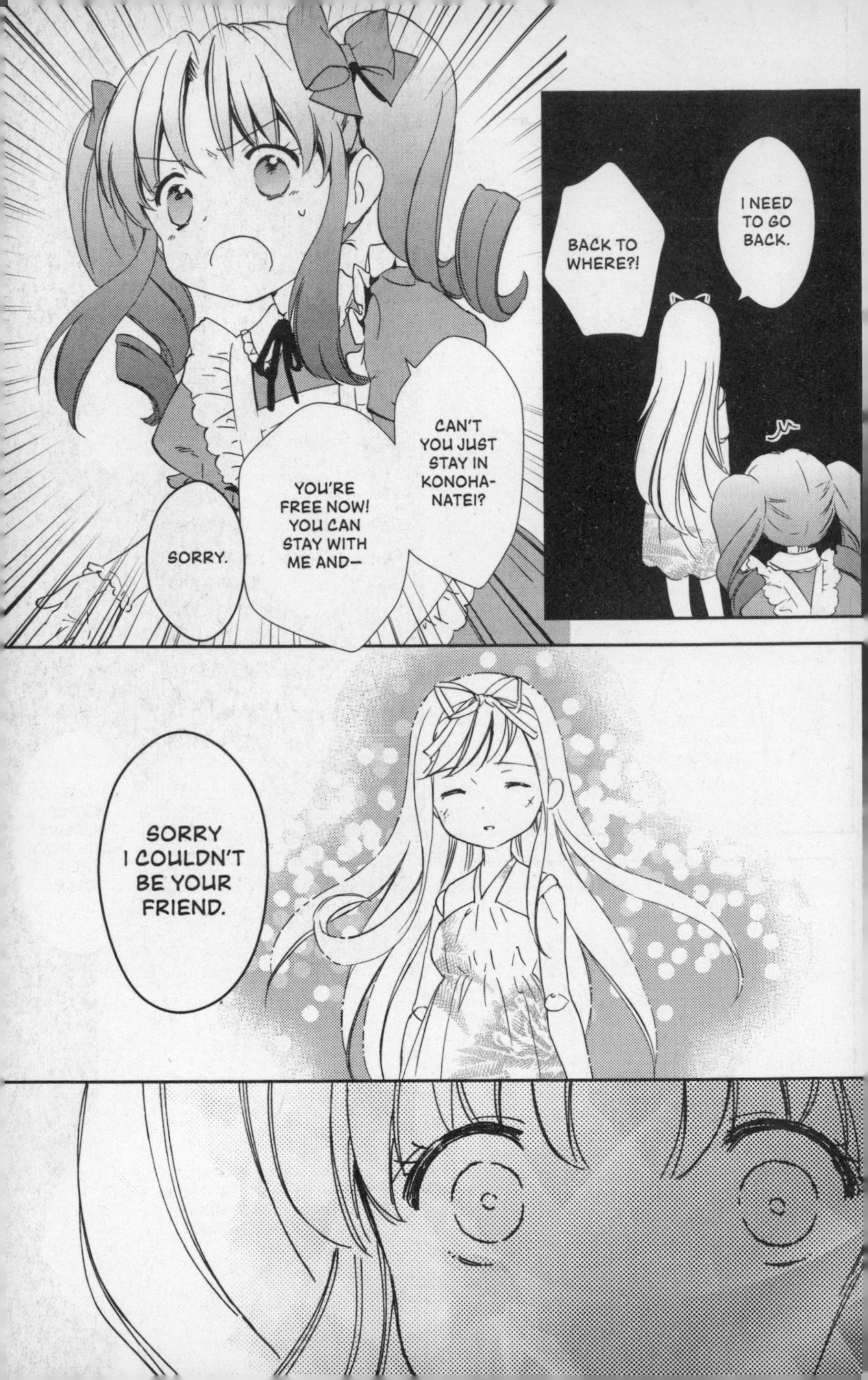
I NEED TO GO BACK.
BACK TO WHERE?!
CAN'T YOU JUST STAY IN KONOHA-NATEI!?
YOU'RE FREE NOW! YOU CAN STAY WITH ME AND—
SORRY.
SORRY I COULDN'T BE YOUR FRIEND.

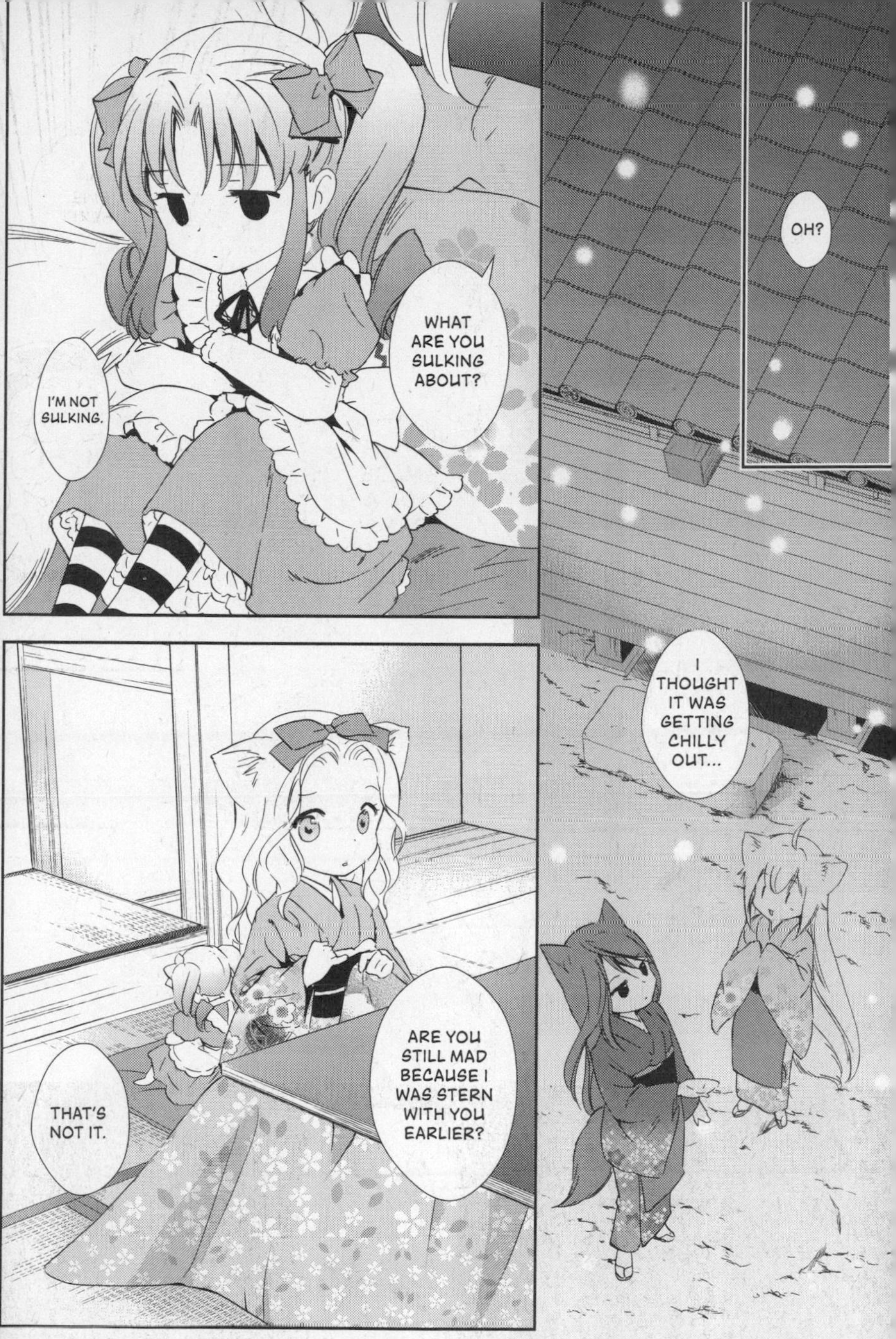
OH?
I THOUGHT IT WAS GETTING CHILLY OUT...
WHAT ARE YOU SULKING ABOUT?
I'M NOT SULKING.
ARE YOU STILL MAD BECAUSE I WAS STERN WITH YOU EARLIER?
THAT'S NOT IT.

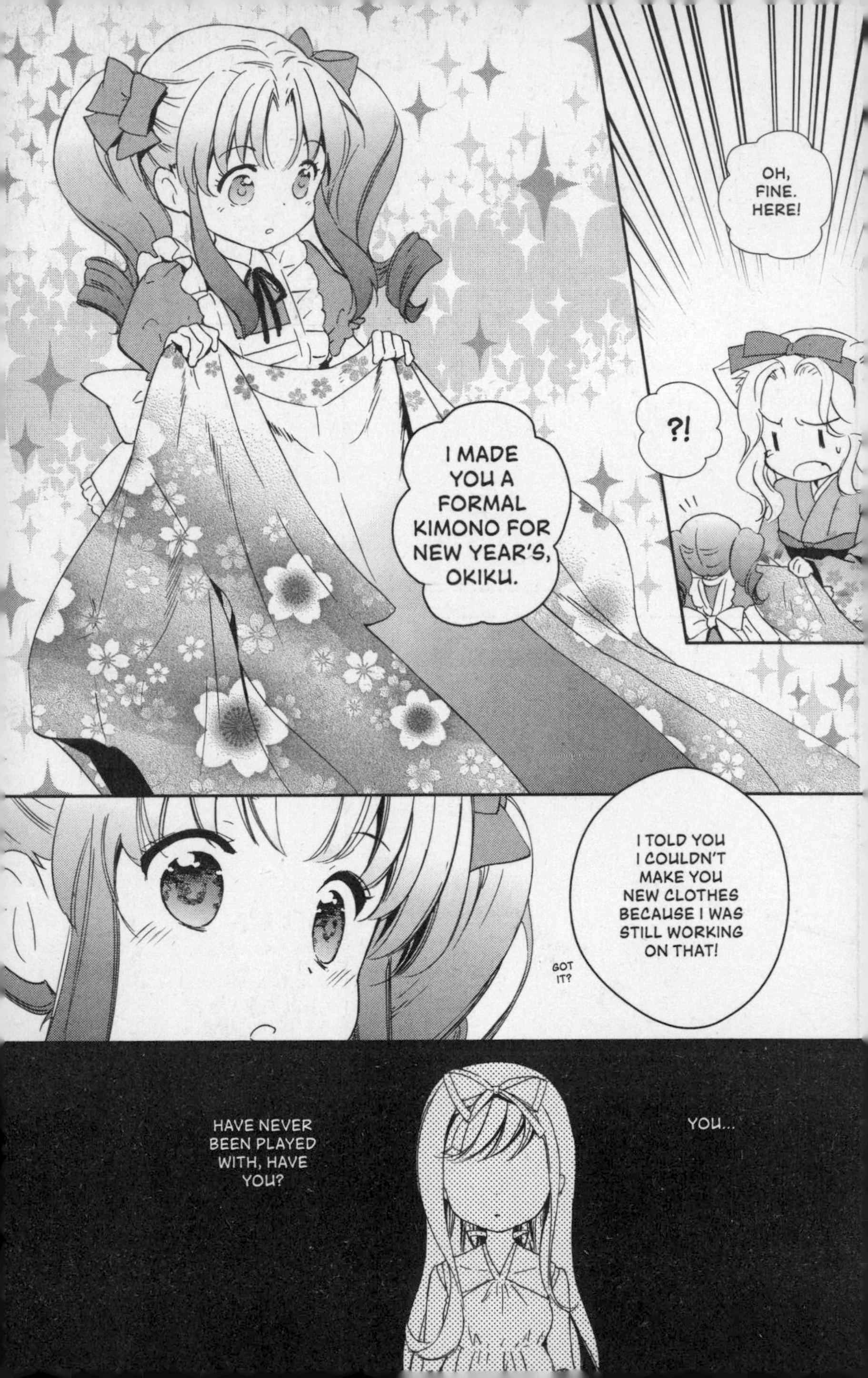
OH, FINE. HERE!
?!
I MADE YOU A FORMAL KIMONO FOR NEW YEAR'S, OKIKU.
I TOLD YOU I COULDN'T MAKE YOU NEW CLOTHES BECAUSE I WAS STILL WORKING ON THAT!
GOT IT?
YOU...
HAVE NEVER BEEN PLAYED WITH, HAVE YOU?

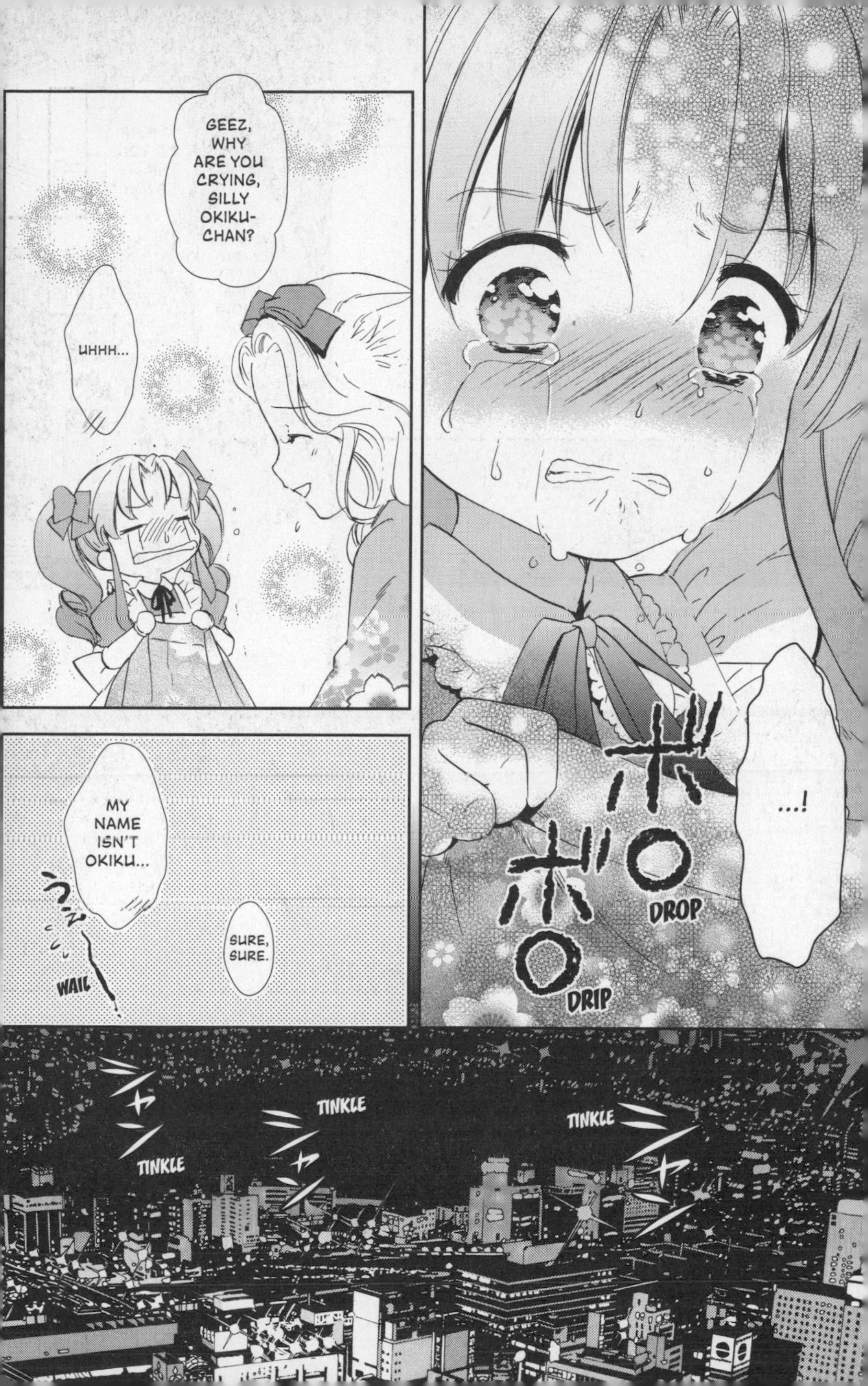
...!
DROP
DRIP
GEEZ, WHY ARE YOU CRYING, SILLY OKIKU-CHAN?
UHHH...
MY NAME ISN'T OKIKU...
WAIL
SURE, SURE.
TINKLE
TINKLE
TINKLE

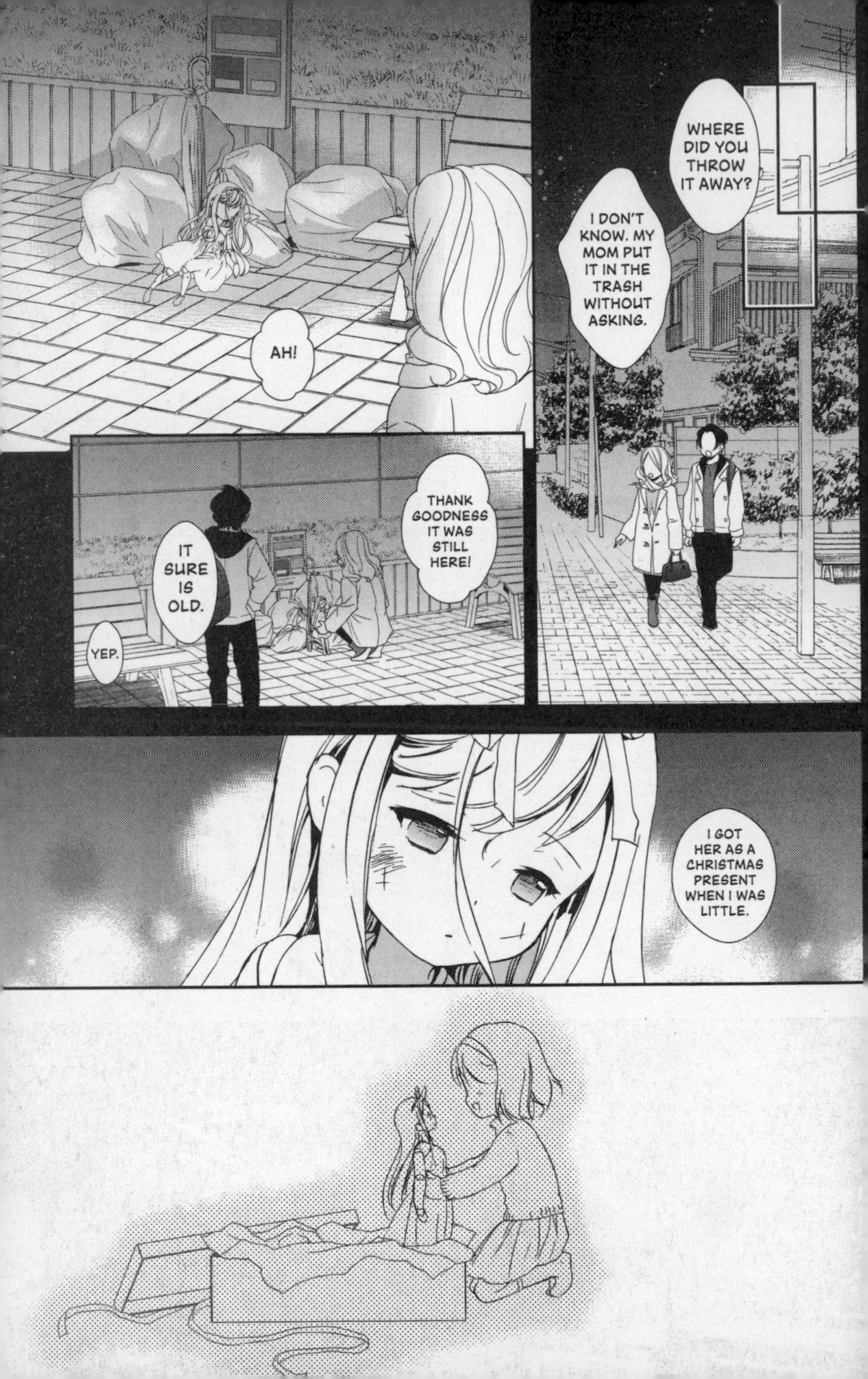
WHERE DID YOU THROW IT AWAY?
I DON'T KNOW. MY MOM PUT IT IN THE TRASH WITHOUT ASKING.
AH!
THANK GOODNESS IT WAS STILL HERE!
IT SURE IS OLD.
YEP.
I GOT HER AS A CHRISTMAS PRESENT WHEN I WAS LITTLE.

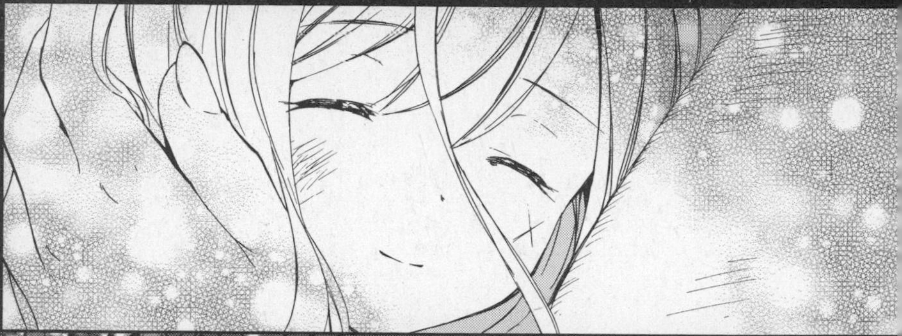

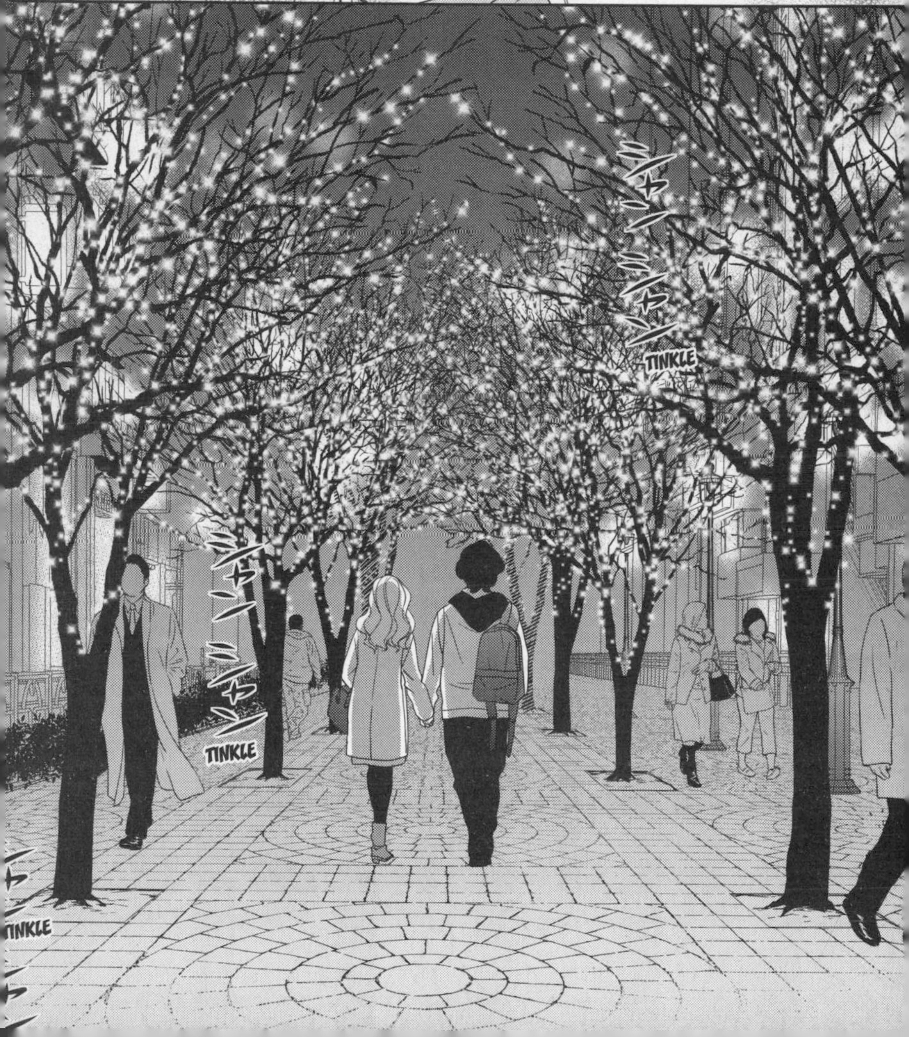
TINKLE
TINKLE
TINKLE

KONOHANA KITAN

Miracle on New Year's Eve

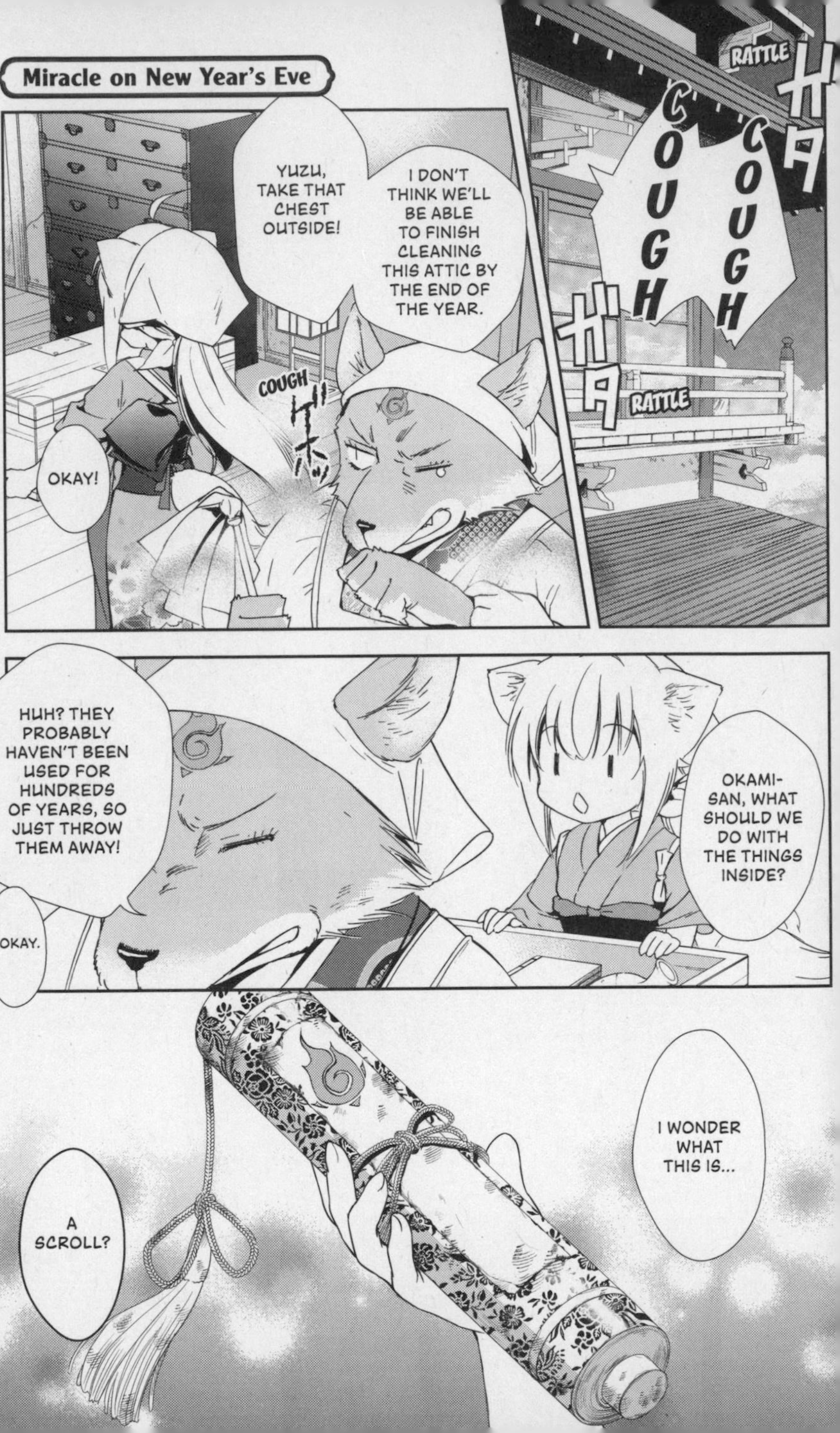
RATTLE
ガタ
COUGH
COUGH
ガタ
RATTLE
I DON'T THINK WE'LL BE ABLE TO FINISH CLEANING THIS ATTIC BY THE END OF THE YEAR.
YUZU, TAKE THAT CHEST OUTSIDE!
COUGH
ゲホッ
OKAY!
OKAMI-SAN, WHAT SHOULD WE DO WITH THE THINGS INSIDE?
HUH? THEY PROBABLY HAVEN'T BEEN USED FOR HUNDREDS OF YEARS, SO JUST THROW THEM AWAY!
...OKAY.
I WONDER WHAT THIS IS...
A SCROLL?

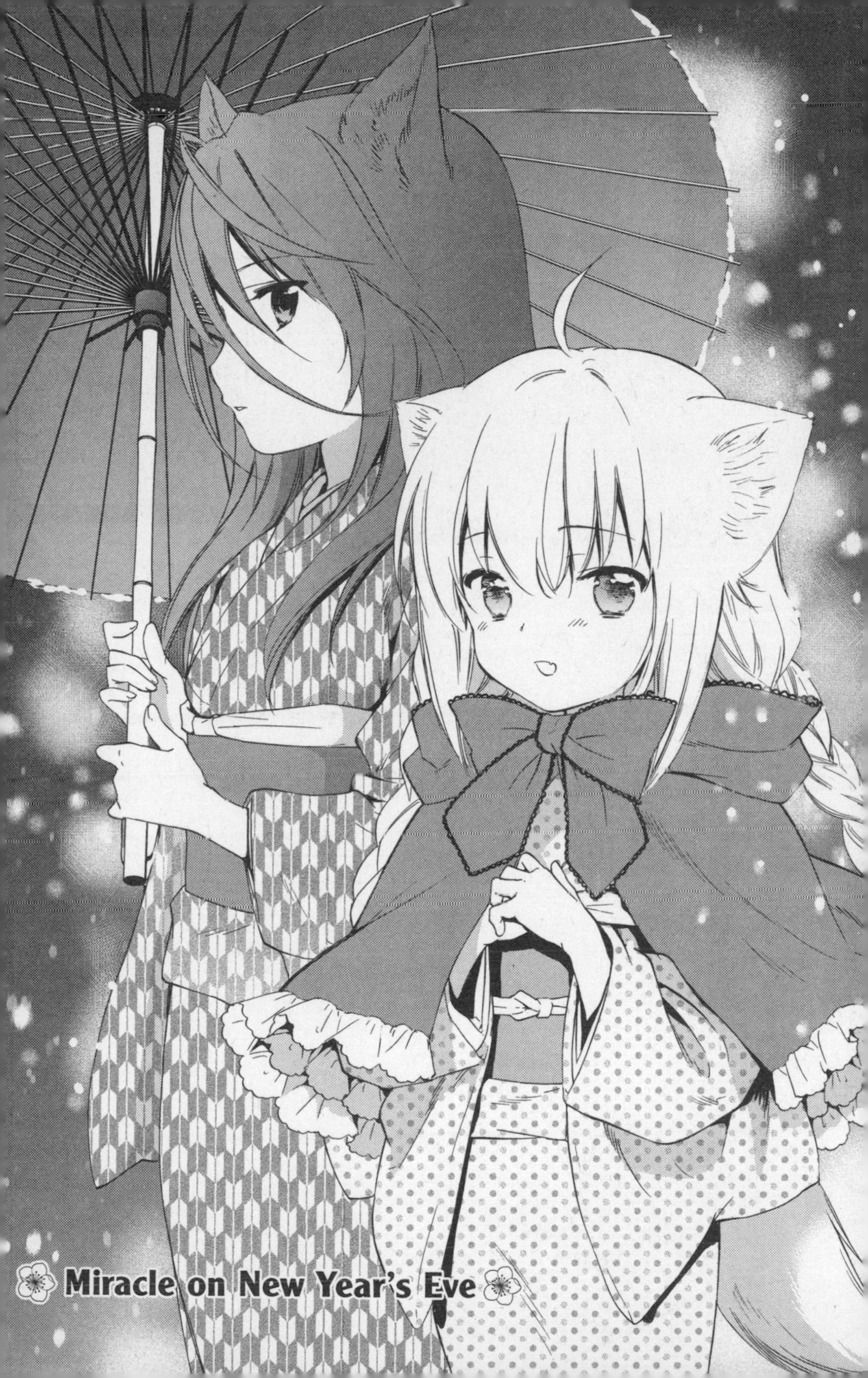

Miracle on New Year's Eve

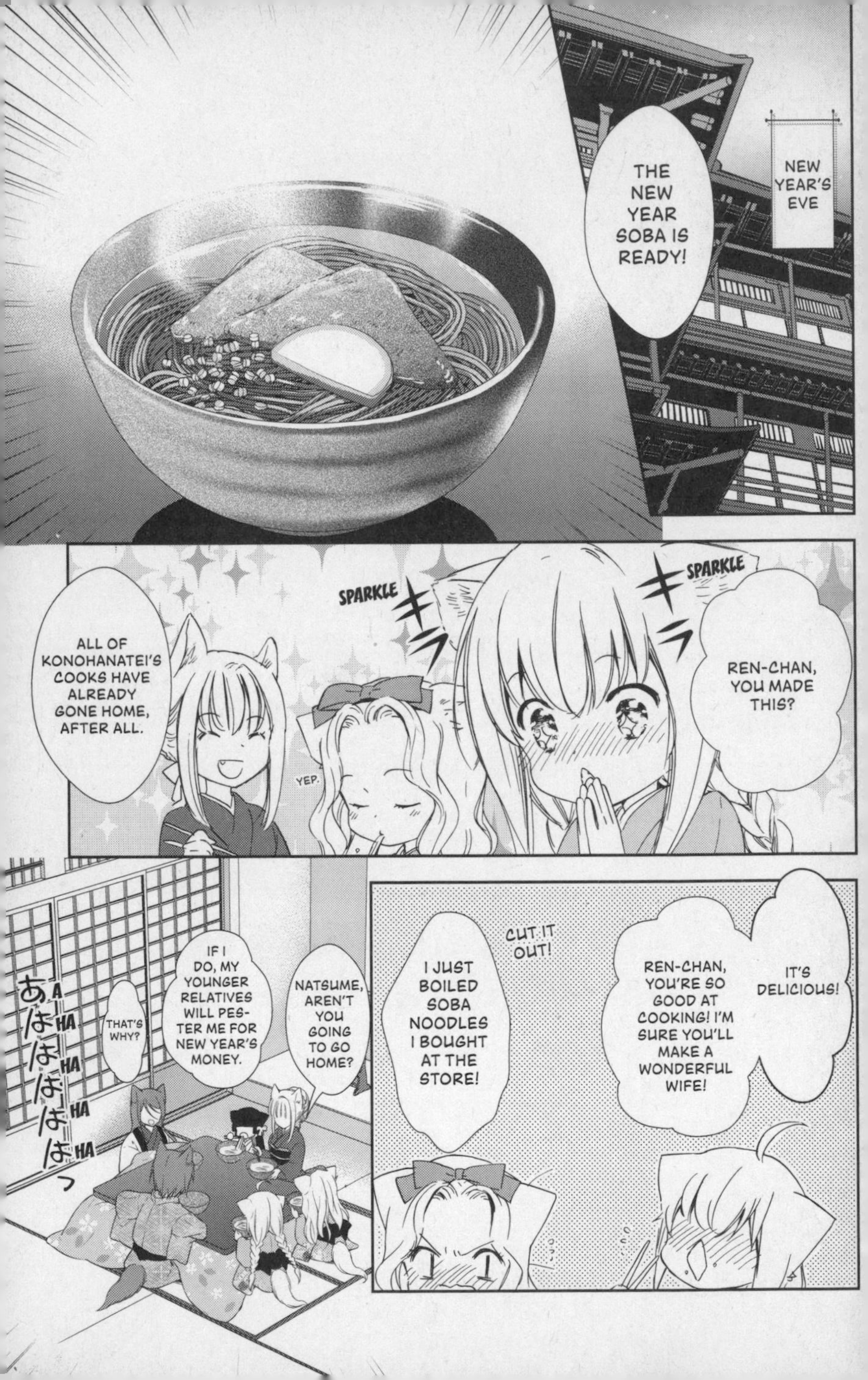
NEW YEAR'S EVE
THE NEW YEAR SOBA IS READY!
SPARKLE
REN-CHAN, YOU MADE THIS?
SPARKLE
YEP.
ALL OF KONOHANATEI'S COOKS HAVE ALREADY GONE HOME, AFTER ALL.
IT'S DELICIOUS!
REN-CHAN, YOU'RE SO GOOD AT COOKING! I'M SURE YOU'LL MAKE A WONDERFUL WIFE!
CUT IT OUT!
I JUST BOILED SOBA NOODLES I BOUGHT AT THE STORE!
NATSUME, AREN'T YOU GOING TO GO HOME?
IF I DO, MY YOUNGER RELATIVES WILL PES-TER ME FOR NEW YEAR'S MONEY.
THAT'S WHY?
あははははっ A HA HA HA HA

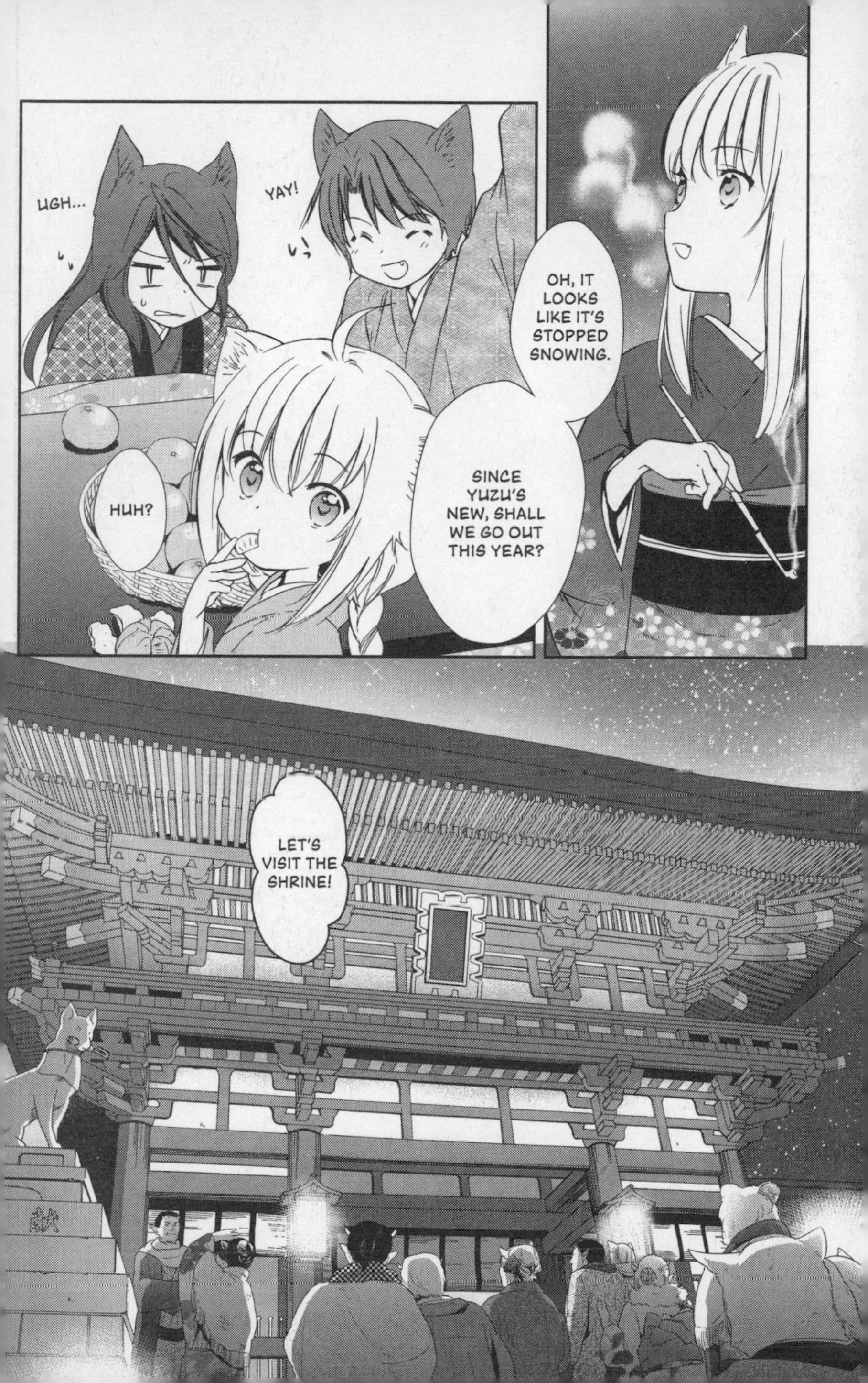
OH, IT LOOKS LIKE IT'S STOPPED SNOWING.
SINCE YUZU'S NEW, SHALL WE GO OUT THIS YEAR?
YAY!
UGH...
HUH?
LET'S VISIT THE SHRINE!

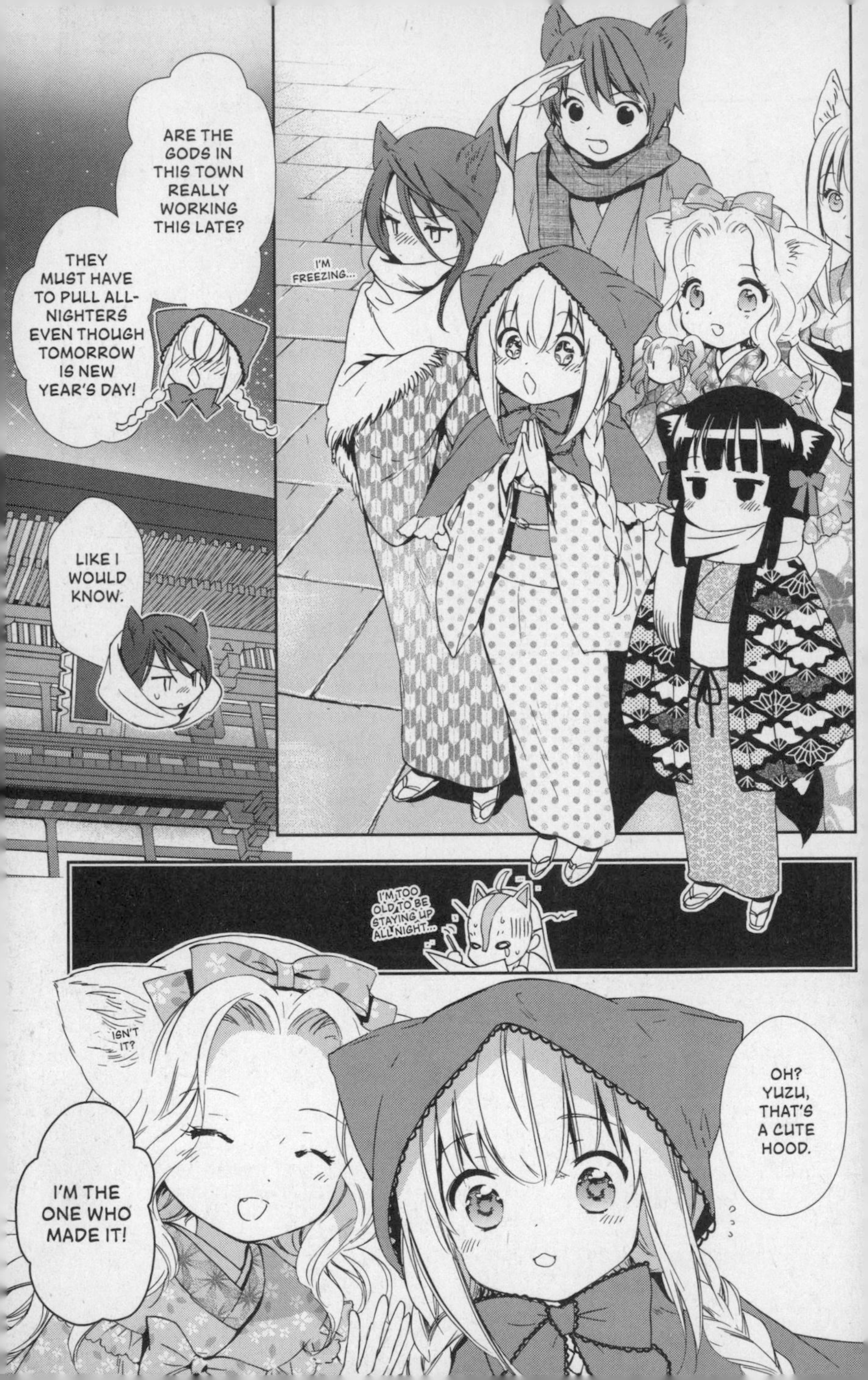
I'M FREEZING...
ARE THE GODS IN THIS TOWN REALLY WORKING THIS LATE?
THEY MUST HAVE TO PULL ALL-NIGHTERS EVEN THOUGH TOMORROW IS NEW YEAR'S DAY!
LIKE I WOULD KNOW.
I'M TOO OLD TO BE STAYING UP ALL NIGHT...
OH? YUZU, THAT'S A CUTE HOOD.
ISN'T IT?
I'M THE ONE WHO MADE IT!

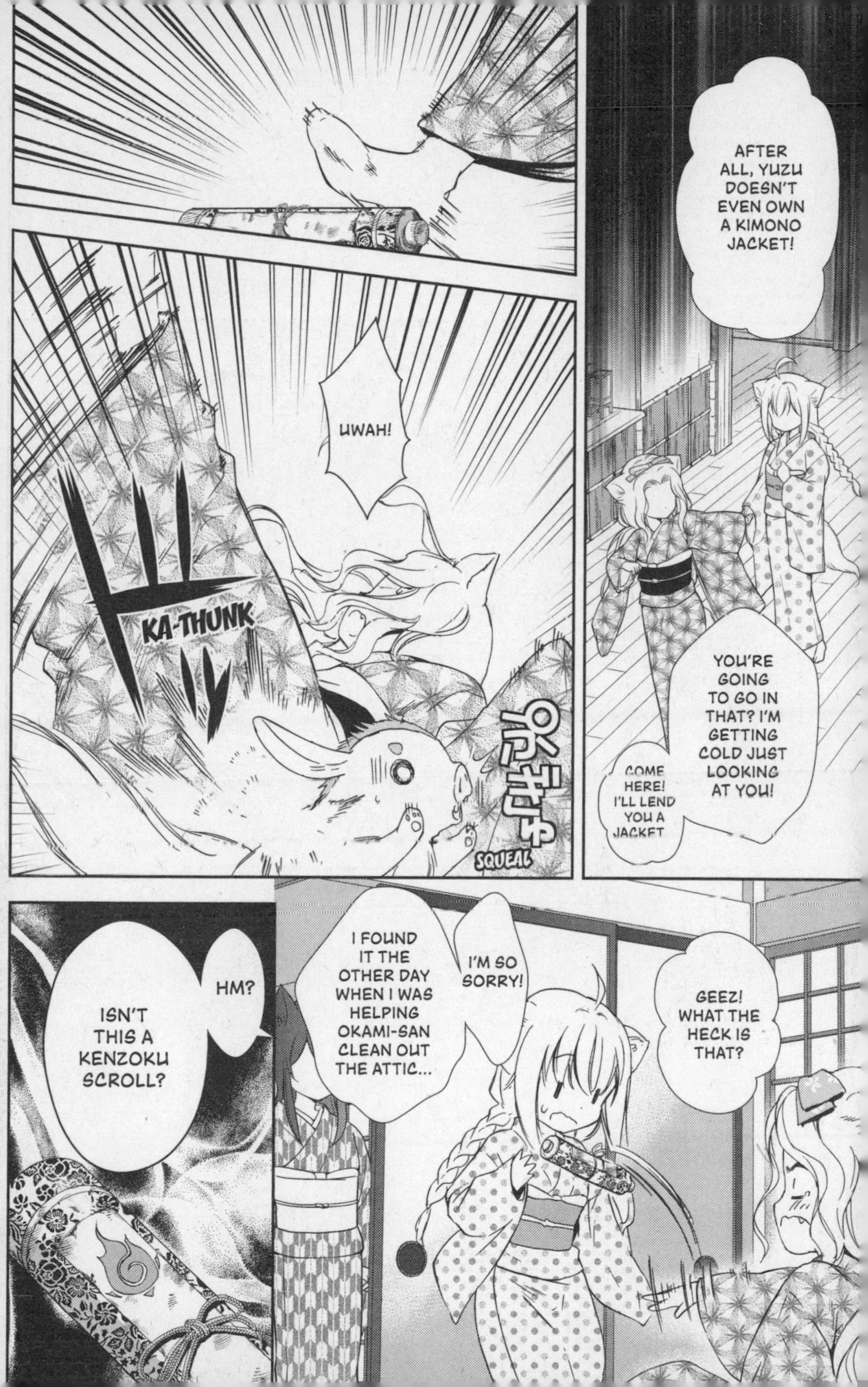
AFTER ALL, YUZU DOESN'T EVEN OWN A KIMONO JACKET!
YOU'RE GOING TO GO IN THAT? I'M GETTING COLD JUST LOOKING AT YOU!
COME HERE! I'LL LEND YOU A JACKET
UWAH!
KA-THUNK
ぴぎゅ
SQUEAL
GEEZ! WHAT THE HECK IS THAT?
I'M SO SORRY!
I FOUND IT THE OTHER DAY WHEN I WAS HELPING OKAMI-SAN CLEAN OUT THE ATTIC...
HM?
ISN'T THIS A KENZOKU SCROLL?

*EACH DEITY HAS DIFFERENT SERVANTS, SUCH AS THE INARI SHRINE HAVING FOXES AND THE ISE GRAND SHRINE HAVING ROOSTERS.

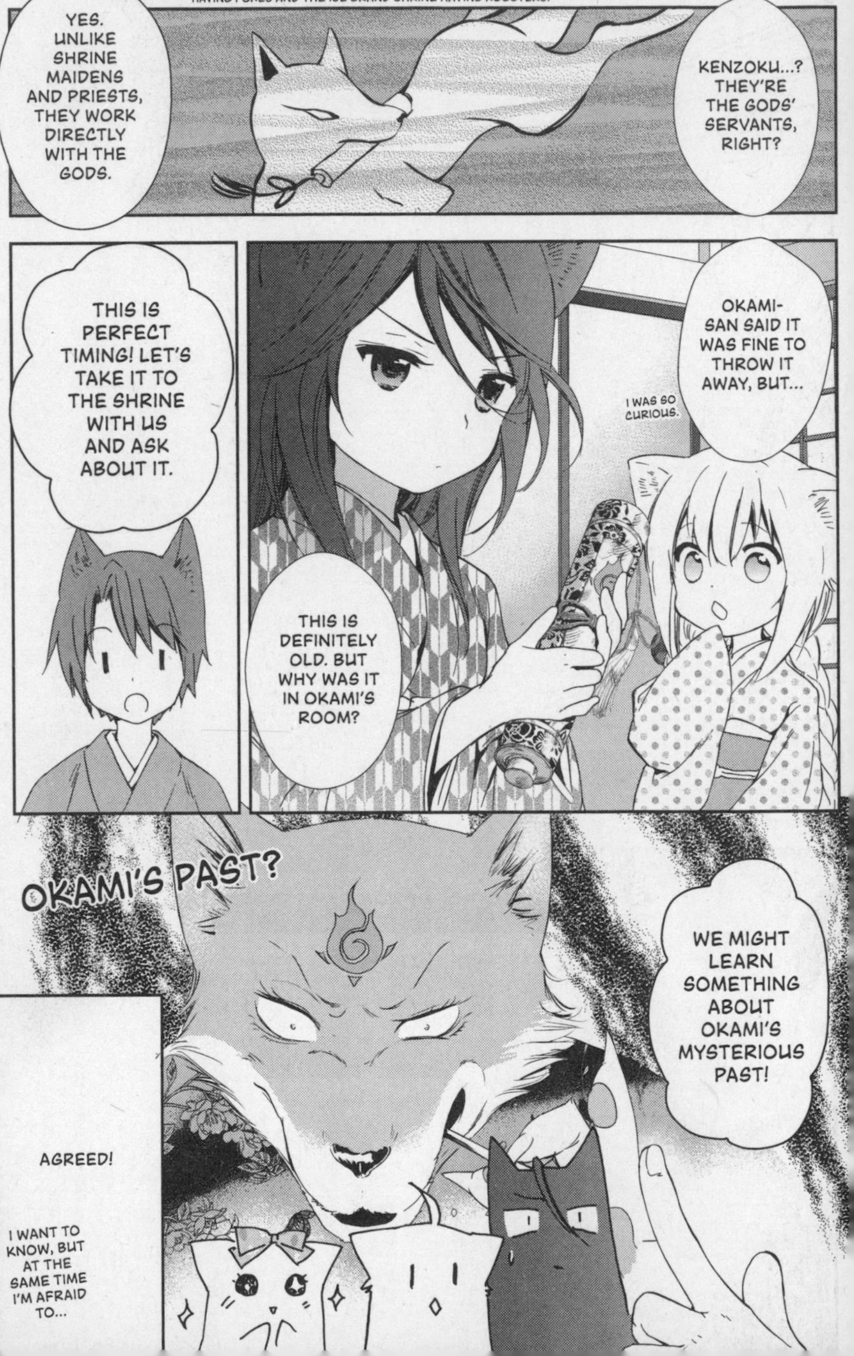
KENZOKU...? THEY'RE THE GODS' SERVANTS, RIGHT?
YES. UNLIKE SHRINE MAIDENS AND PRIESTS, THEY WORK DIRECTLY WITH THE GODS.
OKAMI-SAN SAID IT WAS FINE TO THROW IT AWAY, BUT...
I WAS SO CURIOUS.
THIS IS DEFINITELY OLD. BUT WHY WAS IT IN OKAMI'S ROOM?
THIS IS PERFECT TIMING! LET'S TAKE IT TO THE SHRINE WITH US AND ASK ABOUT IT.
WE MIGHT LEARN SOMETHING ABOUT OKAMI'S MYSTERIOUS PAST!
OKAMI'S PAST?
AGREED!
I WANT TO KNOW, BUT AT THE SAME TIME I'M AFRAID TO...

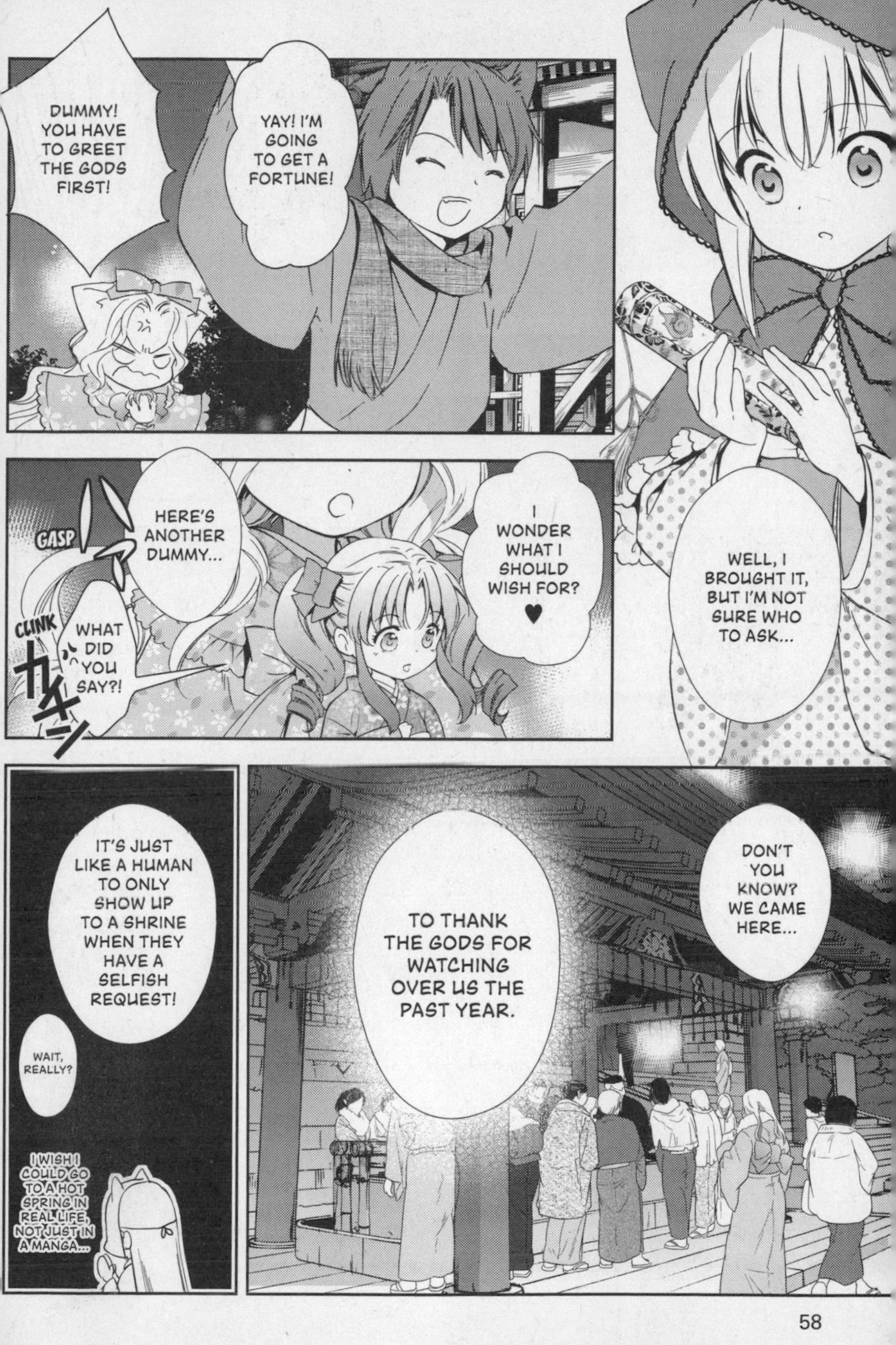
WELL, I BROUGHT IT, BUT I'M NOT SURE WHO TO ASK...
YAY! I'M GOING TO GET A FORTUNE!
DUMMY! YOU HAVE TO GREET THE GODS FIRST!
I WONDER WHAT I SHOULD WISH FOR? ♥
HERE'S ANOTHER DUMMY...
GASP
WHAT DID YOU SAY?!
CLINK
カチーン
DON'T YOU KNOW? WE CAME HERE...
TO THANK THE GODS FOR WATCHING OVER US THE PAST YEAR.
IT'S JUST LIKE A HUMAN TO ONLY SHOW UP TO A SHRINE WHEN THEY HAVE A SELFISH REQUEST!
WAIT, REALLY?
I WISH I COULD GO TO A HOT SPRING IN REAL LIFE, NOT JUST IN A MANGA...

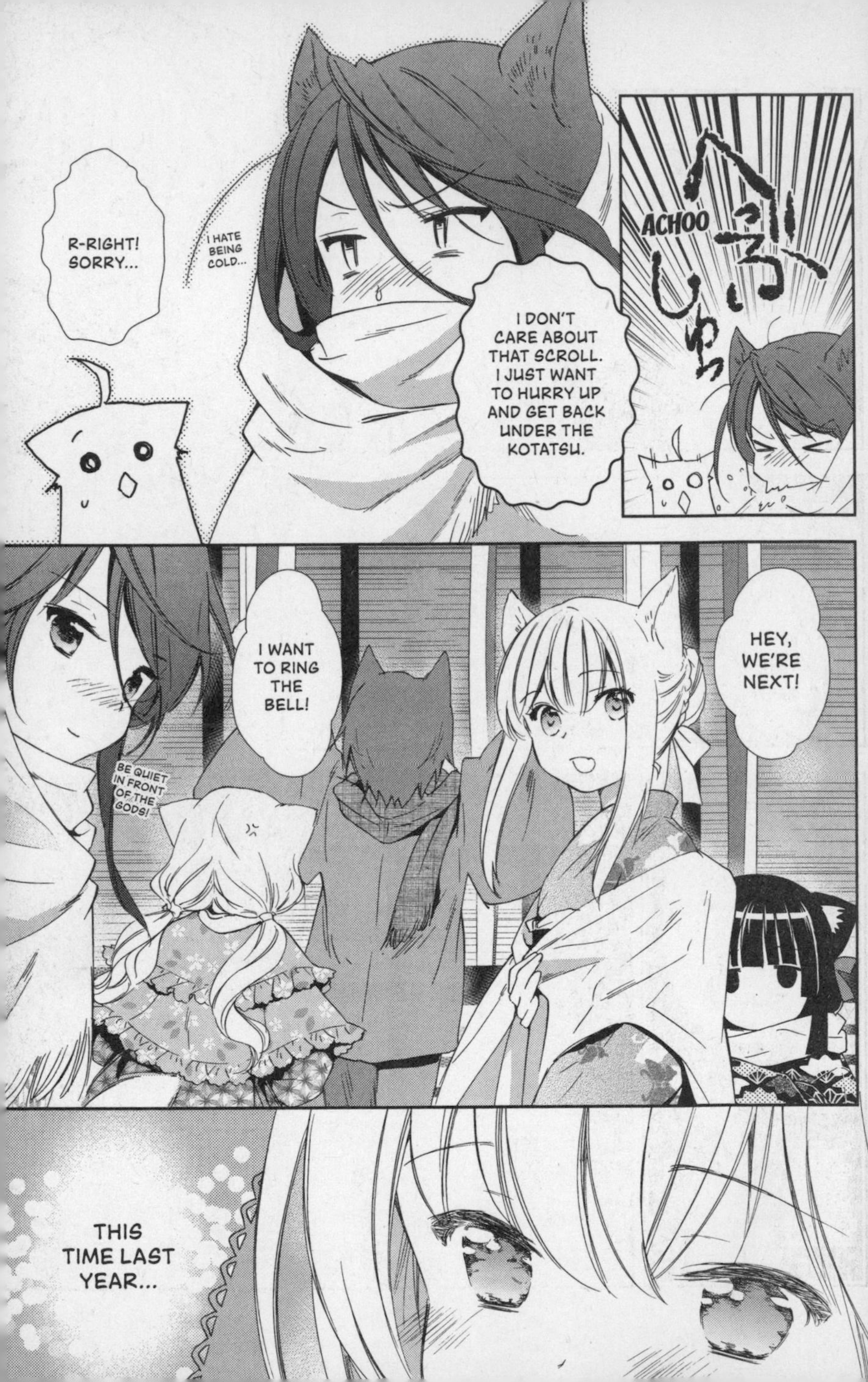
ACHOO
I DON'T CARE ABOUT THAT SCROLL. I JUST WANT TO HURRY UP AND GET BACK UNDER THE KOTATSU.
I HATE BEING COLD...
R-RIGHT! SORRY...
HEY, WE'RE NEXT!
I WANT TO RING THE BELL!
BE QUIET IN FRONT OF THE GODS!
THIS TIME LAST YEAR...

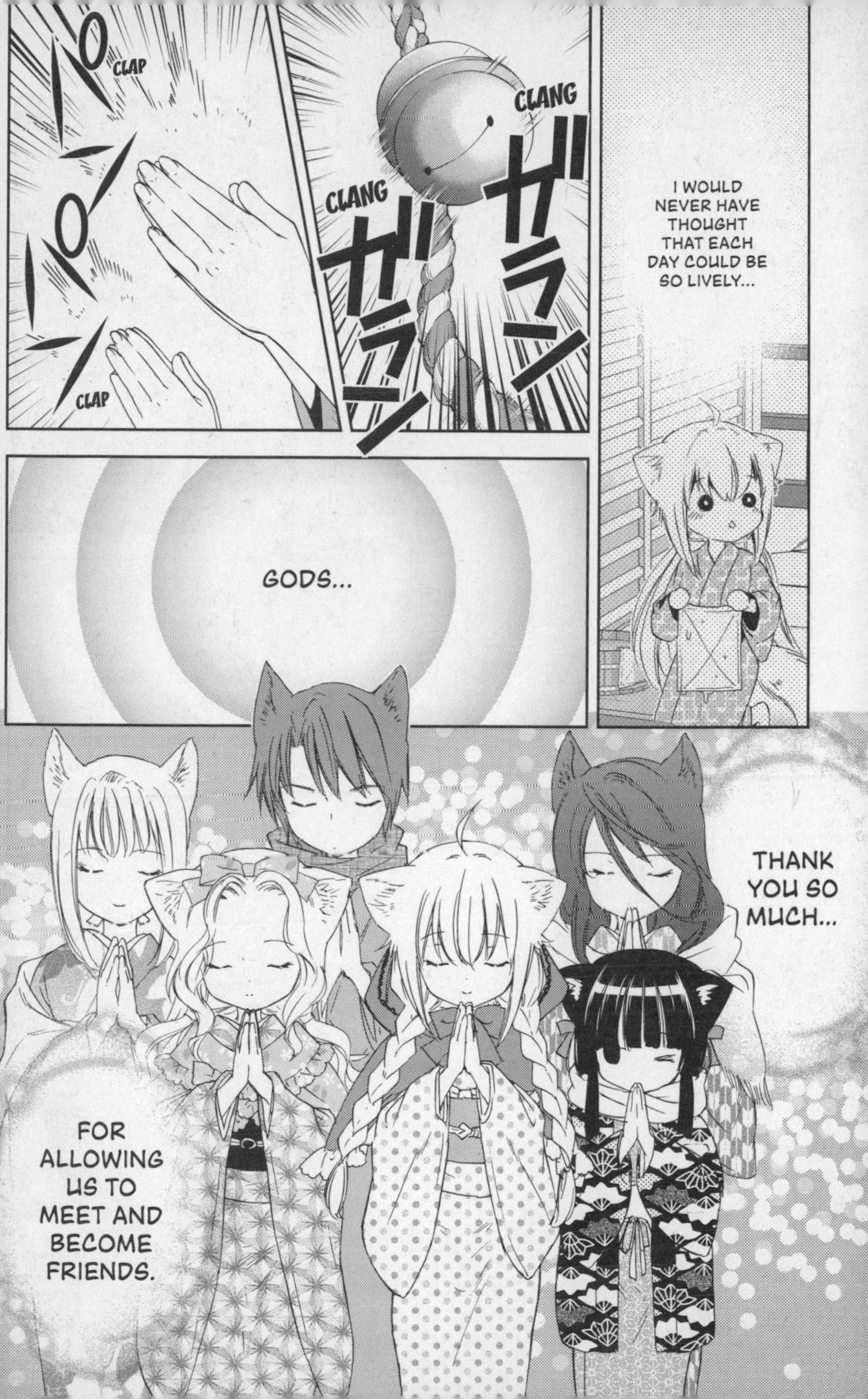
I WOULD NEVER HAVE THOUGHT THAT EACH DAY COULD BE SO LIVELY...
ガラン
CLANG
ガラン
CLANG
パン
CLAP
パン
CLAP
GODS...
THANK YOU SO MUCH...
FOR ALLOWING US TO MEET AND BECOME FRIENDS.

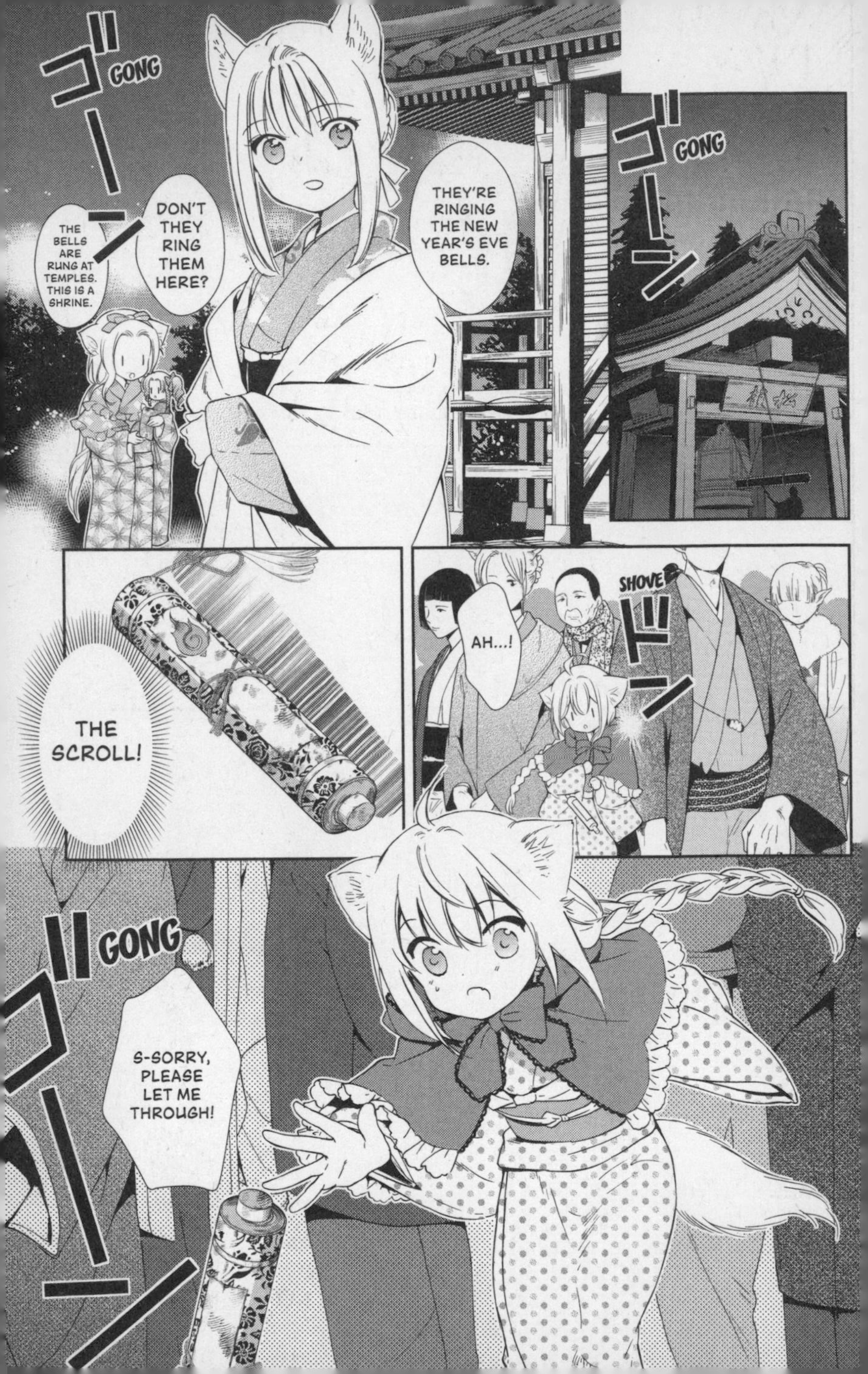
GONG
GONG
THEY'RE RINGING THE NEW YEAR'S EVE BELLS.
DON'T THEY RING THEM HERE?
THE BELLS ARE RUNG AT TEMPLES. THIS IS A SHRINE.
SHOVE
AH...!
THE SCROLL!
GONG
S-SORRY, PLEASE LET ME THROUGH!

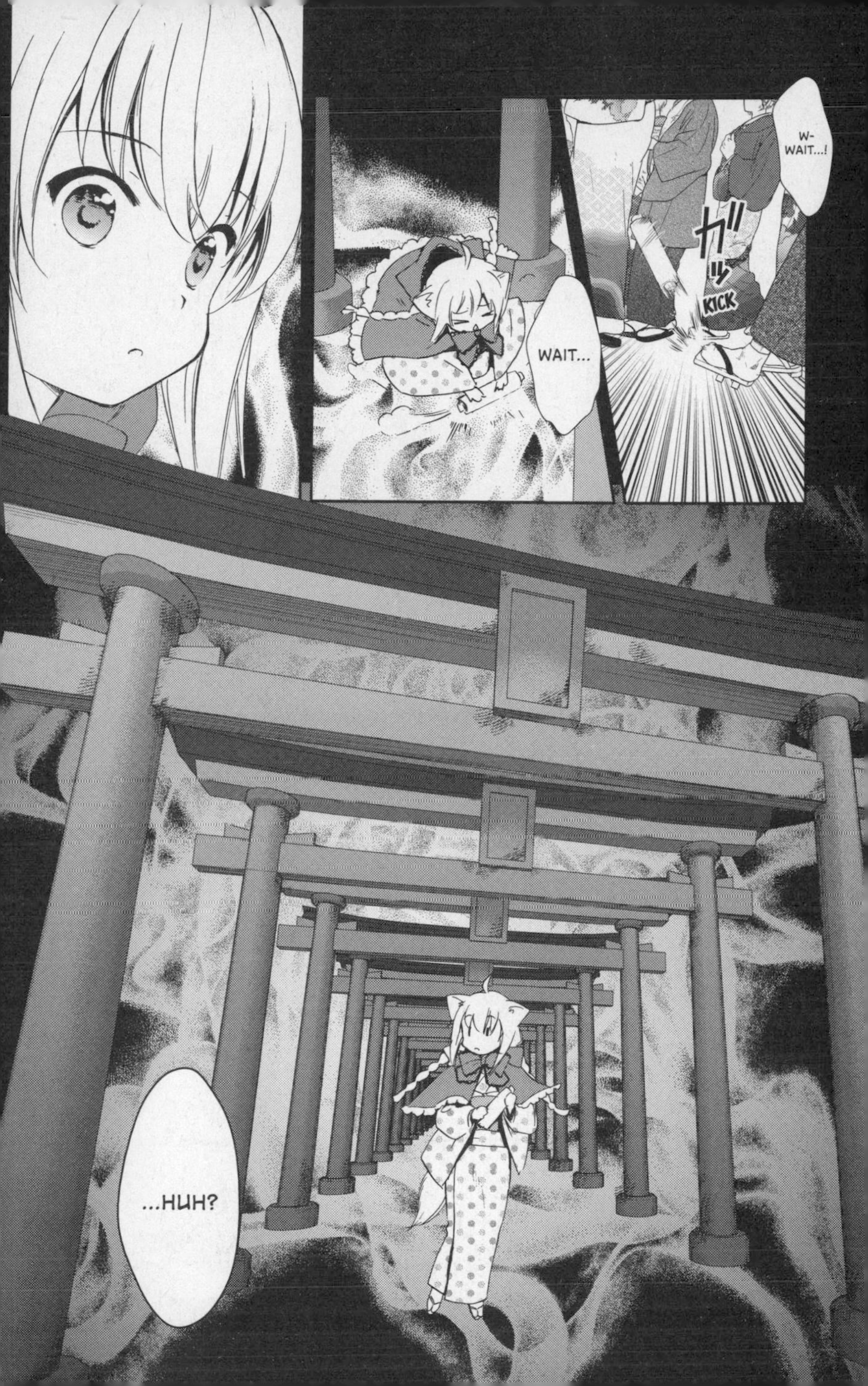
W-
WAIT...!
ガッ
KICK
WAIT...
...HUH?

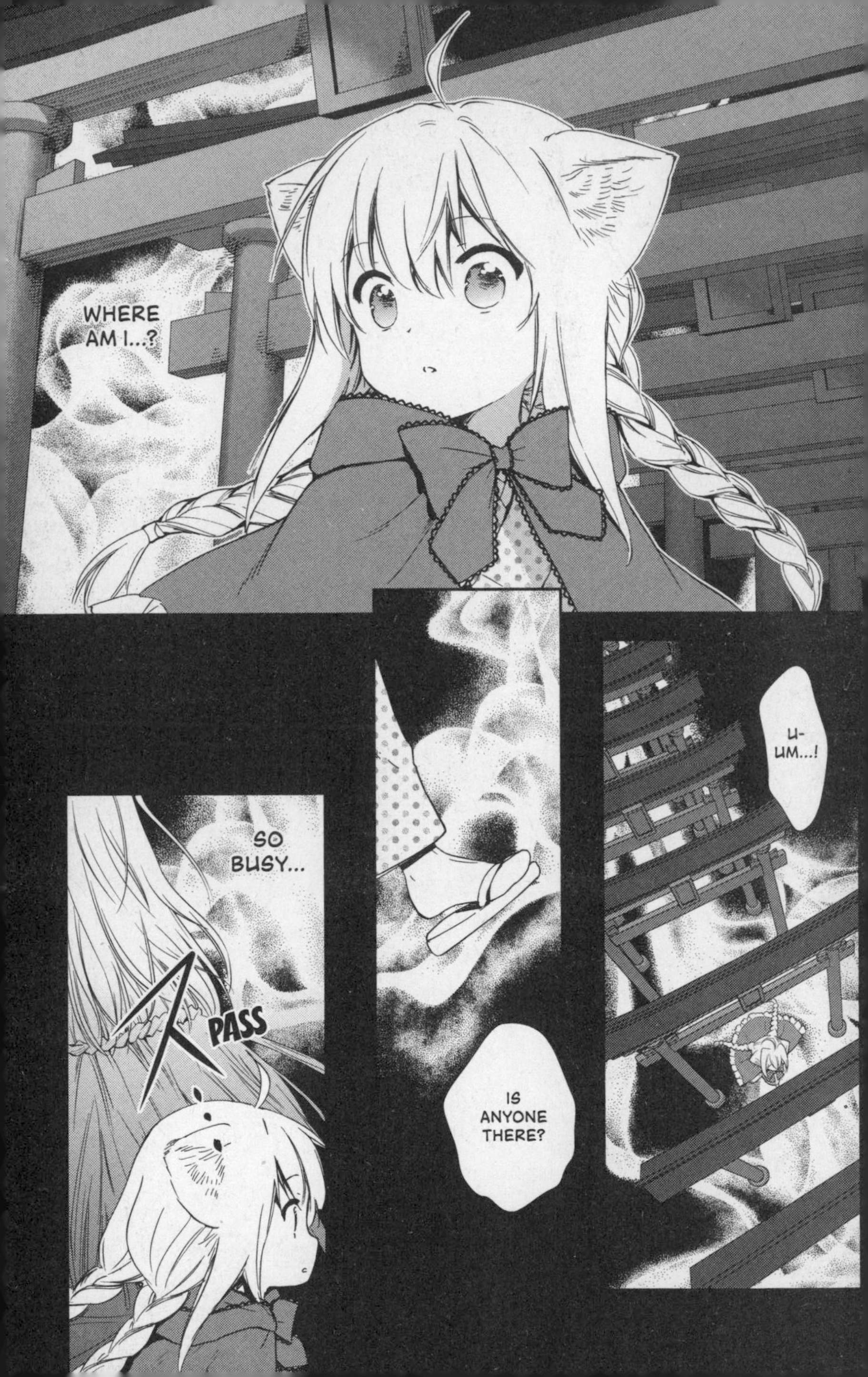
WHERE AM I...?
U-UM...!
IS ANYONE THERE?
SO BUSY...
PASS

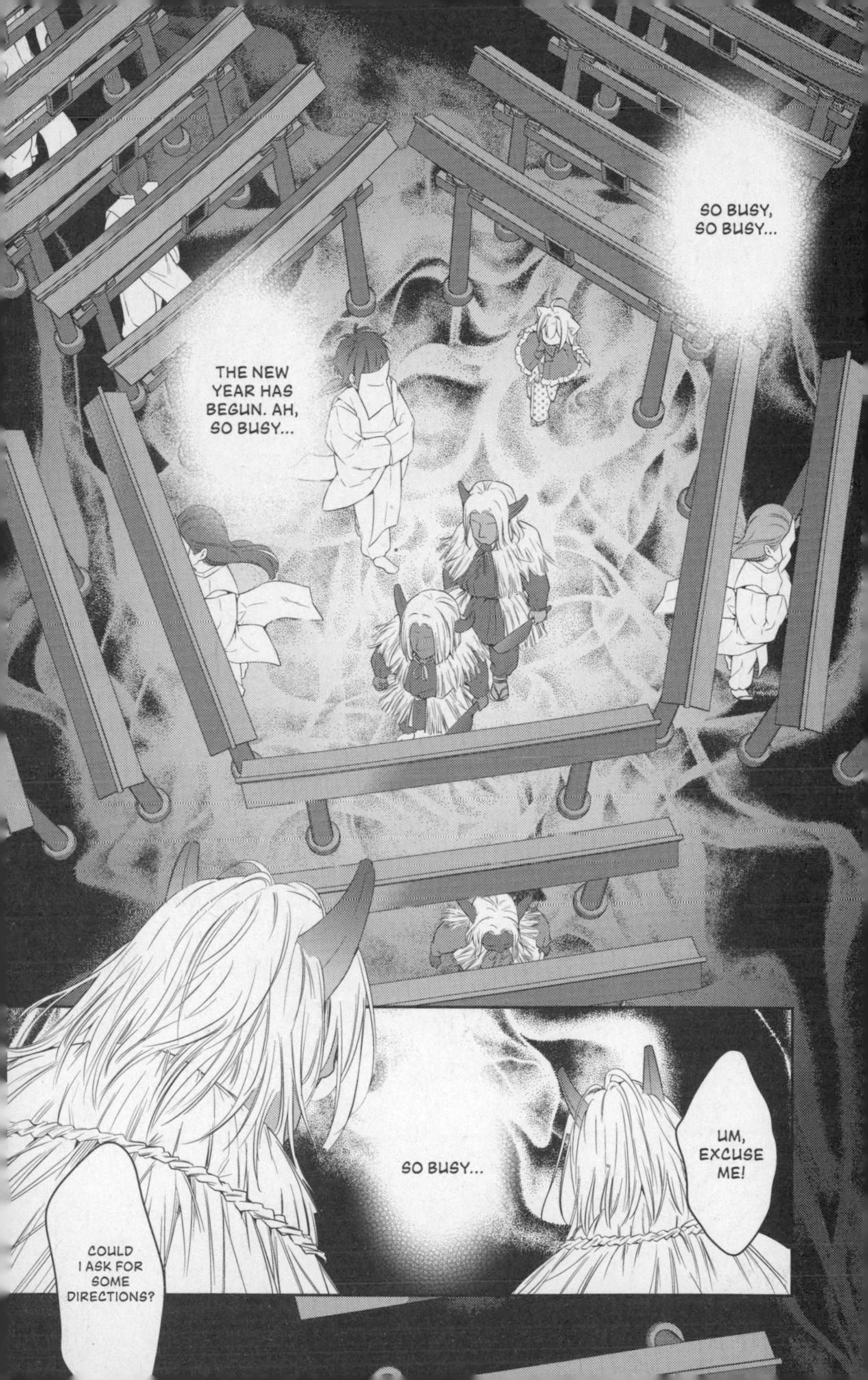
SO BUSY, SO BUSY...
THE NEW YEAR HAS BEGUN. AH, SO BUSY...
UM, EXCUSE ME!
SO BUSY...
COULD I ASK FOR SOME DIRECTIONS?

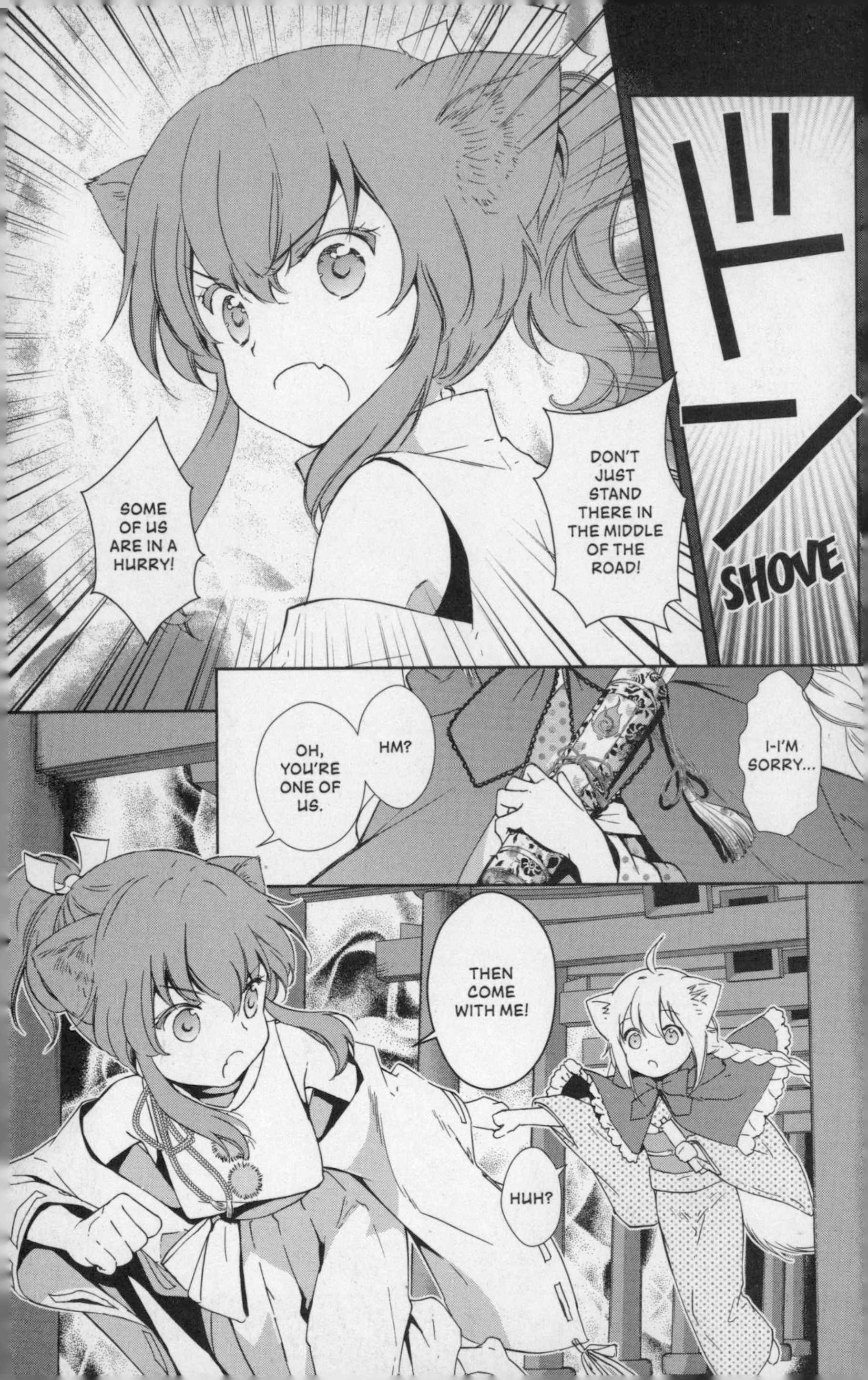
SHOVE
DON'T JUST STAND THERE IN THE MIDDLE OF THE ROAD!
SOME OF US ARE IN A HURRY!
I-I'M SORRY...
HM?
OH, YOU'RE ONE OF US.
THEN COME WITH ME!
HUH?

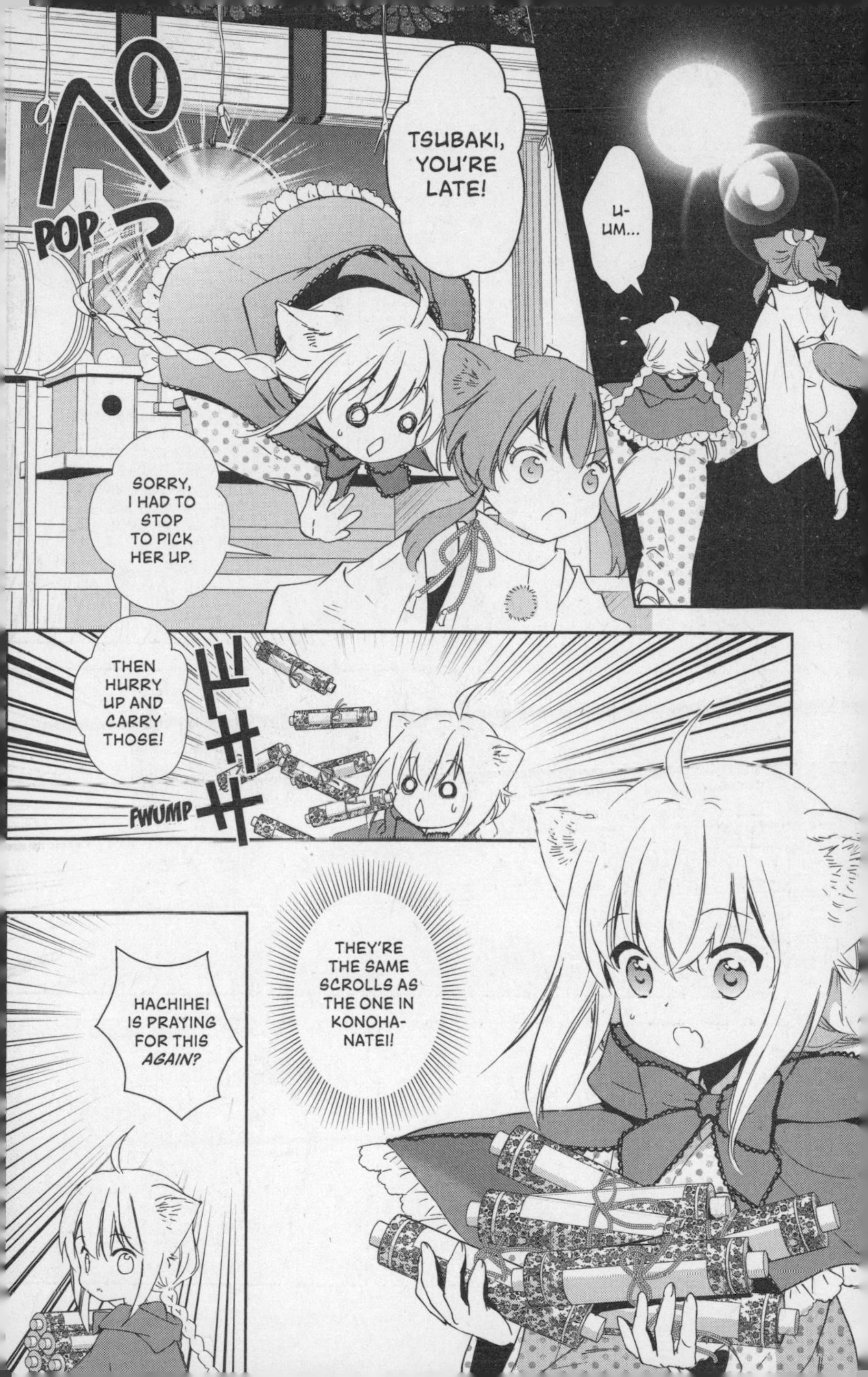
U-UM...
TSUBAKI, YOU'RE LATE!
POP
SORRY, I HAD TO STOP TO PICK HER UP.
THEN HURRY UP AND CARRY THOSE!
FWUMP
THEY'RE THE SAME SCROLLS AS THE ONE IN KONOHA-NATEI!
HACHIHEI IS PRAYING FOR THIS *AGAIN?*

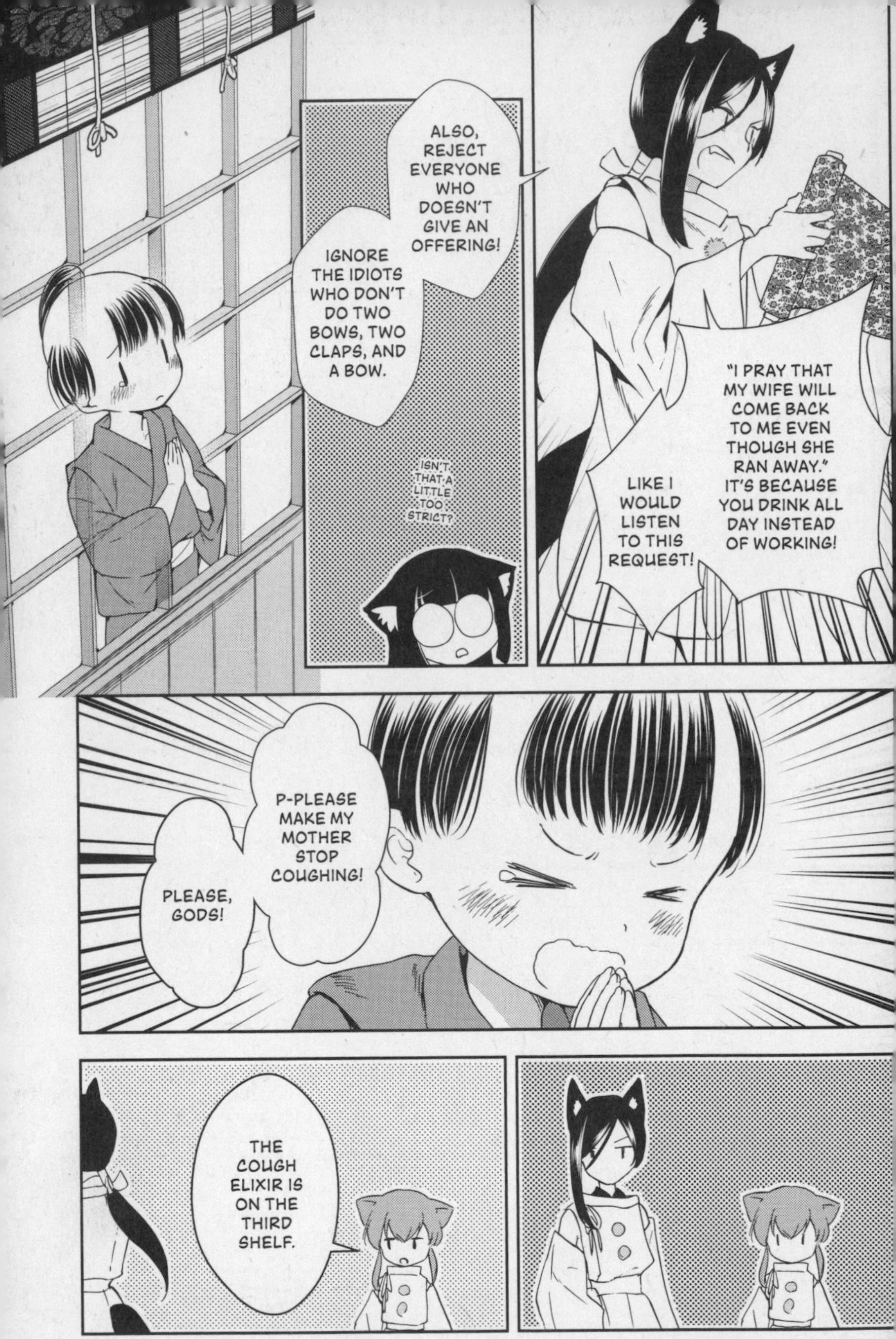
"I PRAY THAT MY WIFE WILL COME BACK TO ME EVEN THOUGH SHE RAN AWAY." IT'S BECAUSE YOU DRINK ALL DAY INSTEAD OF WORKING!
LIKE I WOULD LISTEN TO THIS REQUEST!
ALSO, REJECT EVERYONE WHO DOESN'T GIVE AN OFFERING!
IGNORE THE IDIOTS WHO DON'T DO TWO BOWS, TWO CLAPS, AND A BOW.
ISN'T THAT A LITTLE TOO STRICT?
P-PLEASE MAKE MY MOTHER STOP COUGHING!
PLEASE, GODS!
THE COUGH ELIXIR IS ON THE THIRD SHELF.

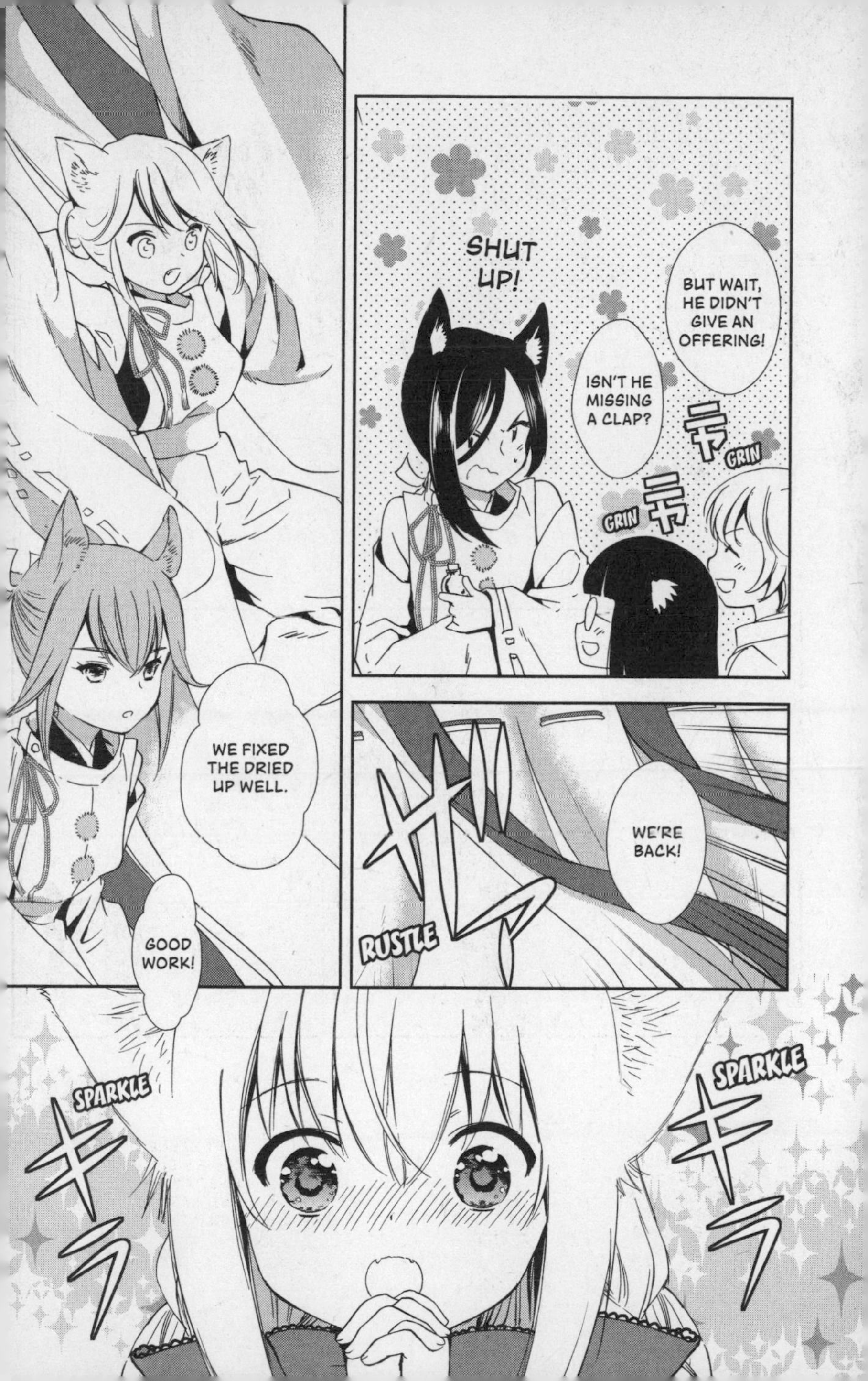
BUT WAIT, HE DIDN'T GIVE AN OFFERING!
ISN'T HE MISSING A CLAP?
SHUT UP!
GRIN
GRIN
WE'RE BACK!
RUSTLE
WE FIXED THE DRIED UP WELL.
GOOD WORK!
SPARKLE
SPARKLE

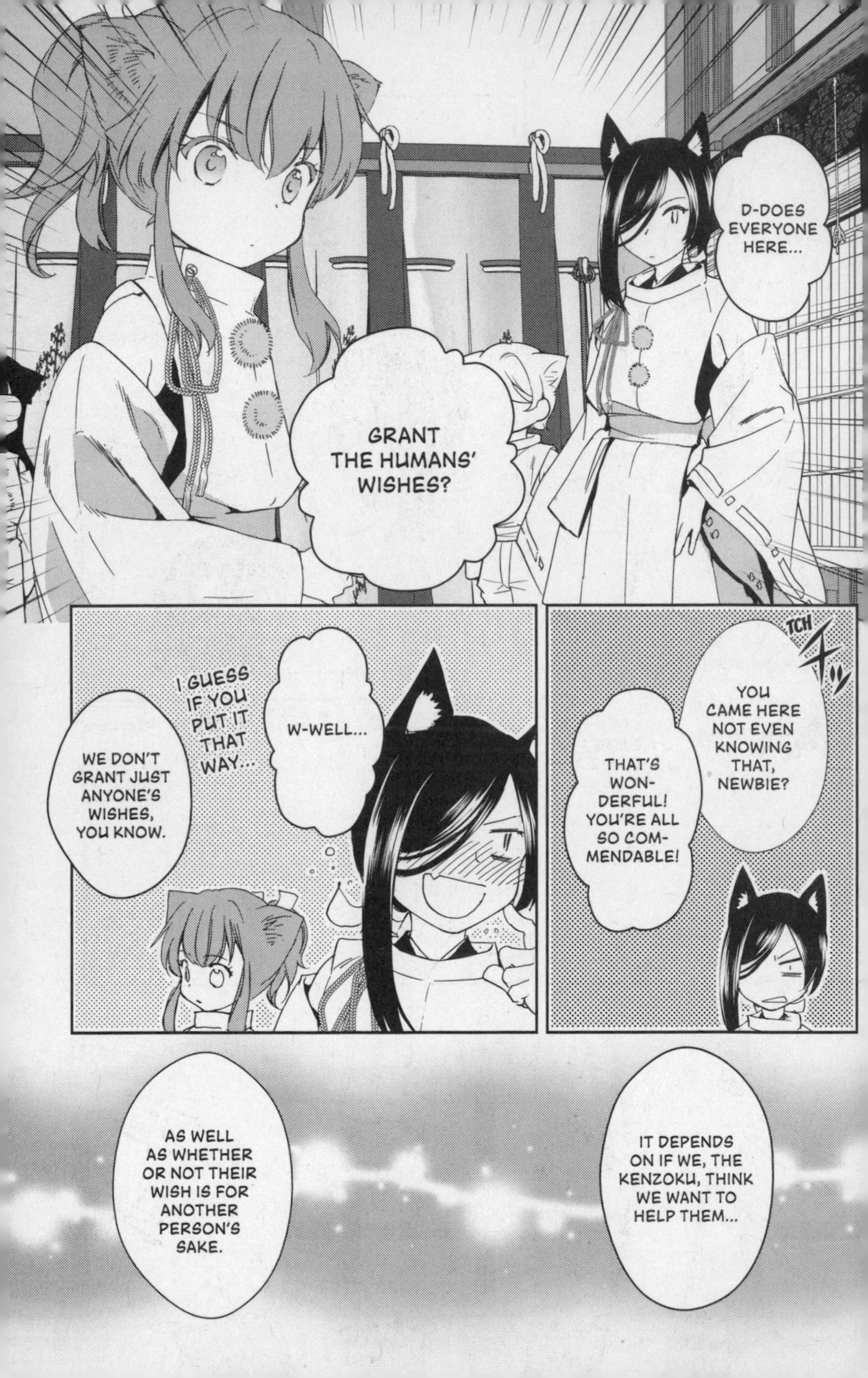

D-DOES EVERYONE HERE...
GRANT THE HUMANS' WISHES?
TCH
YOU CAME HERE NOT EVEN KNOWING THAT, NEWBIE?
THAT'S WONDERFUL! YOU'RE ALL SO COMMENDABLE!
W-WELL...
I GUESS IF YOU PUT IT THAT WAY...
WE DON'T GRANT JUST ANYONE'S WISHES, YOU KNOW.
IT DEPENDS ON IF WE, THE KENZOKU, THINK WE WANT TO HELP THEM...
AS WELL AS WHETHER OR NOT THEIR WISH IS FOR ANOTHER PERSON'S SAKE.

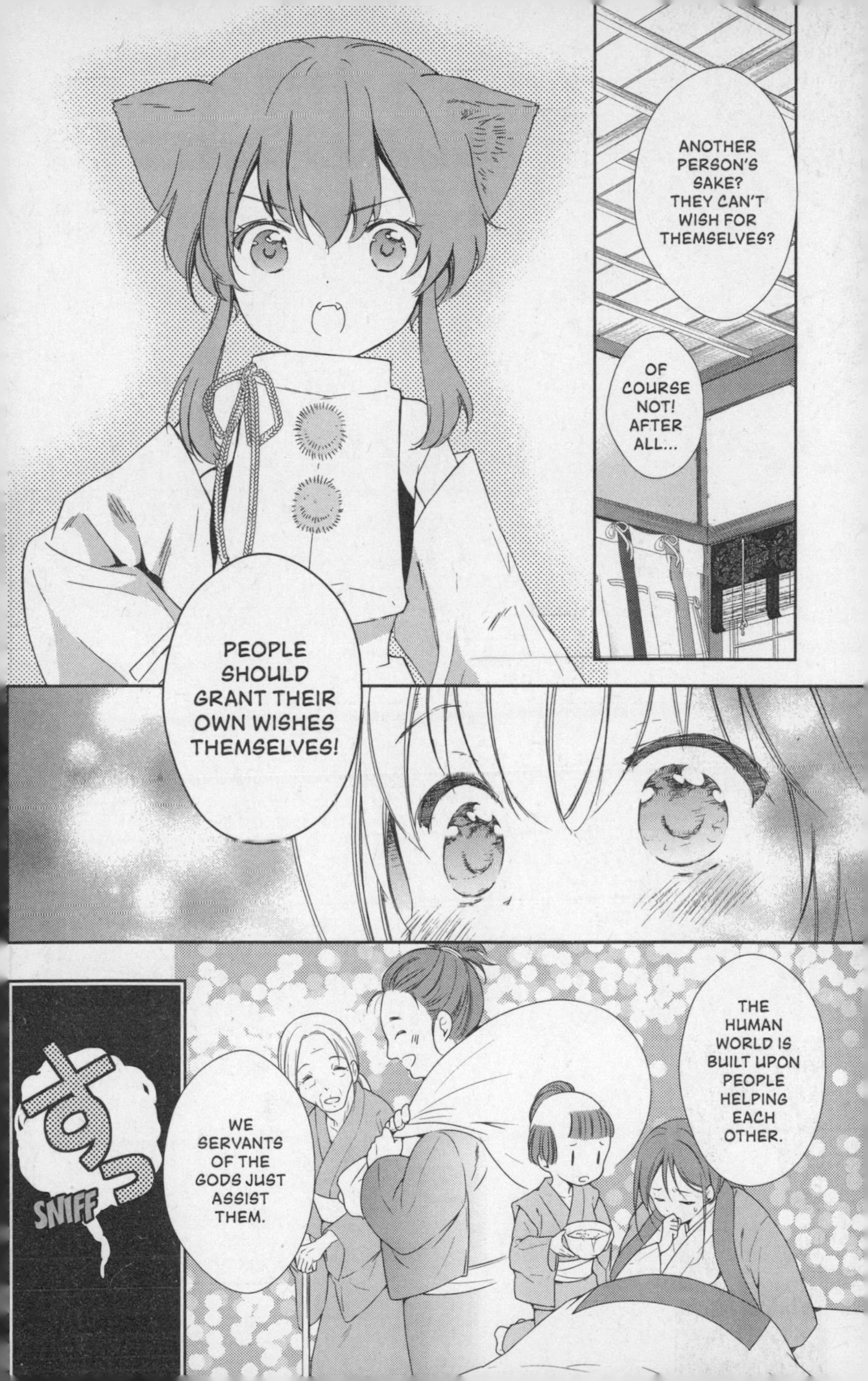
ANOTHER PERSON'S SAKE? THEY CAN'T WISH FOR THEMSELVES?
OF COURSE NOT! AFTER ALL...
PEOPLE SHOULD GRANT THEIR OWN WISHES THEMSELVES!
THE HUMAN WORLD IS BUILT UPON PEOPLE HELPING EACH OTHER.
WE SERVANTS OF THE GODS JUST ASSIST THEM.
すん
SNIFF

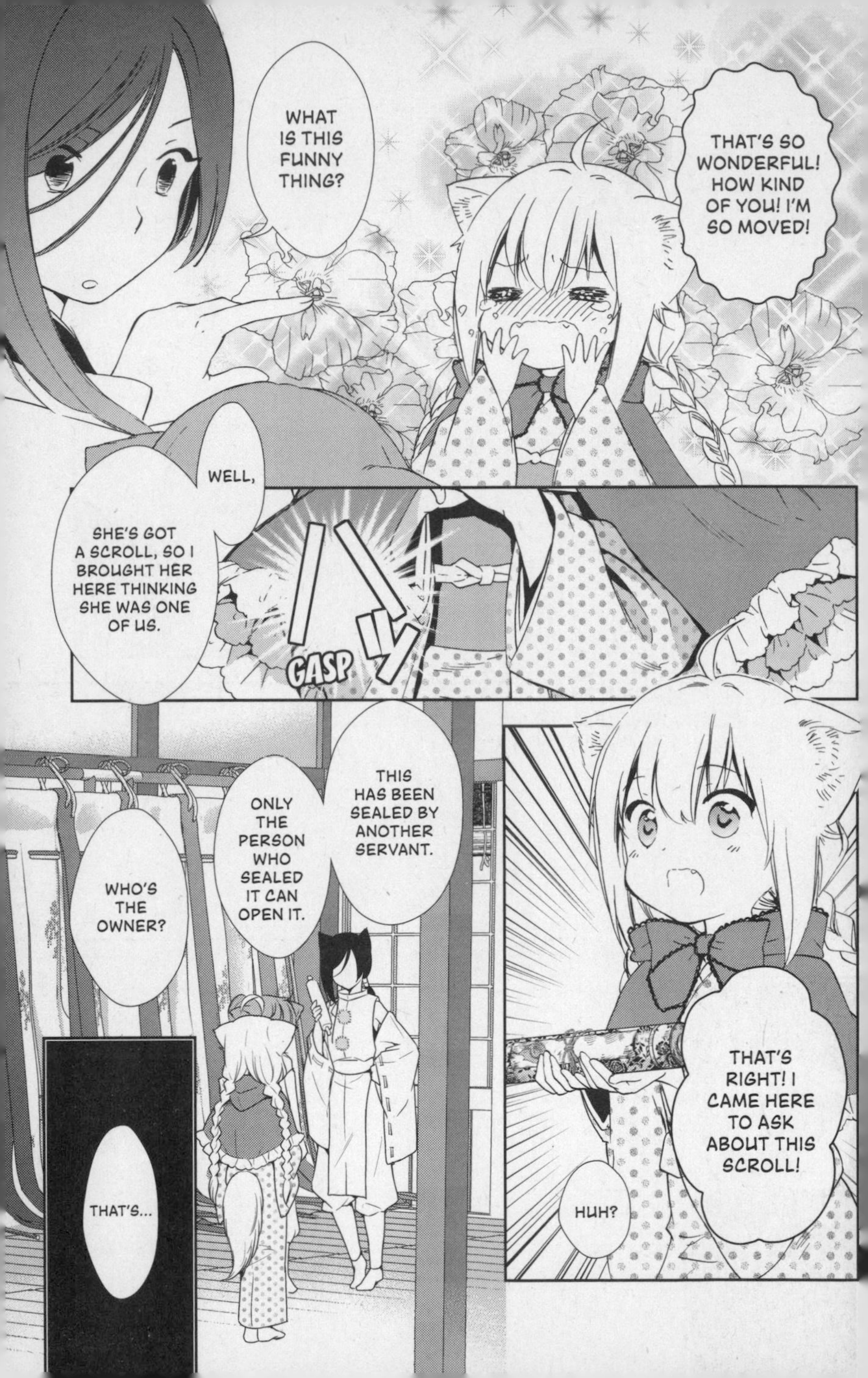
THAT'S SO WONDERFUL! HOW KIND OF YOU! I'M SO MOVED!
WHAT IS THIS FUNNY THING?
WELL,
SHE'S GOT A SCROLL, SO I BROUGHT HER HERE THINKING SHE WAS ONE OF US.
GASP
THAT'S RIGHT! I CAME HERE TO ASK ABOUT THIS SCROLL!
HUH?
THIS HAS BEEN SEALED BY ANOTHER SERVANT.
ONLY THE PERSON WHO SEALED IT CAN OPEN IT.
WHO'S THE OWNER?
THAT'S...

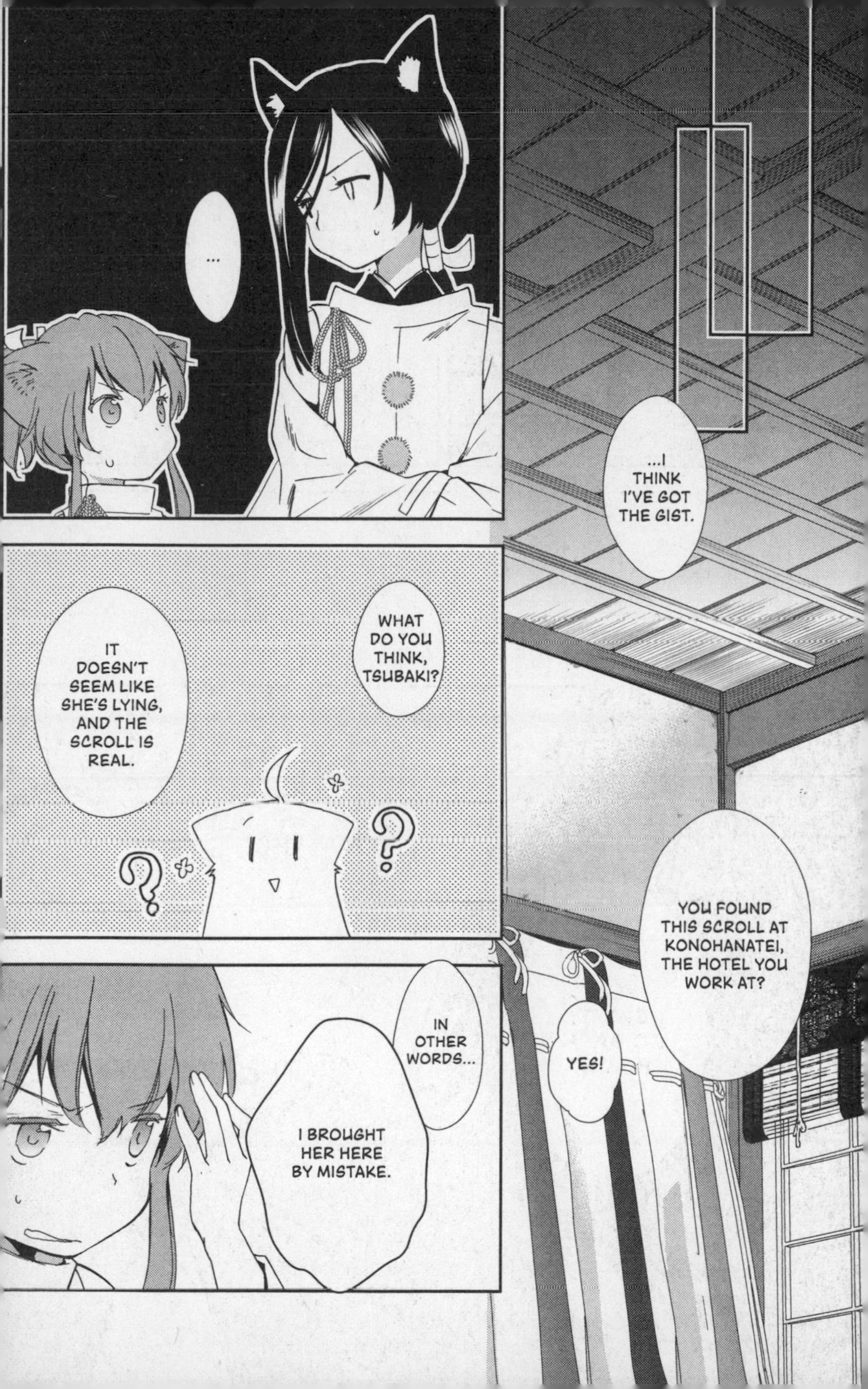
...I THINK I'VE GOT THE GIST.
YOU FOUND THIS SCROLL AT KONOHANATEI, THE HOTEL YOU WORK AT?
YES!
...
WHAT DO YOU THINK, TSUBAKI?
IT DOESN'T SEEM LIKE SHE'S LYING, AND THE SCROLL IS REAL.
IN OTHER WORDS...
I BROUGHT HER HERE BY MISTAKE.

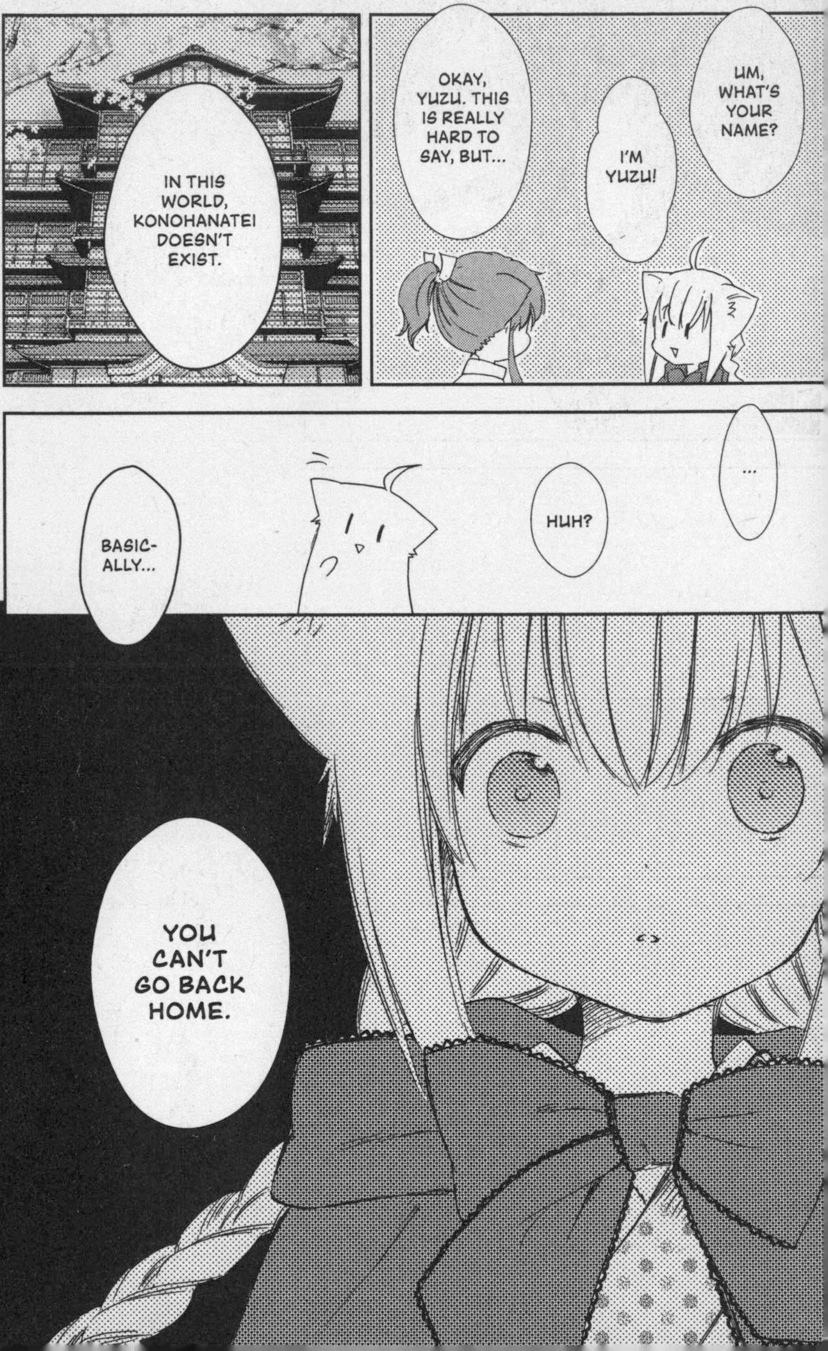
UM, WHAT'S YOUR NAME?
I'M YUZU!
OKAY, YUZU. THIS IS REALLY HARD TO SAY, BUT...
IN THIS WORLD, KONOHANATEI DOESN'T EXIST.
...
HUH?
BASIC-ALLY...
YOU CAN'T GO BACK HOME.

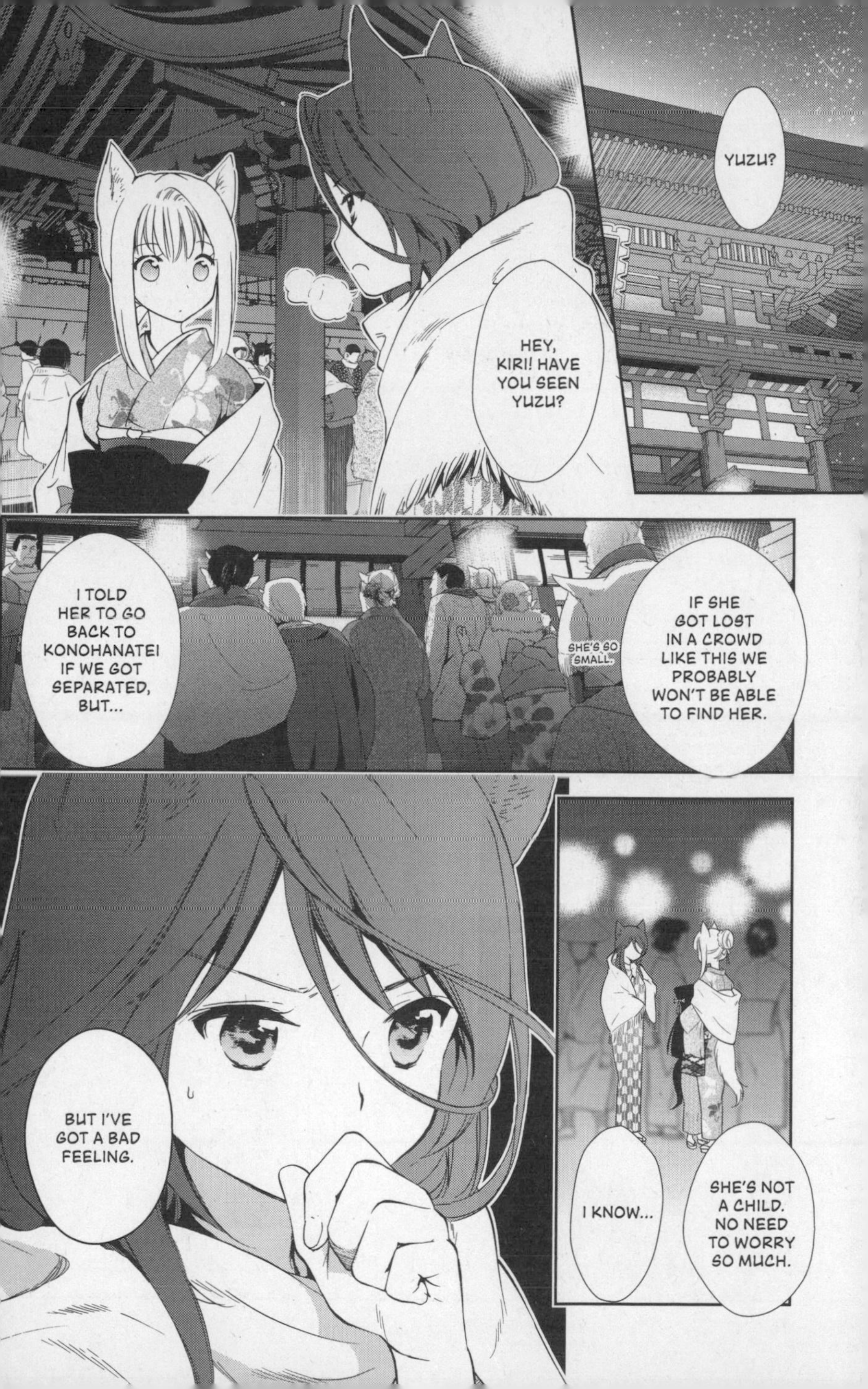
YUZU?
HEY, KIRI! HAVE YOU SEEN YUZU?
IF SHE GOT LOST IN A CROWD LIKE THIS WE PROBABLY WON'T BE ABLE TO FIND HER.
SHE'S SO SMALL.
I TOLD HER TO GO BACK TO KONOHANATEI IF WE GOT SEPARATED, BUT...
SHE'S NOT A CHILD. NO NEED TO WORRY SO MUCH.
I KNOW...
BUT I'VE GOT A BAD FEELING.

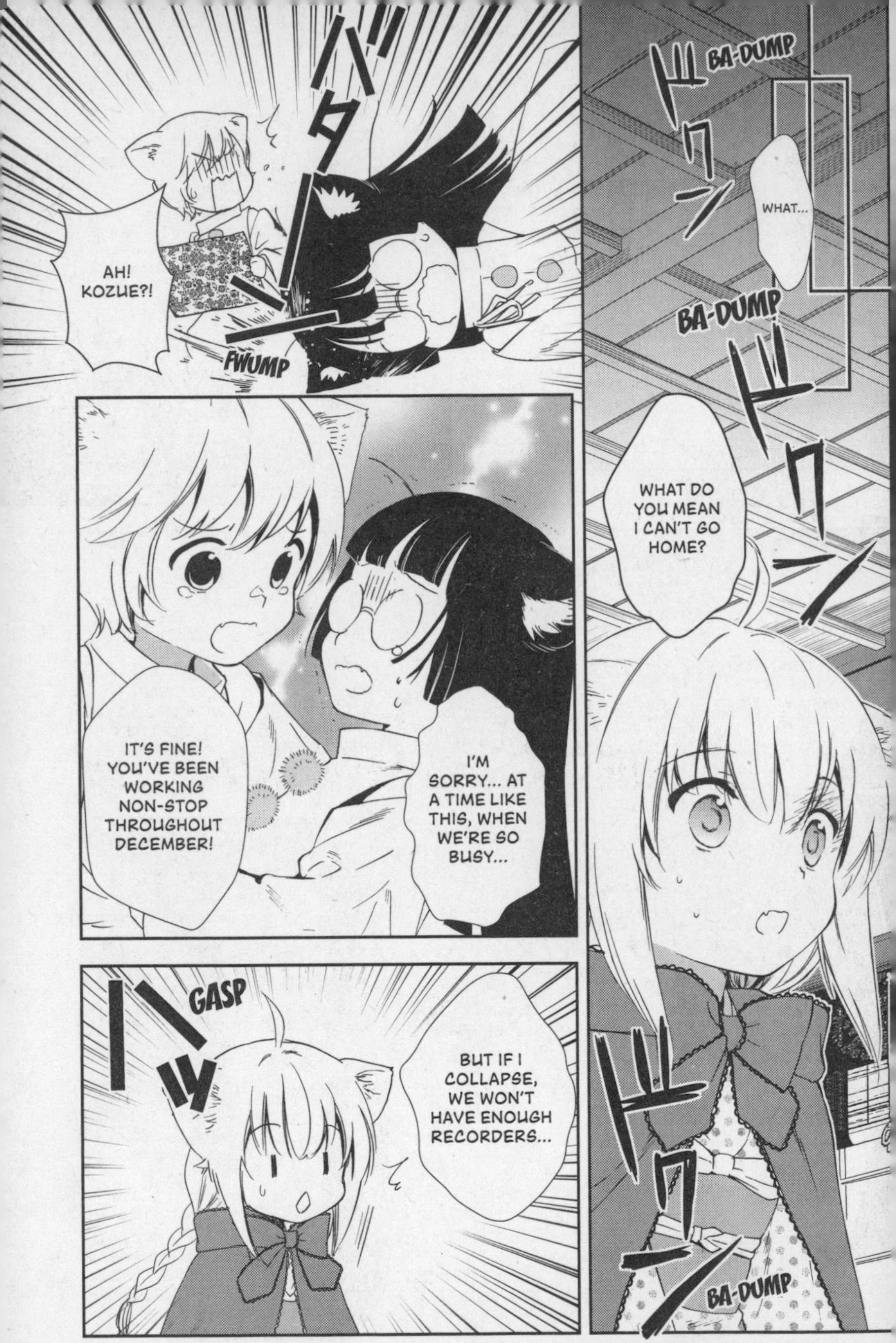
BA-DUMP
WHAT...
BA-DUMP
WHAT DO YOU MEAN I CAN'T GO HOME?
BA-DUMP
AH! KOZUE?!
FWUMP
I'M SORRY... AT A TIME LIKE THIS, WHEN WE'RE SO BUSY...
IT'S FINE! YOU'VE BEEN WORKING NON-STOP THROUGHOUT DECEMBER!
BUT IF I COLLAPSE, WE WON'T HAVE ENOUGH RECORDERS...
GASP

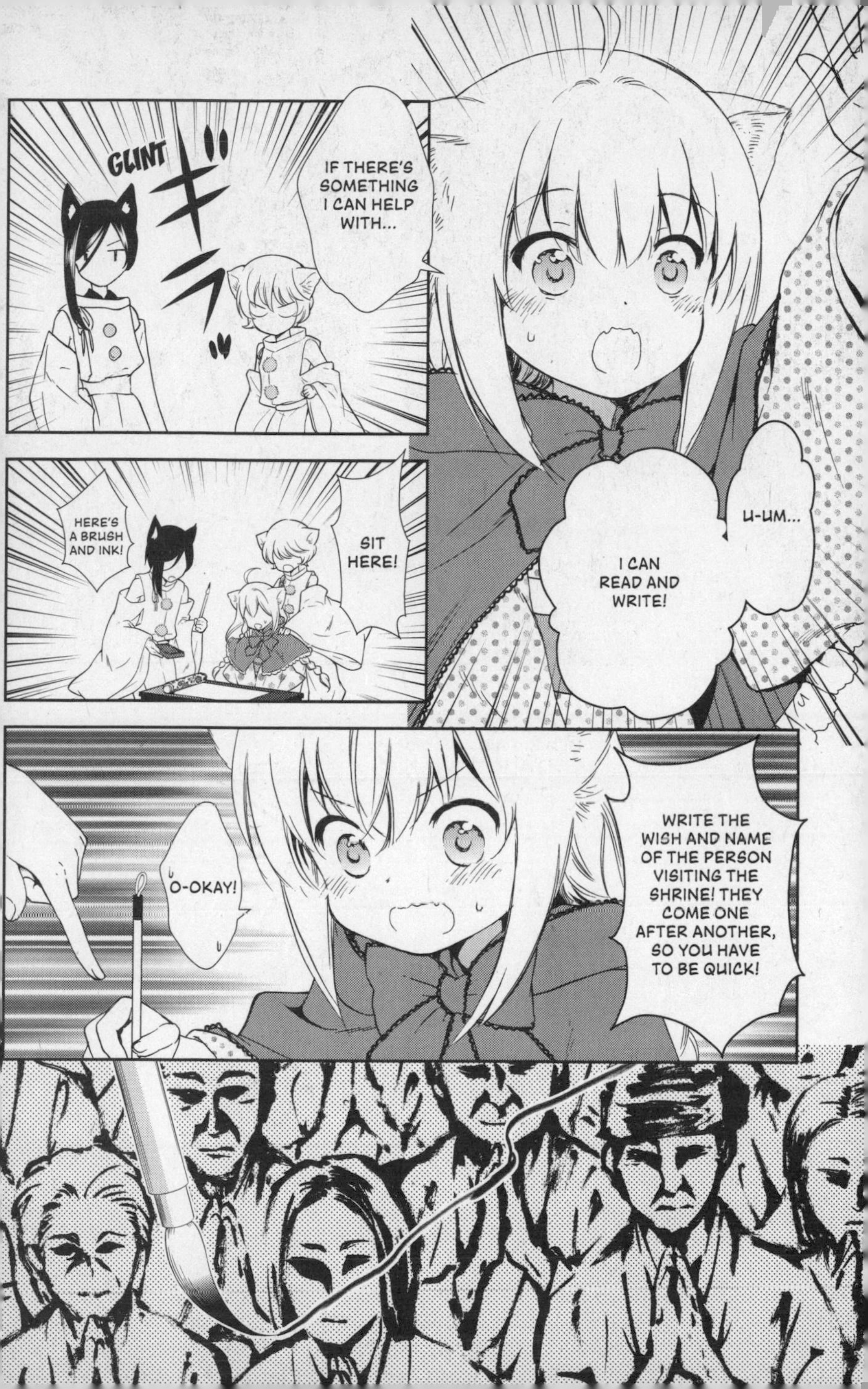
U-UM...
I CAN READ AND WRITE!
IF THERE'S SOMETHING I CAN HELP WITH...
GLINT
SIT HERE!
HERE'S A BRUSH AND INK!
WRITE THE WISH AND NAME OF THE PERSON VISITING THE SHRINE! THEY COME ONE AFTER ANOTHER, SO YOU HAVE TO BE QUICK!
O-OKAY!

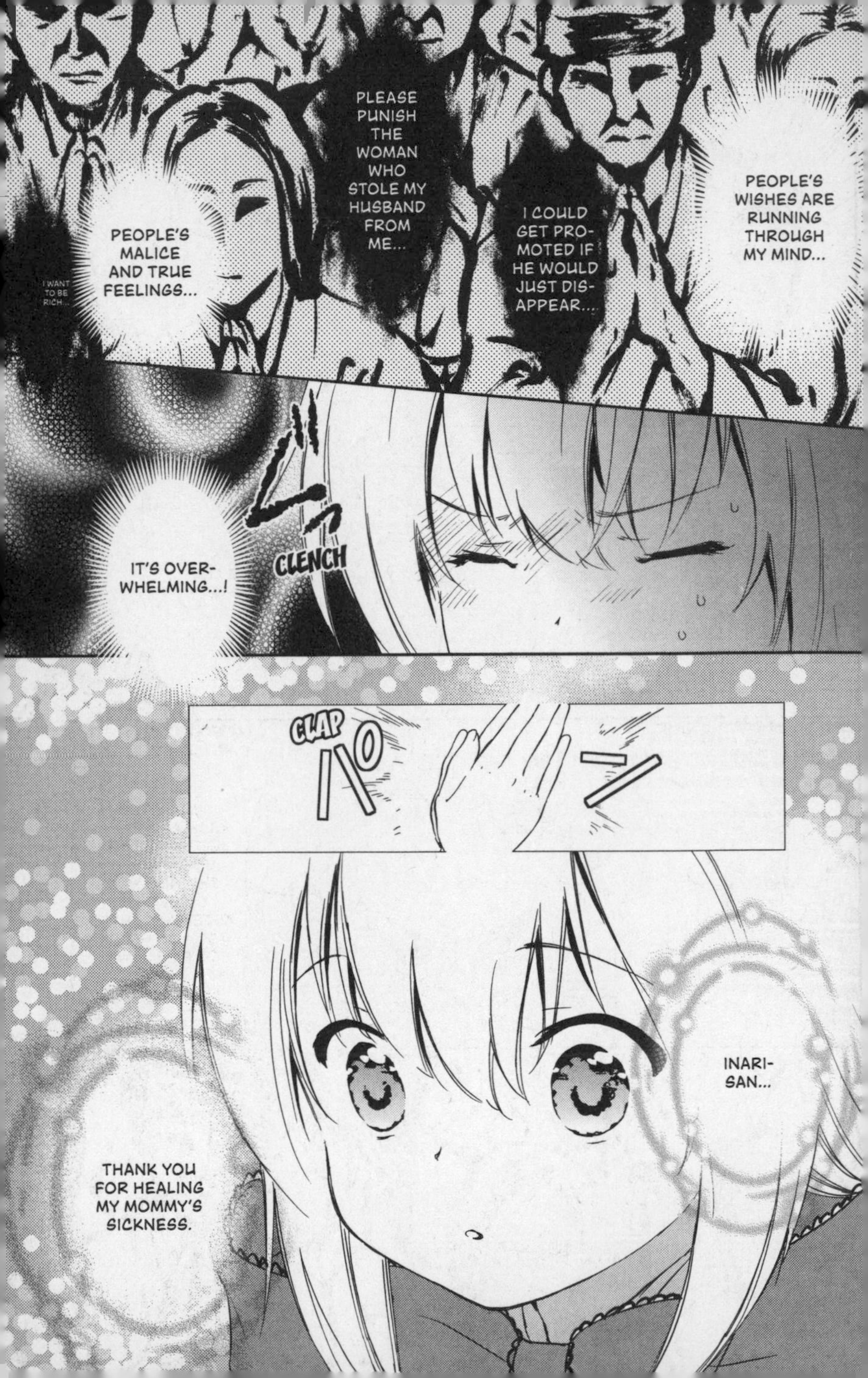
PEOPLE'S WISHES ARE RUNNING THROUGH MY MIND...
I COULD GET PRO-MOTED IF HE WOULD JUST DIS-APPEAR...
PLEASE PUNISH THE WOMAN WHO STOLE MY HUSBAND FROM ME...
PEOPLE'S MALICE AND TRUE FEELINGS...
I WANT TO BE RICH...
CLENCH
IT'S OVER-WHELMING...!
CLAP
INARI-SAN...
THANK YOU FOR HEALING MY MOMMY'S SICKNESS.

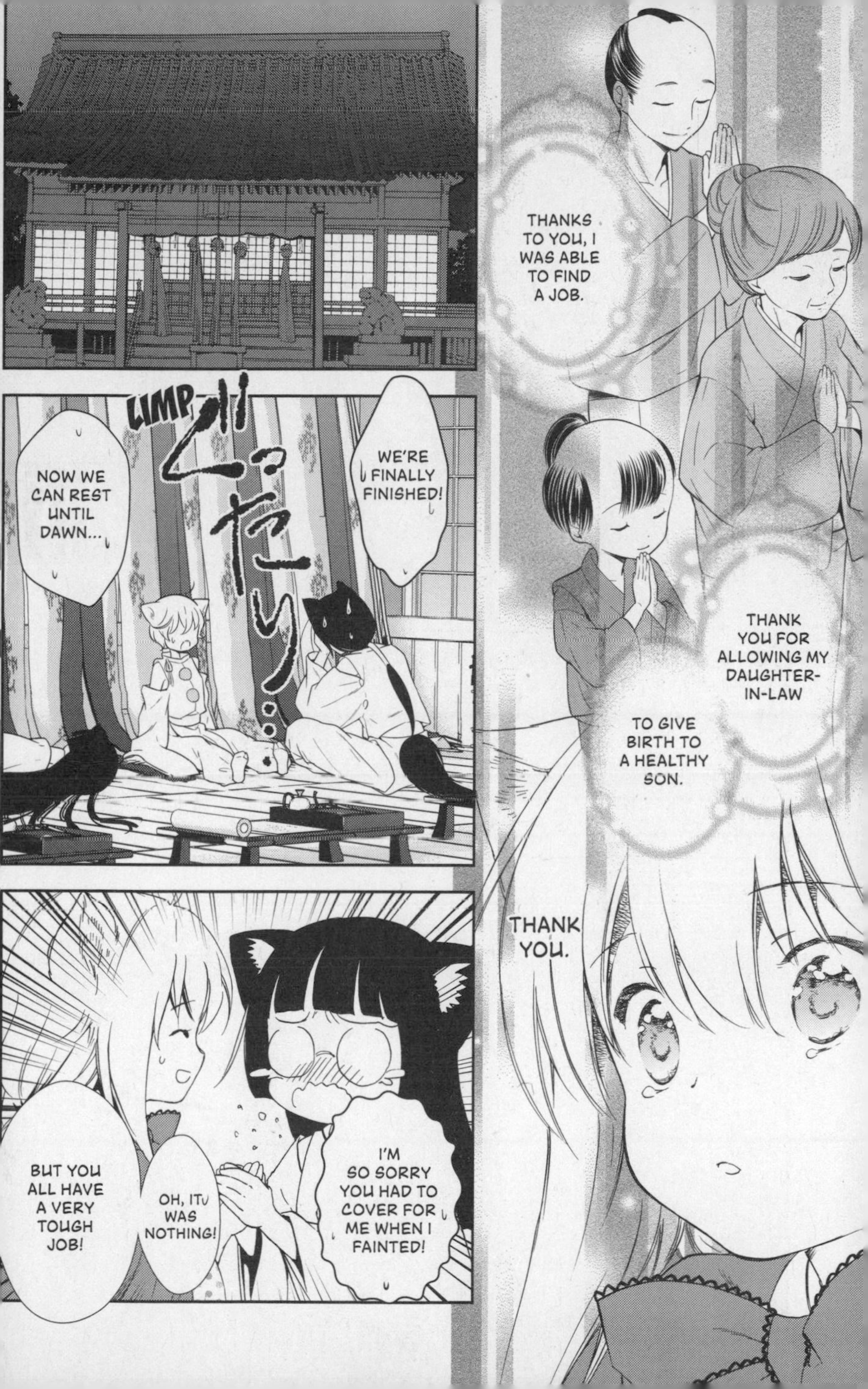
THANKS TO YOU, I WAS ABLE TO FIND A JOB.
THANK YOU FOR ALLOWING MY DAUGHTER-IN-LAW
TO GIVE BIRTH TO A HEALTHY SON.
THANK YOU.
LIMP
ぐったり…
WE'RE FINALLY FINISHED!
NOW WE CAN REST UNTIL DAWN...
I'M SO SORRY YOU HAD TO COVER FOR ME WHEN I FAINTED!
OH, IT WAS NOTHING!
BUT YOU ALL HAVE A VERY TOUGH JOB!

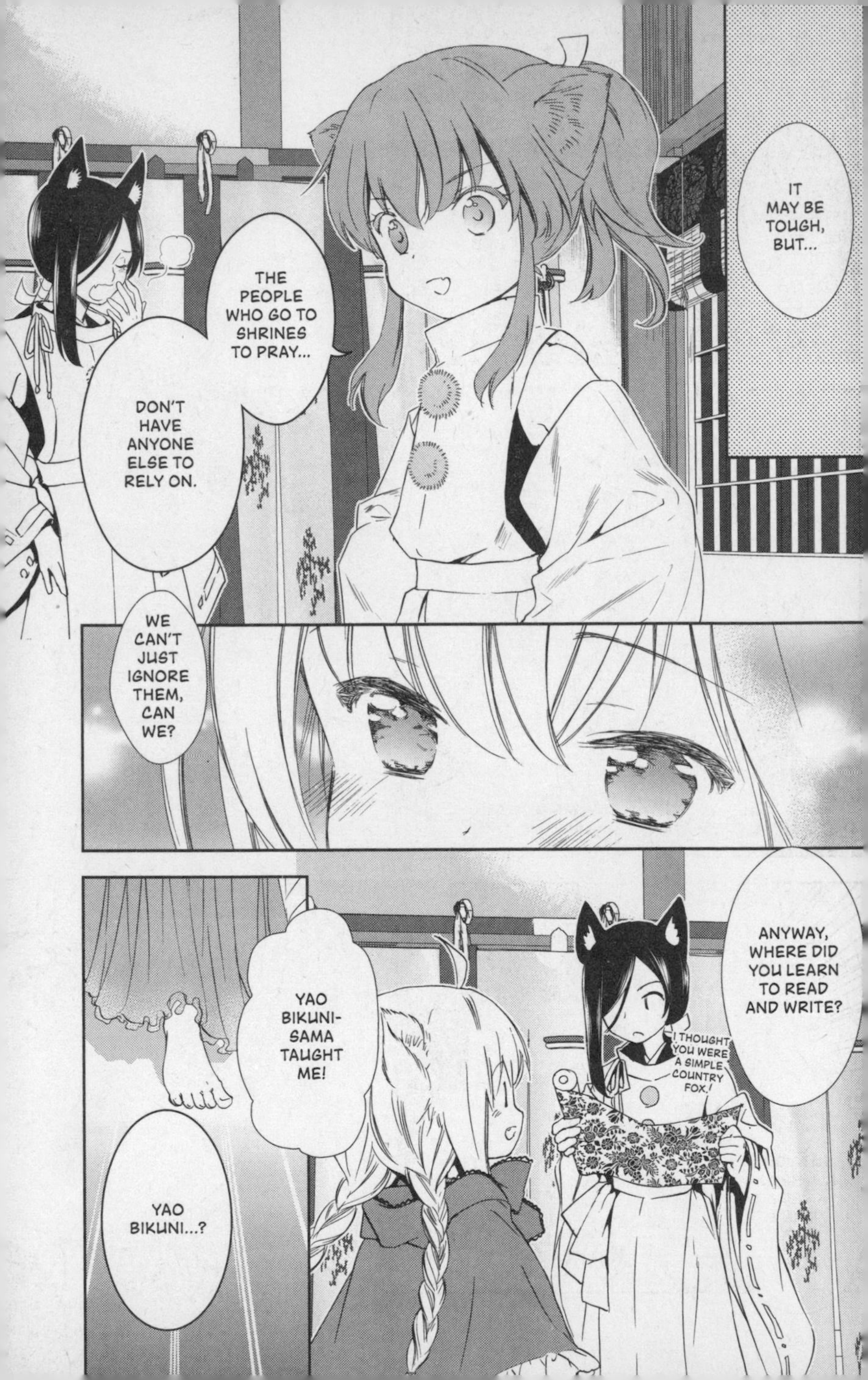
IT MAY BE TOUGH, BUT...
THE PEOPLE WHO GO TO SHRINES TO PRAY...
DON'T HAVE ANYONE ELSE TO RELY ON.
WE CAN'T JUST IGNORE THEM, CAN WE?
ANYWAY, WHERE DID YOU LEARN TO READ AND WRITE?
I THOUGHT YOU WERE A SIMPLE COUNTRY FOX!
YAO BIKUNI-SAMA TAUGHT ME!
YAO BIKUNI...?

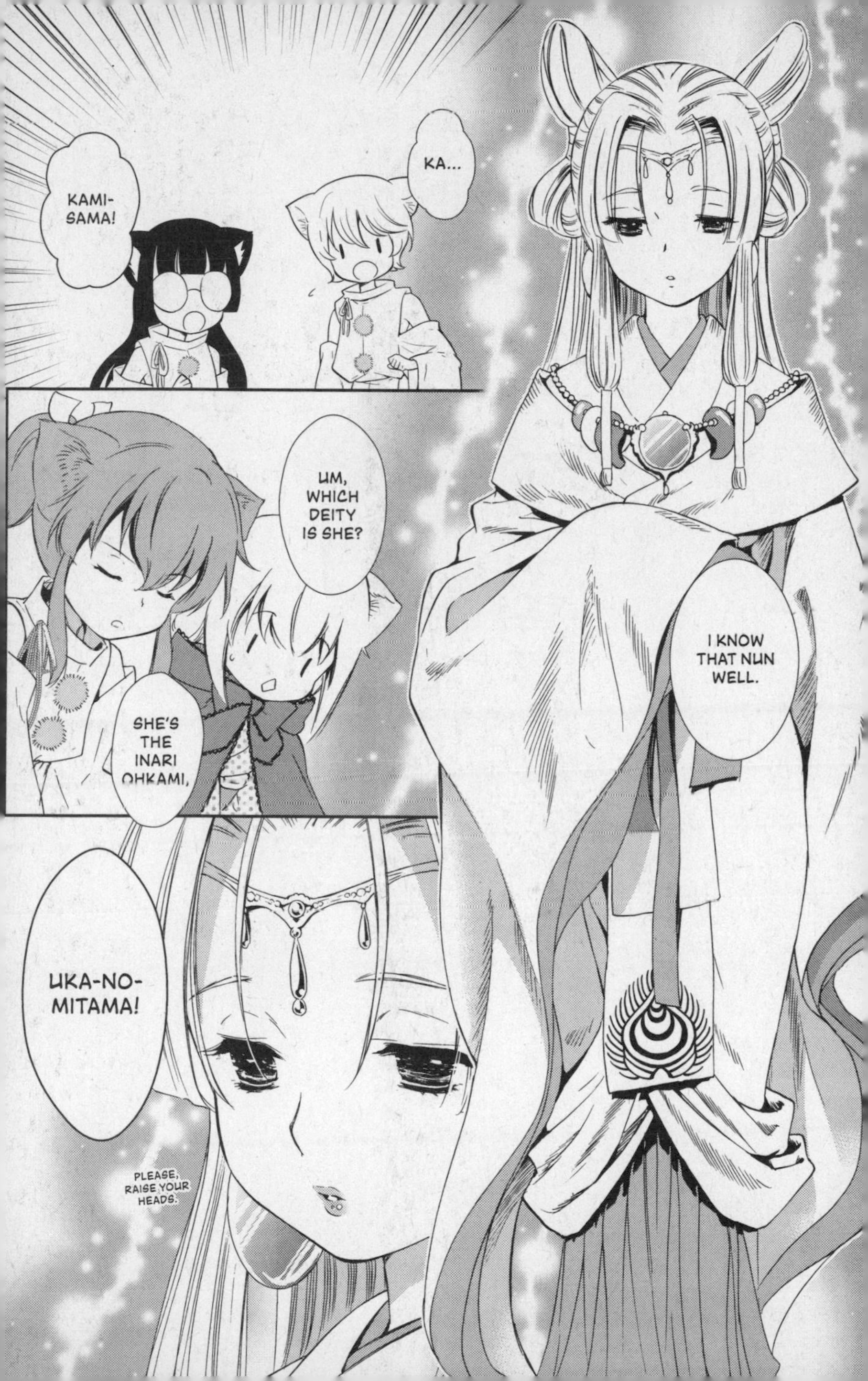
I KNOW THAT NUN WELL.
KA...
KAMI-SAMA!
UM, WHICH DEITY IS SHE?
SHE'S THE INARI OHKAMI,
UKA-NO-MITAMA!
PLEASE, RAISE YOUR HEADS.

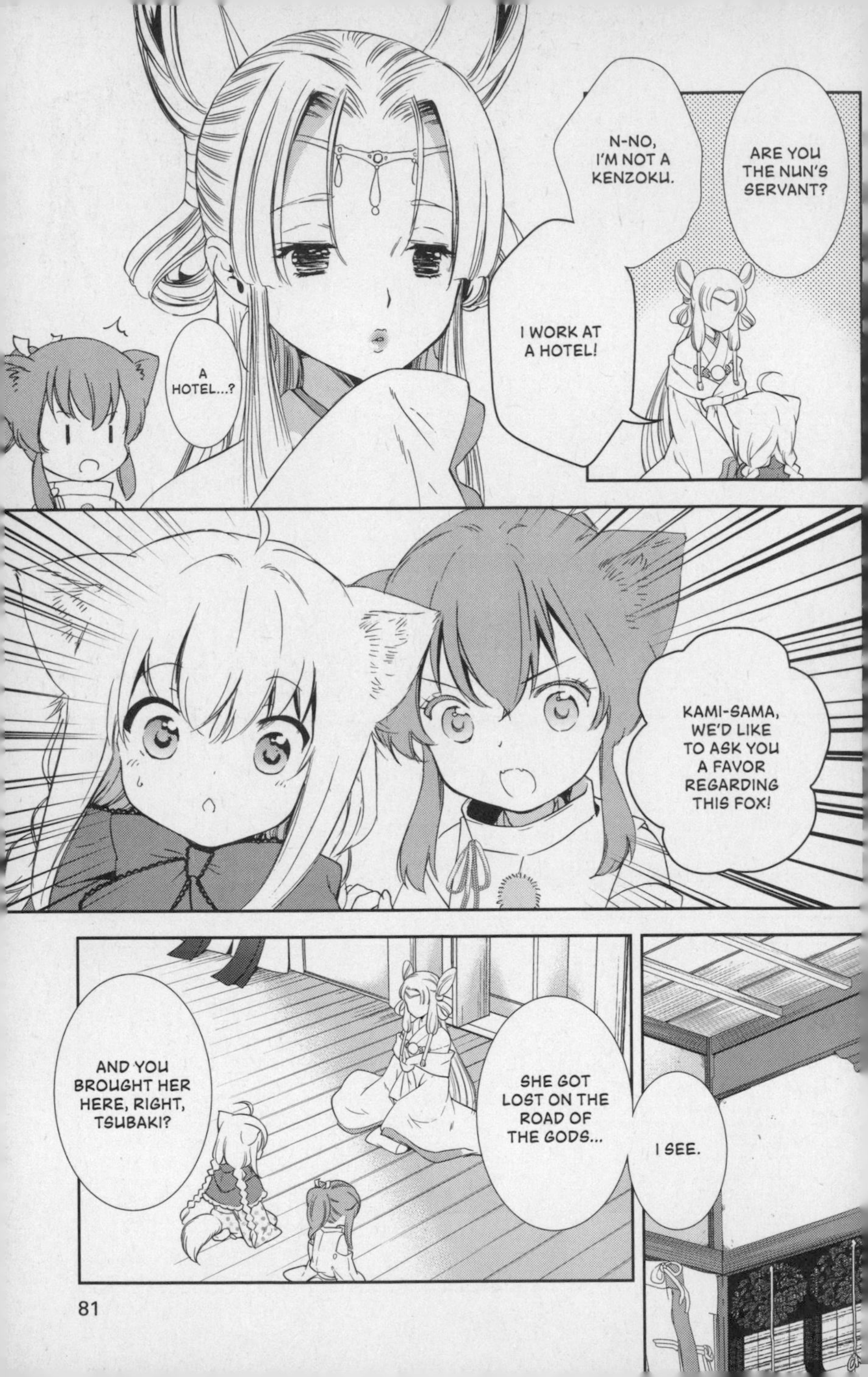
ARE YOU THE NUN'S SERVANT?
N-NO, I'M NOT A KENZOKU.
I WORK AT A HOTEL!
A HOTEL...?
KAMI-SAMA, WE'D LIKE TO ASK YOU A FAVOR REGARDING THIS FOX!
I SEE.
SHE GOT LOST ON THE ROAD OF THE GODS...
AND YOU BROUGHT HER HERE, RIGHT, TSUBAKI?

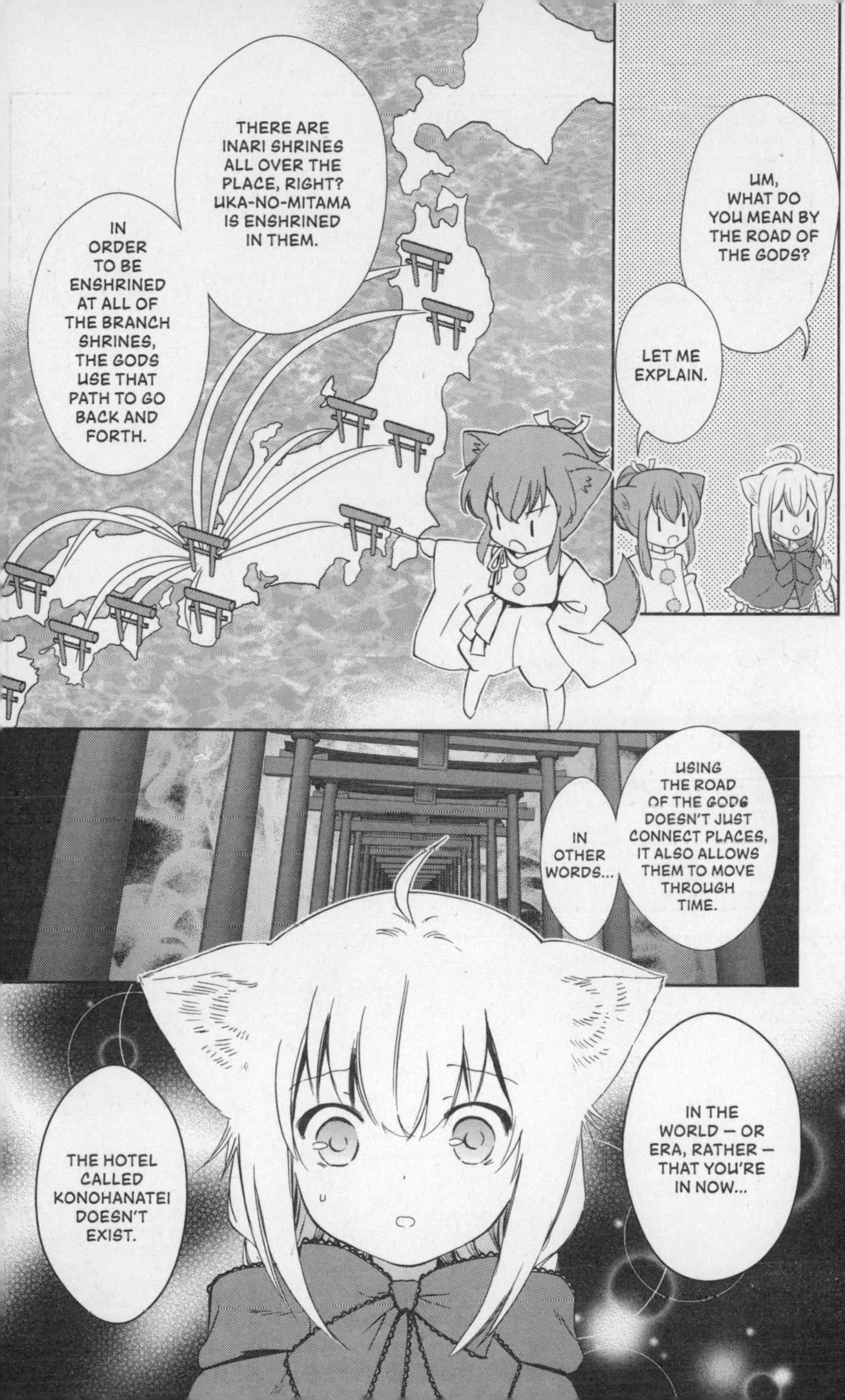
UM, WHAT DO YOU MEAN BY THE ROAD OF THE GODS?
LET ME EXPLAIN.
THERE ARE INARI SHRINES ALL OVER THE PLACE, RIGHT? UKA-NO-MITAMA IS ENSHRINED IN THEM.
IN ORDER TO BE ENSHRINED AT ALL OF THE BRANCH SHRINES, THE GODS USE THAT PATH TO GO BACK AND FORTH.
USING THE ROAD OF THE GODS DOESN'T JUST CONNECT PLACES, IT ALSO ALLOWS THEM TO MOVE THROUGH TIME.
IN OTHER WORDS...
IN THE WORLD — OR ERA, RATHER — THAT YOU'RE IN NOW...
THE HOTEL CALLED KONOHANATEI DOESN'T EXIST.

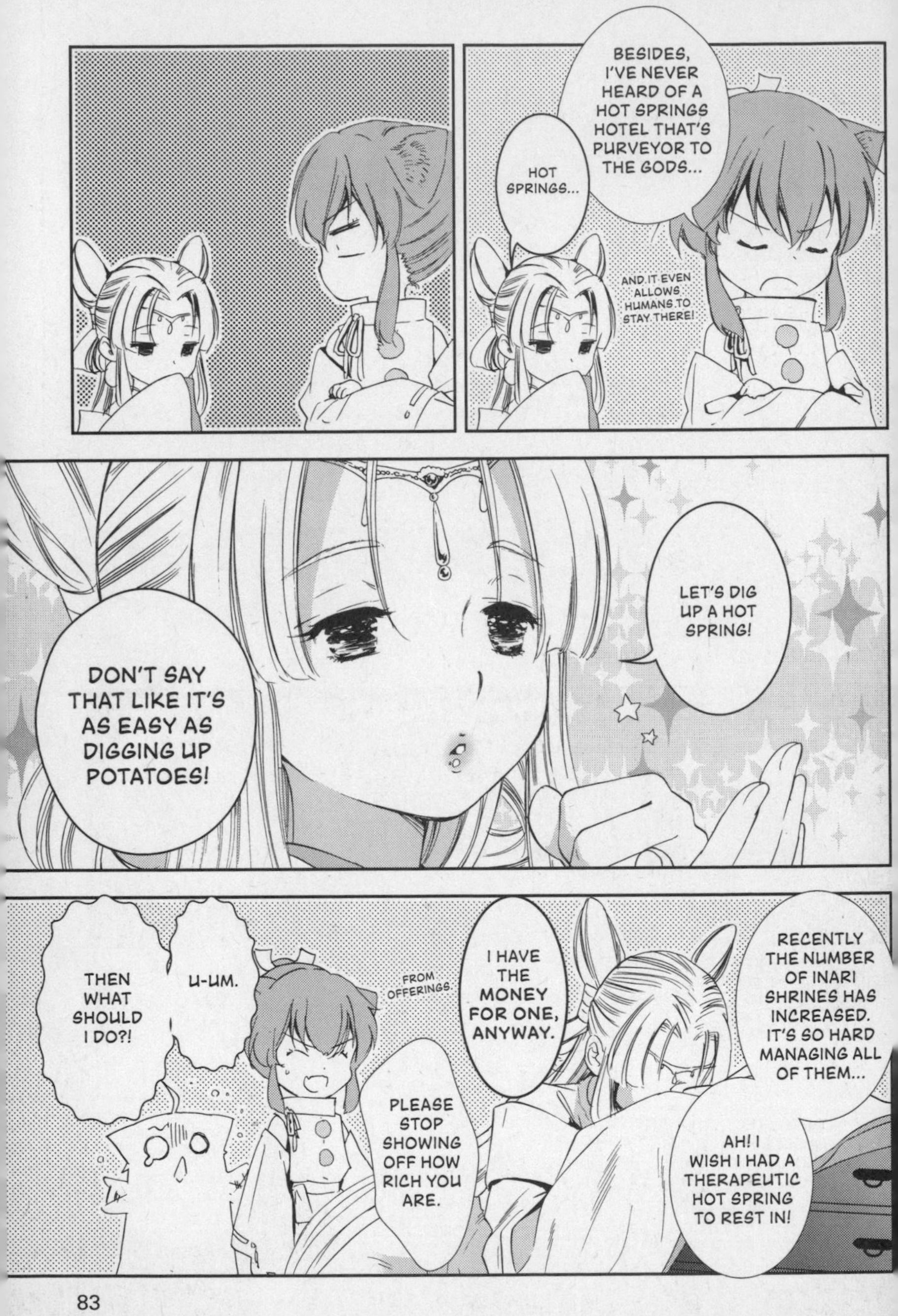
BESIDES, I'VE NEVER HEARD OF A HOT SPRINGS HOTEL THAT'S PURVEYOR TO THE GODS...
HOT SPRINGS...
AND IT EVEN ALLOWS HUMANS TO STAY THERE!
LET'S DIG UP A HOT SPRING!
DON'T SAY THAT LIKE IT'S AS EASY AS DIGGING UP POTATOES!
RECENTLY THE NUMBER OF INARI SHRINES HAS INCREASED. IT'S SO HARD MANAGING ALL OF THEM...
AH! I WISH I HAD A THERAPEUTIC HOT SPRING TO REST IN!
I HAVE THE MONEY FOR ONE, ANYWAY.
FROM OFFERINGS.
PLEASE STOP SHOWING OFF HOW RICH YOU ARE.
U-UM.
THEN WHAT SHOULD I DO?!

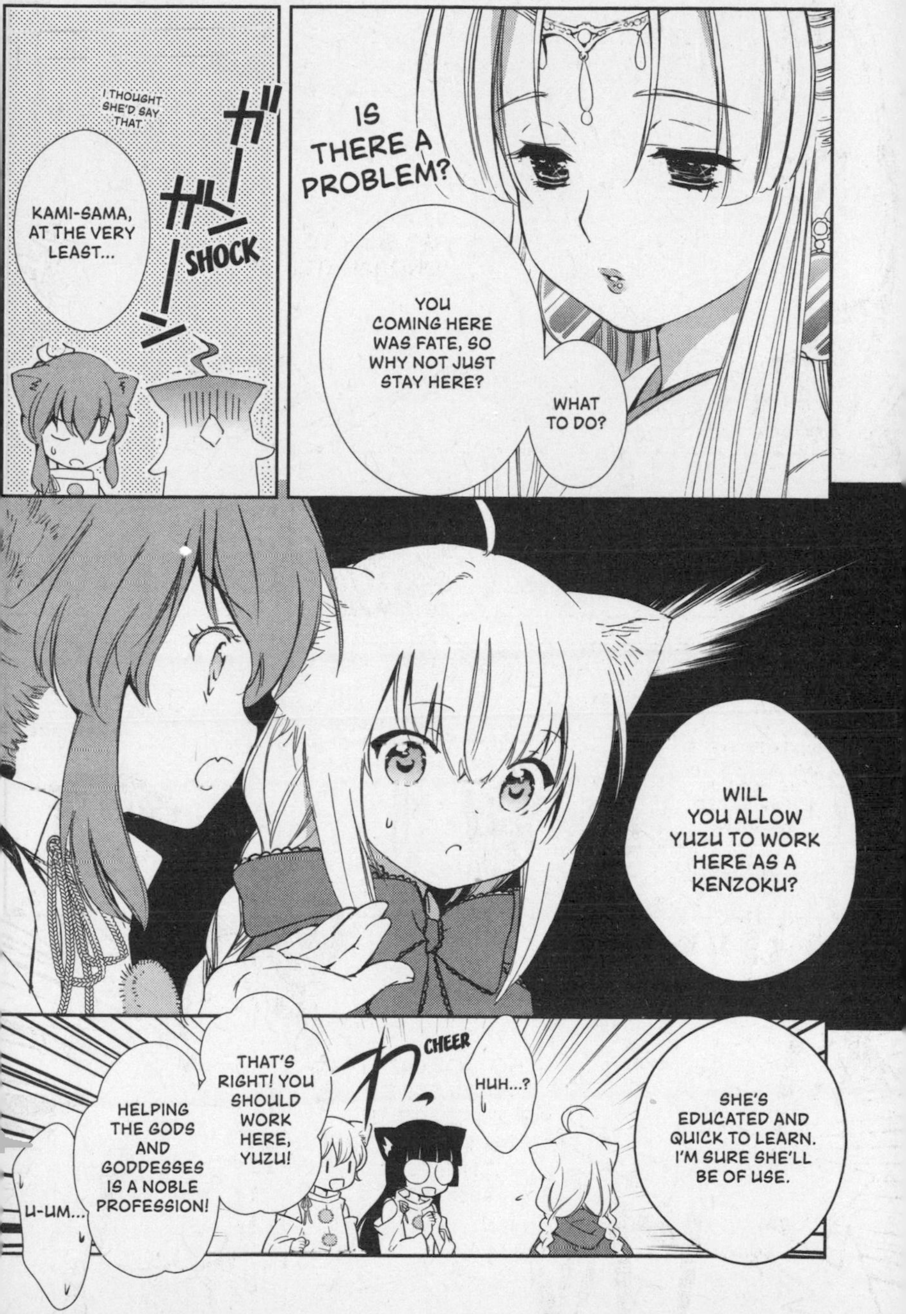
IS THERE A PROBLEM?
YOU COMING HERE WAS FATE, SO WHY NOT JUST STAY HERE?
WHAT TO DO?
SHOCK
I THOUGHT SHE'D SAY THAT
KAMI-SAMA, AT THE VERY LEAST...
WILL YOU ALLOW YUZU TO WORK HERE AS A KENZOKU?
SHE'S EDUCATED AND QUICK TO LEARN. I'M SURE SHE'LL BE OF USE.
HUH...?
CHEER
THAT'S RIGHT! YOU SHOULD WORK HERE, YUZU!
HELPING THE GODS AND GODDESSES IS A NOBLE PROFESSION!
U-UM...

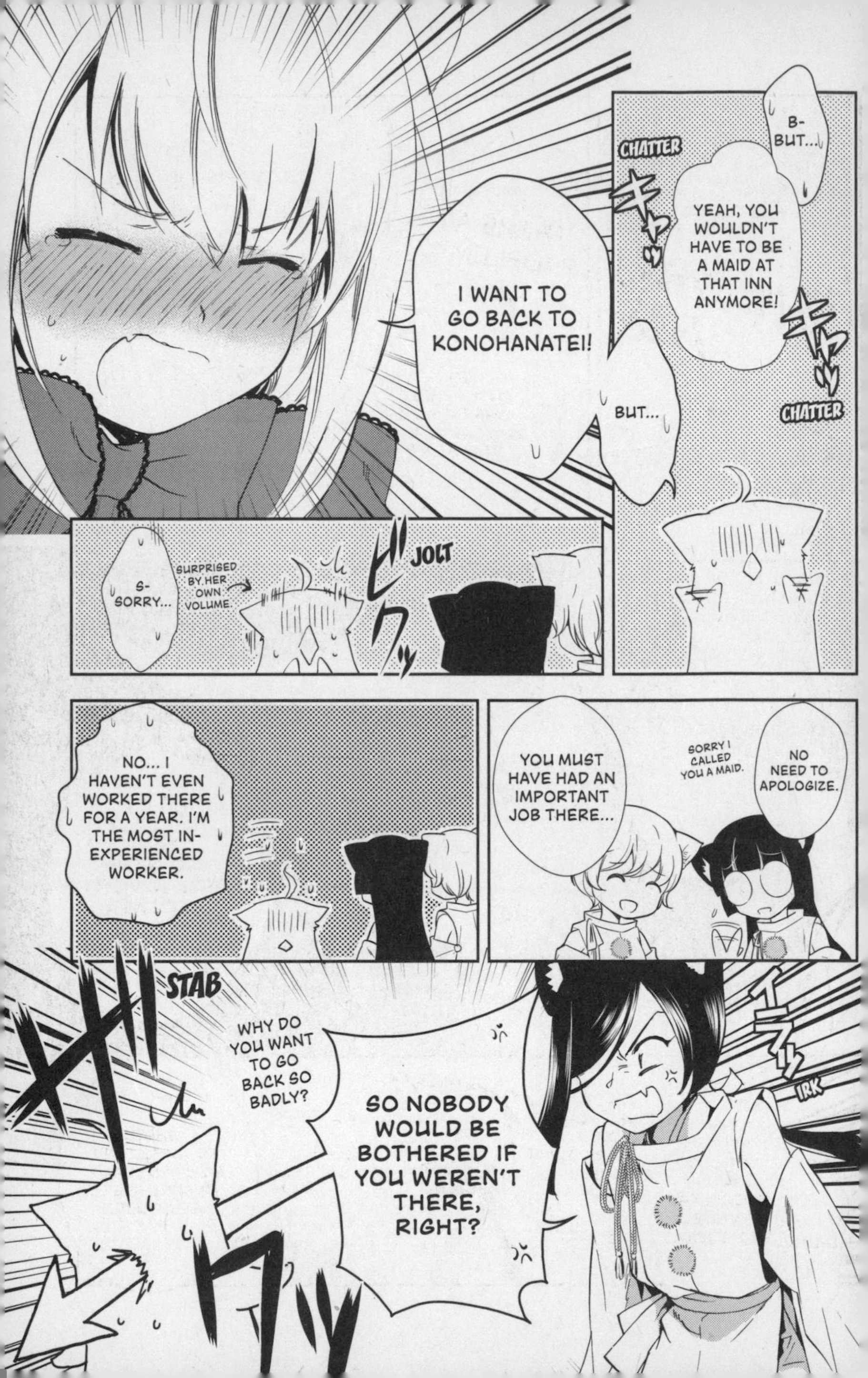
B-BUT...
CHATTER
YEAH, YOU WOULDN'T HAVE TO BE A MAID AT THAT INN ANYMORE!
CHATTER
BUT...
I WANT TO GO BACK TO KONOHANATEI!
JOLT
SURPRISED BY HER OWN VOLUME.
S-SORRY...
NO NEED TO APOLOGIZE.
SORRY I CALLED YOU A MAID.
YOU MUST HAVE HAD AN IMPORTANT JOB THERE...
NO... I HAVEN'T EVEN WORKED THERE FOR A YEAR. I'M THE MOST IN-EXPERIENCED WORKER.
IRK
SO NOBODY WOULD BE BOTHERED IF YOU WEREN'T THERE, RIGHT?
WHY DO YOU WANT TO GO BACK SO BADLY?
STAB

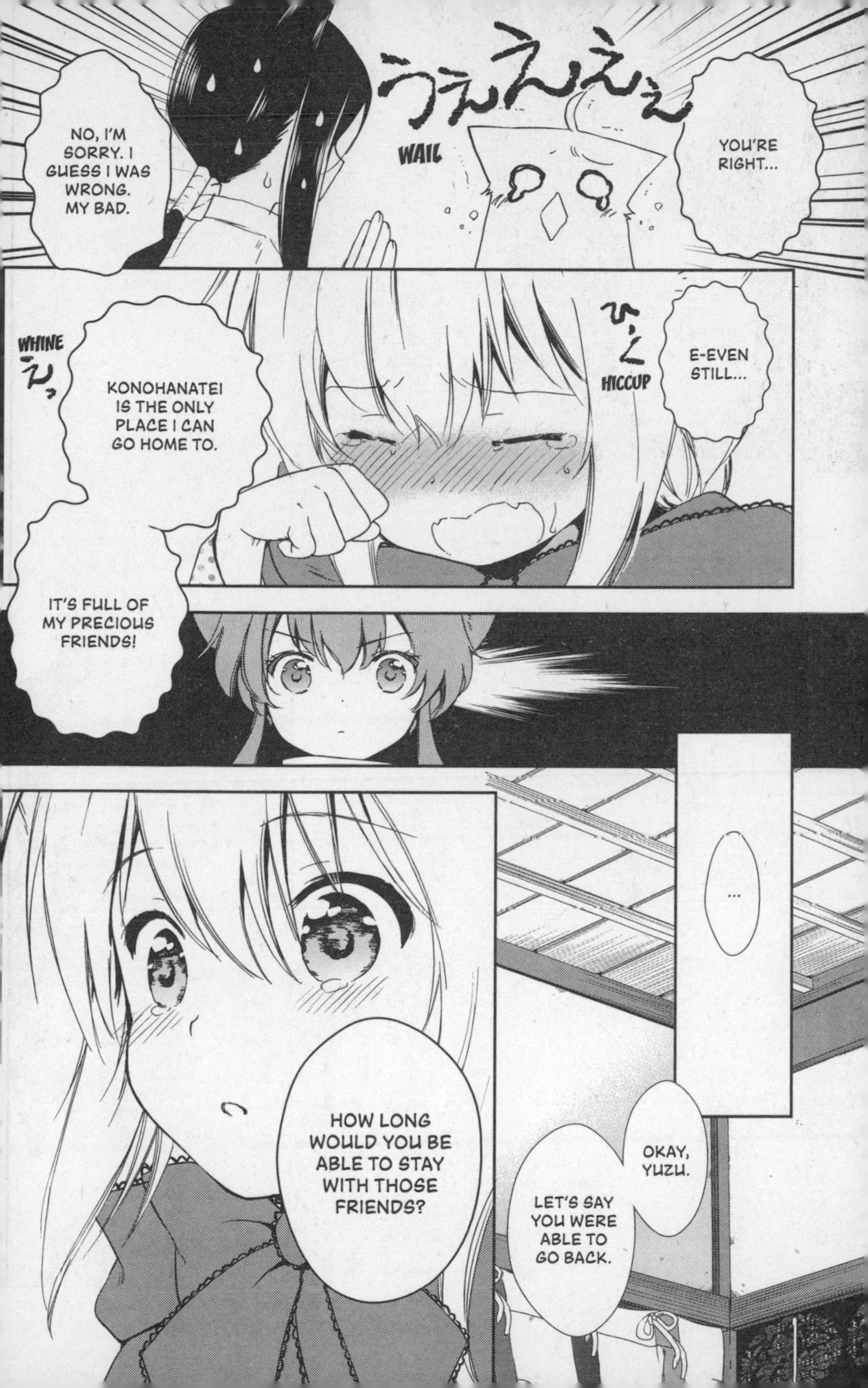
YOU'RE RIGHT...
WAIL
NO, I'M SORRY. I GUESS I WAS WRONG. MY BAD.
E-EVEN STILL...
ひっく
HICCUP
KONOHANATEI IS THE ONLY PLACE I CAN GO HOME TO.
WHINE
えっ
IT'S FULL OF MY PRECIOUS FRIENDS!
...
OKAY, YUZU.
LET'S SAY YOU WERE ABLE TO GO BACK.
HOW LONG WOULD YOU BE ABLE TO STAY WITH THOSE FRIENDS?

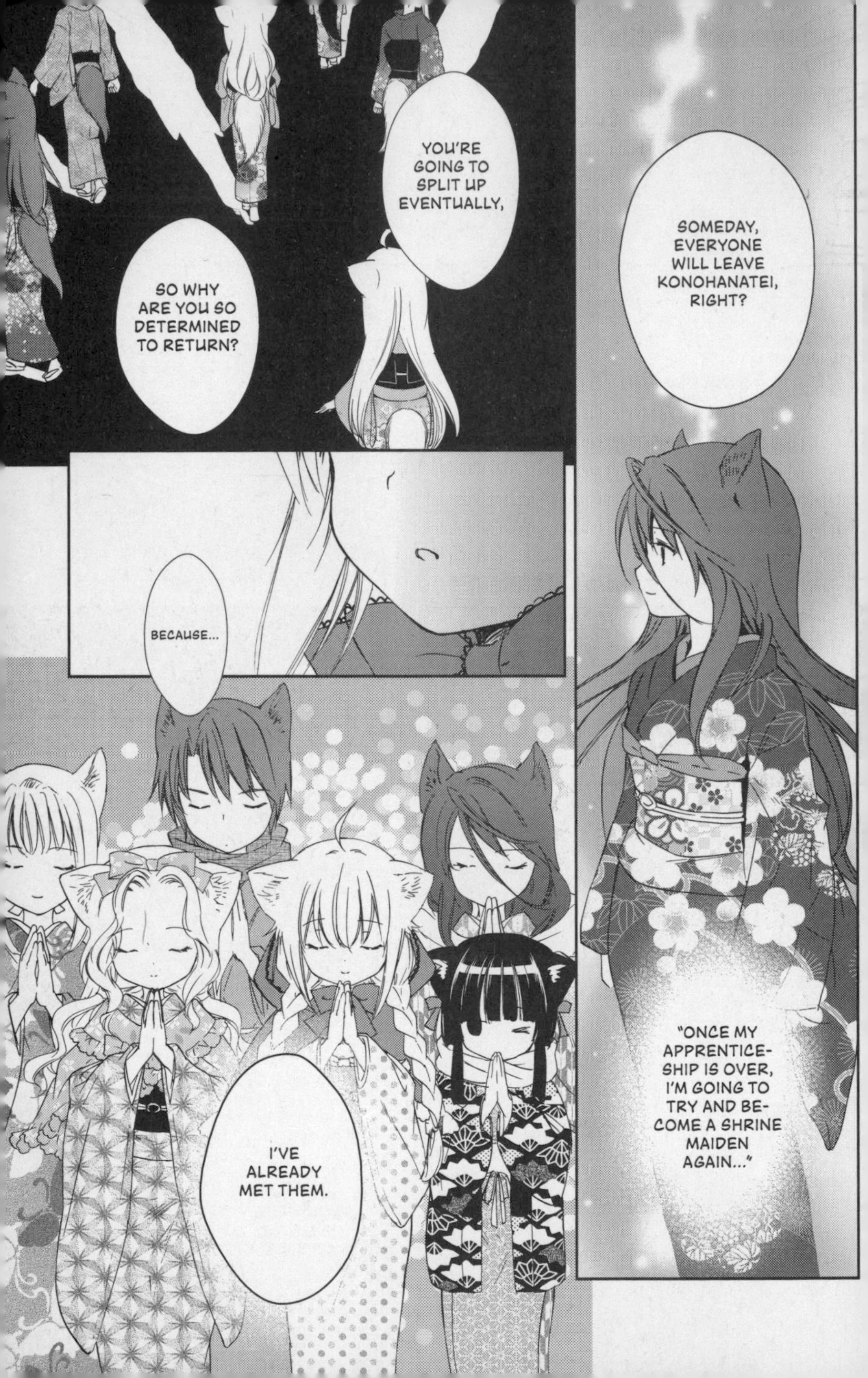
SOMEDAY, EVERYONE WILL LEAVE KONOHANATEI, RIGHT?
"ONCE MY APPRENTICE-SHIP IS OVER, I'M GOING TO TRY AND BE-COME A SHRINE MAIDEN AGAIN..."
YOU'RE GOING TO SPLIT UP EVENTUALLY,
SO WHY ARE YOU SO DETERMINED TO RETURN?
BECAUSE...
I'VE ALREADY MET THEM.

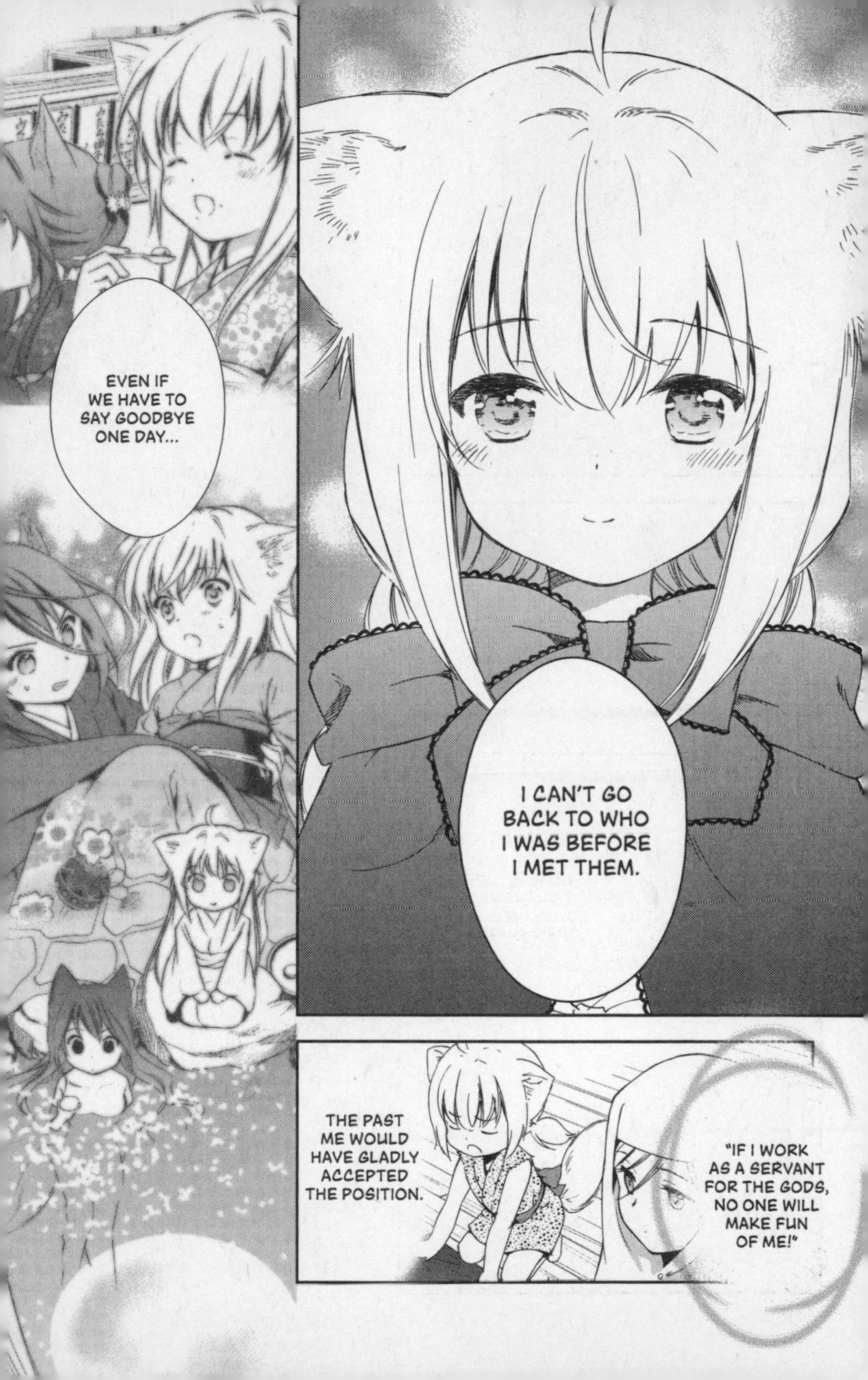
I CAN'T GO BACK TO WHO I WAS BEFORE I MET THEM.
"IF I WORK AS A SERVANT FOR THE GODS, NO ONE WILL MAKE FUN OF ME!"
THE PAST ME WOULD HAVE GLADLY ACCEPTED THE POSITION.
EVEN IF WE HAVE TO SAY GOODBYE ONE DAY...

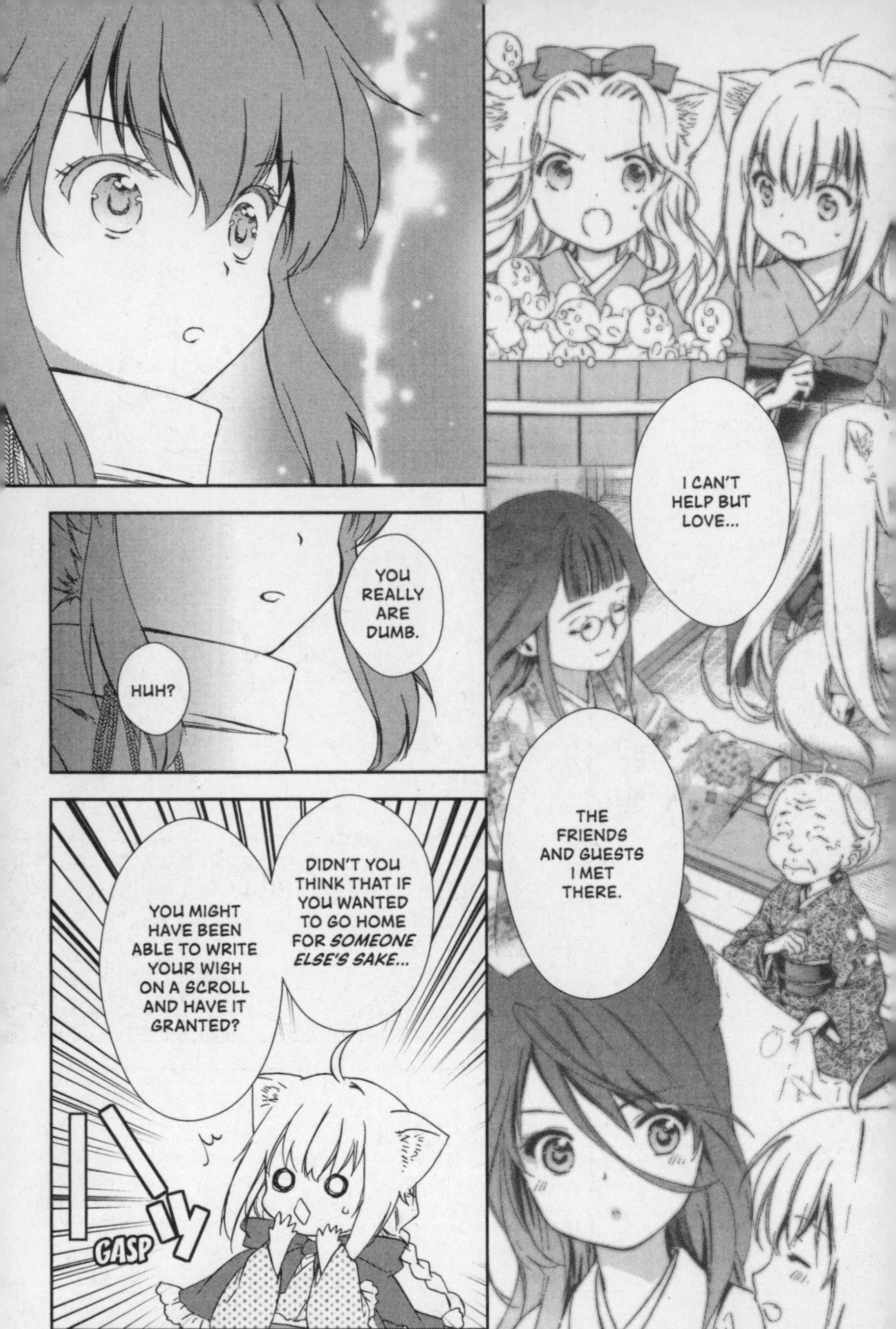
I CAN'T HELP BUT LOVE...
THE FRIENDS AND GUESTS I MET THERE.
YOU REALLY ARE DUMB.
HUH?
DIDN'T YOU THINK THAT IF YOU WANTED TO GO HOME FOR *SOMEONE ELSE'S SAKE*...
YOU MIGHT HAVE BEEN ABLE TO WRITE YOUR WISH ON A SCROLL AND HAVE IT GRANTED?
GASP

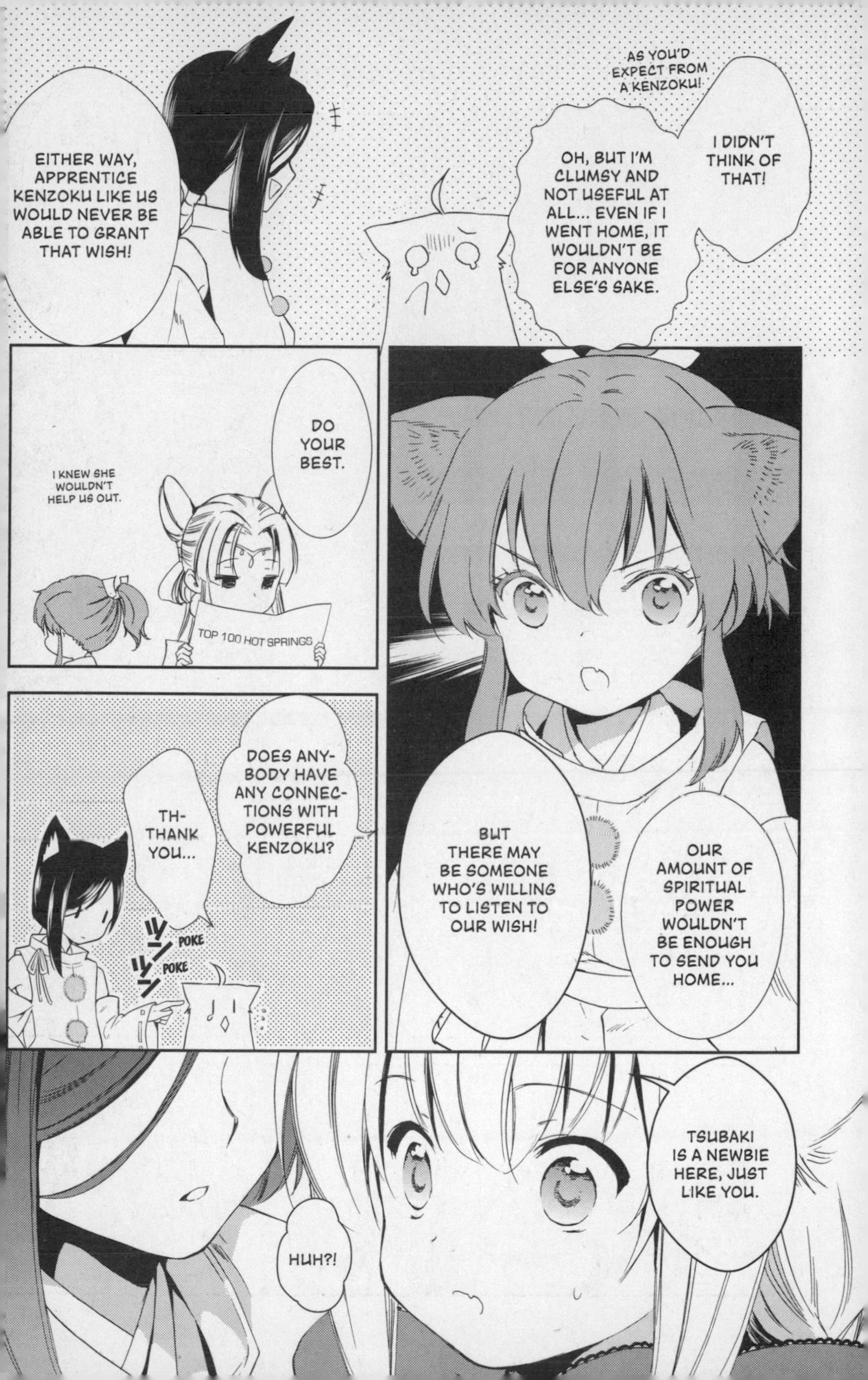
AS YOU'D EXPECT FROM A KENZOKU!
I DIDN'T THINK OF THAT!
OH, BUT I'M CLUMSY AND NOT USEFUL AT ALL... EVEN IF I WENT HOME, IT WOULDN'T BE FOR ANYONE ELSE'S SAKE.
EITHER WAY, APPRENTICE KENZOKU LIKE US WOULD NEVER BE ABLE TO GRANT THAT WISH!
OUR AMOUNT OF SPIRITUAL POWER WOULDN'T BE ENOUGH TO SEND YOU HOME...
BUT THERE MAY BE SOMEONE WHO'S WILLING TO LISTEN TO OUR WISH!
DO YOUR BEST.
I KNEW SHE WOULDN'T HELP US OUT.
TOP 100 HOT SPRINGS
DOES ANY-BODY HAVE ANY CONNEC-TIONS WITH POWERFUL KENZOKU?
TH-THANK YOU...
POKE
POKE
TSUBAKI IS A NEWBIE HERE, JUST LIKE YOU.
HUH?!

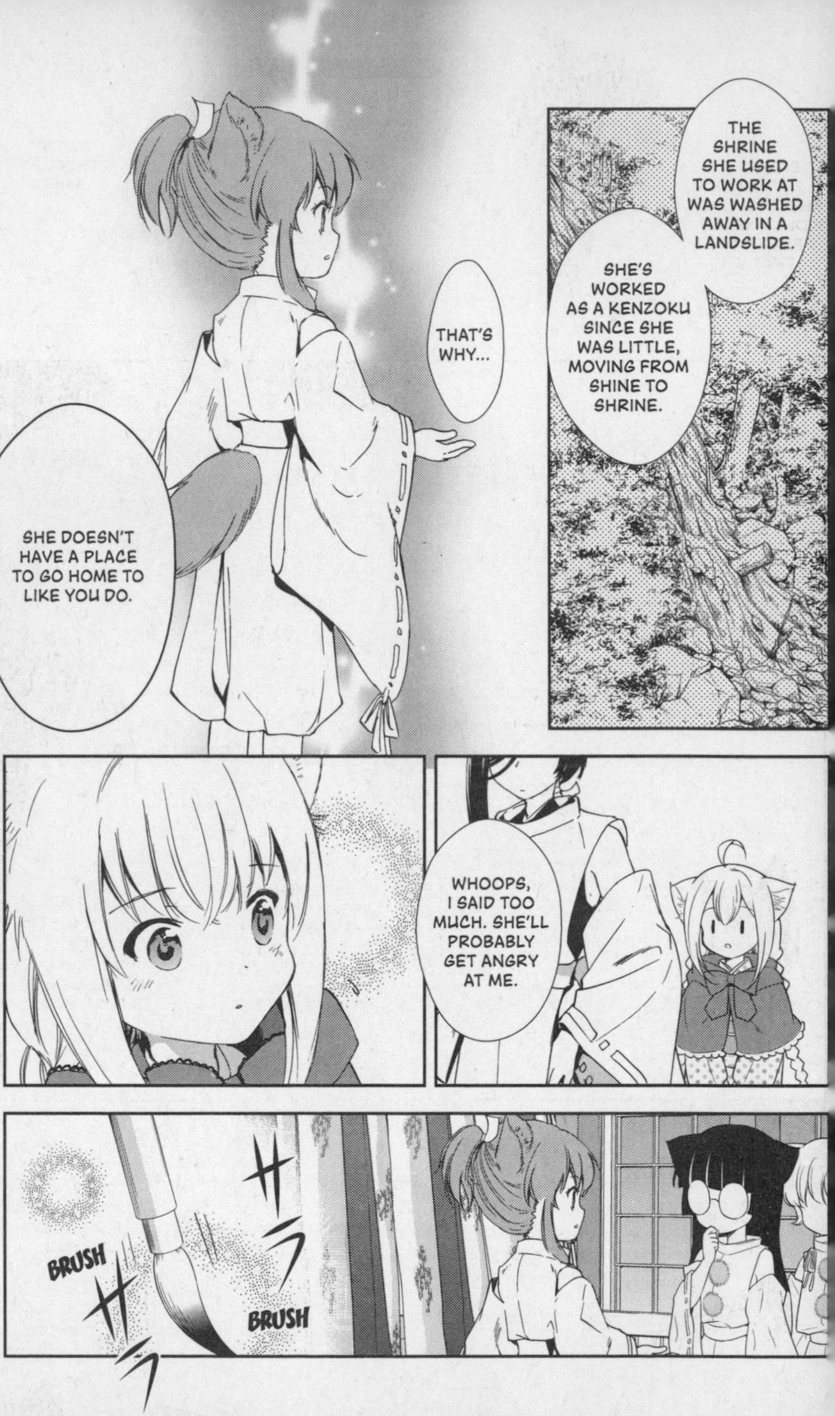
THE SHRINE SHE USED TO WORK AT WAS WASHED AWAY IN A LANDSLIDE.
SHE'S WORKED AS A KENZOKU SINCE SHE WAS LITTLE, MOVING FROM SHINE TO SHRINE.
THAT'S WHY...
SHE DOESN'T HAVE A PLACE TO GO HOME TO LIKE YOU DO.
WHOOPS, I SAID TOO MUCH. SHE'LL PROBABLY GET ANGRY AT ME.
BRUSH
BRUSH

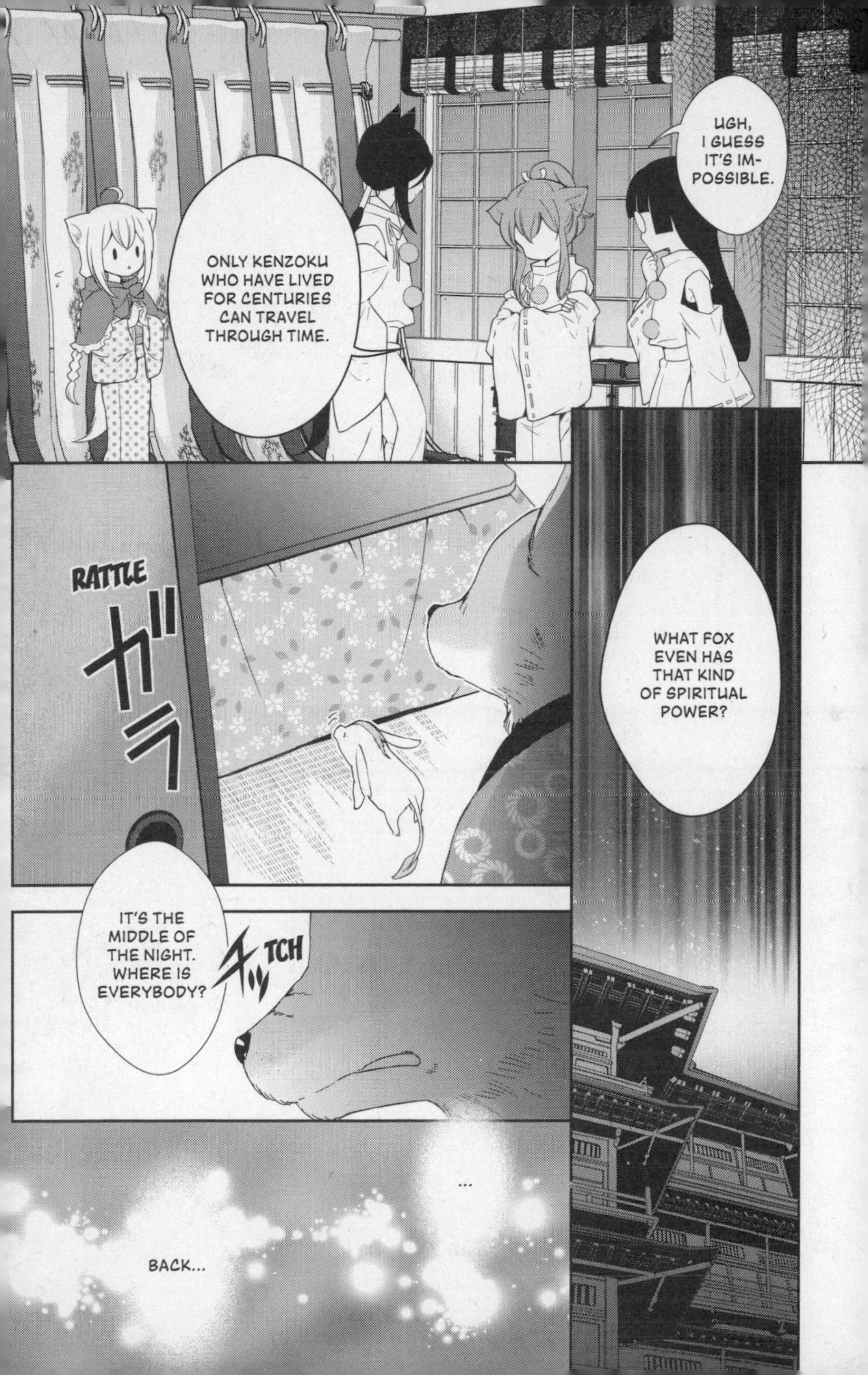
UGH, I GUESS IT'S IM-POSSIBLE.
ONLY KENZOKU WHO HAVE LIVED FOR CENTURIES CAN TRAVEL THROUGH TIME.
WHAT FOX EVEN HAS THAT KIND OF SPIRITUAL POWER?
RATTLE
ガラ
IT'S THE MIDDLE OF THE NIGHT. WHERE IS EVERYBODY?
チッ
TCH
...
BACK...

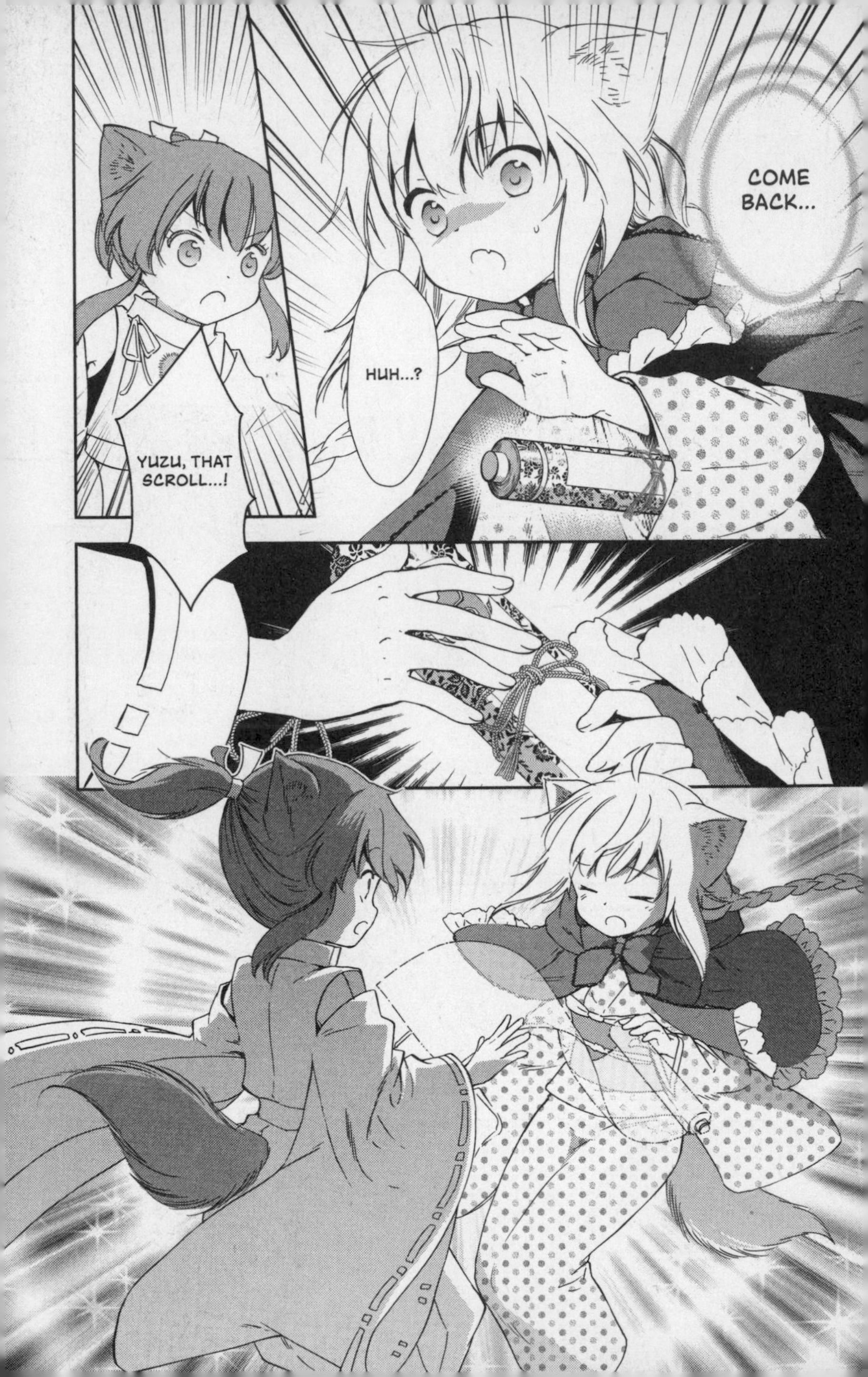
COME BACK...
HUH...?
YUZU, THAT SCROLL...!

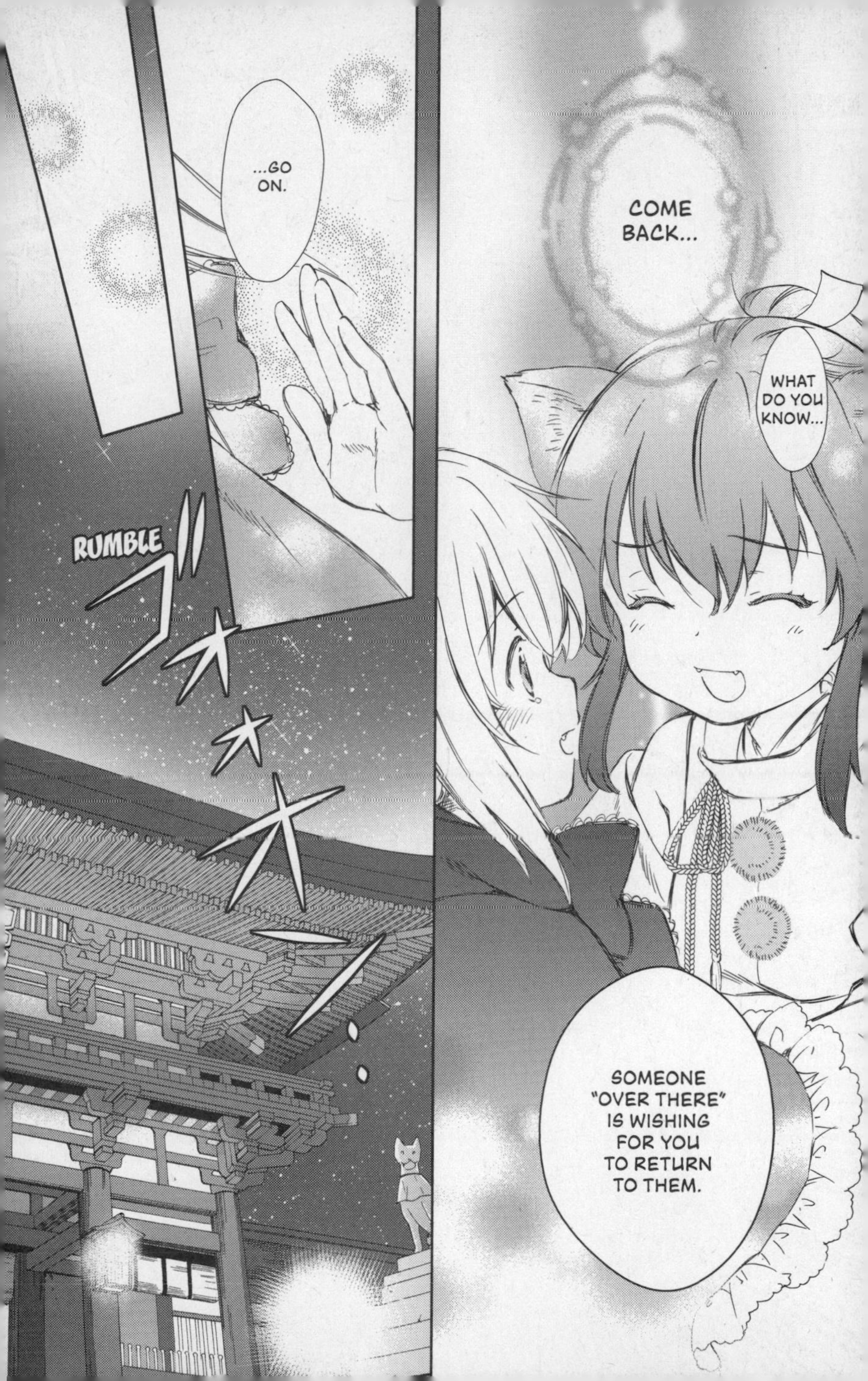
COME BACK...
WHAT DO YOU KNOW...
SOMEONE "OVER THERE" IS WISHING FOR YOU TO RETURN TO THEM.
...GO ON.
RUMBLE

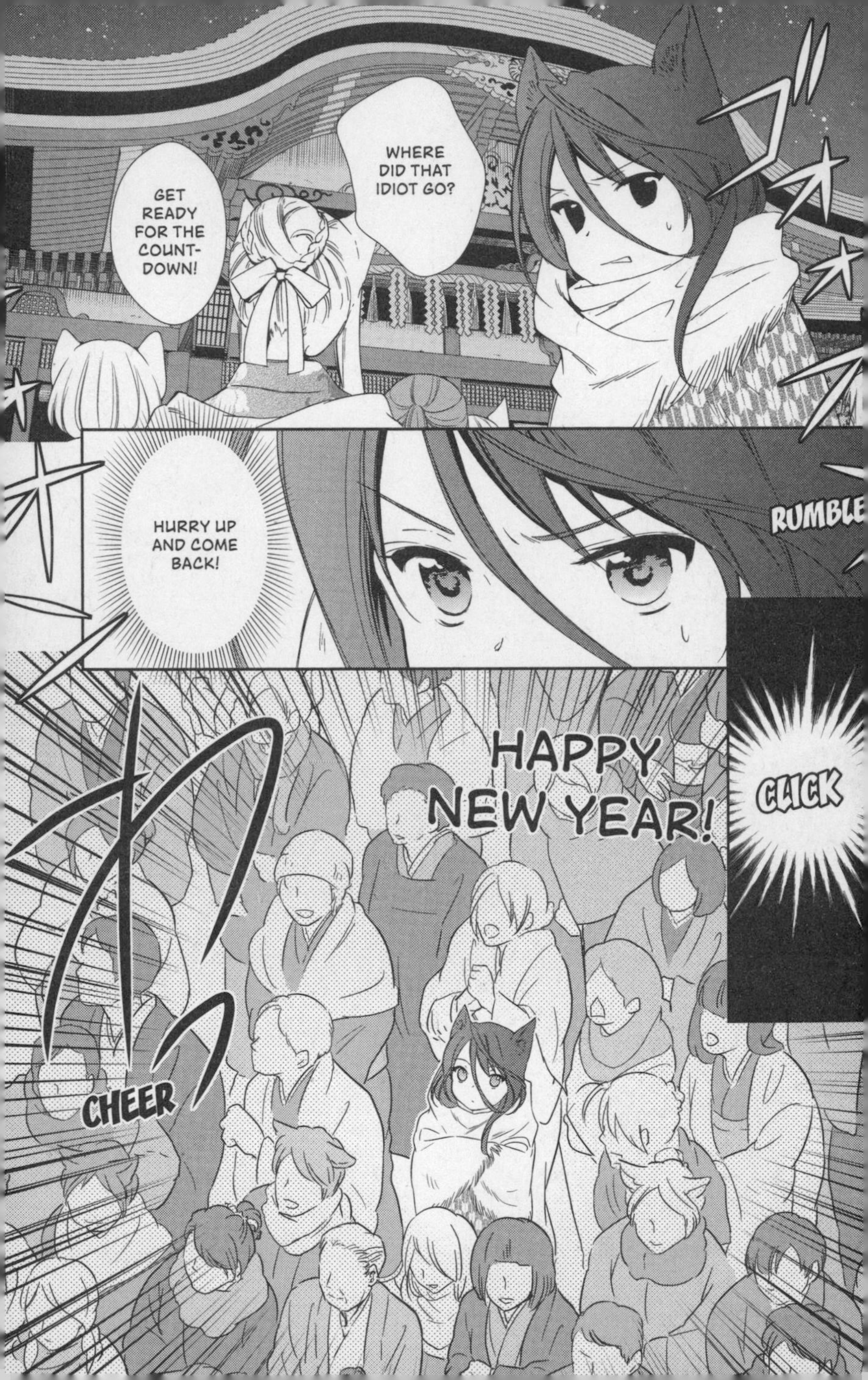
WHERE DID THAT IDIOT GO?
GET READY FOR THE COUNT-DOWN!
RUMBLE
HURRY UP AND COME BACK!
CLICK
HAPPY NEW YEAR!
CHEER

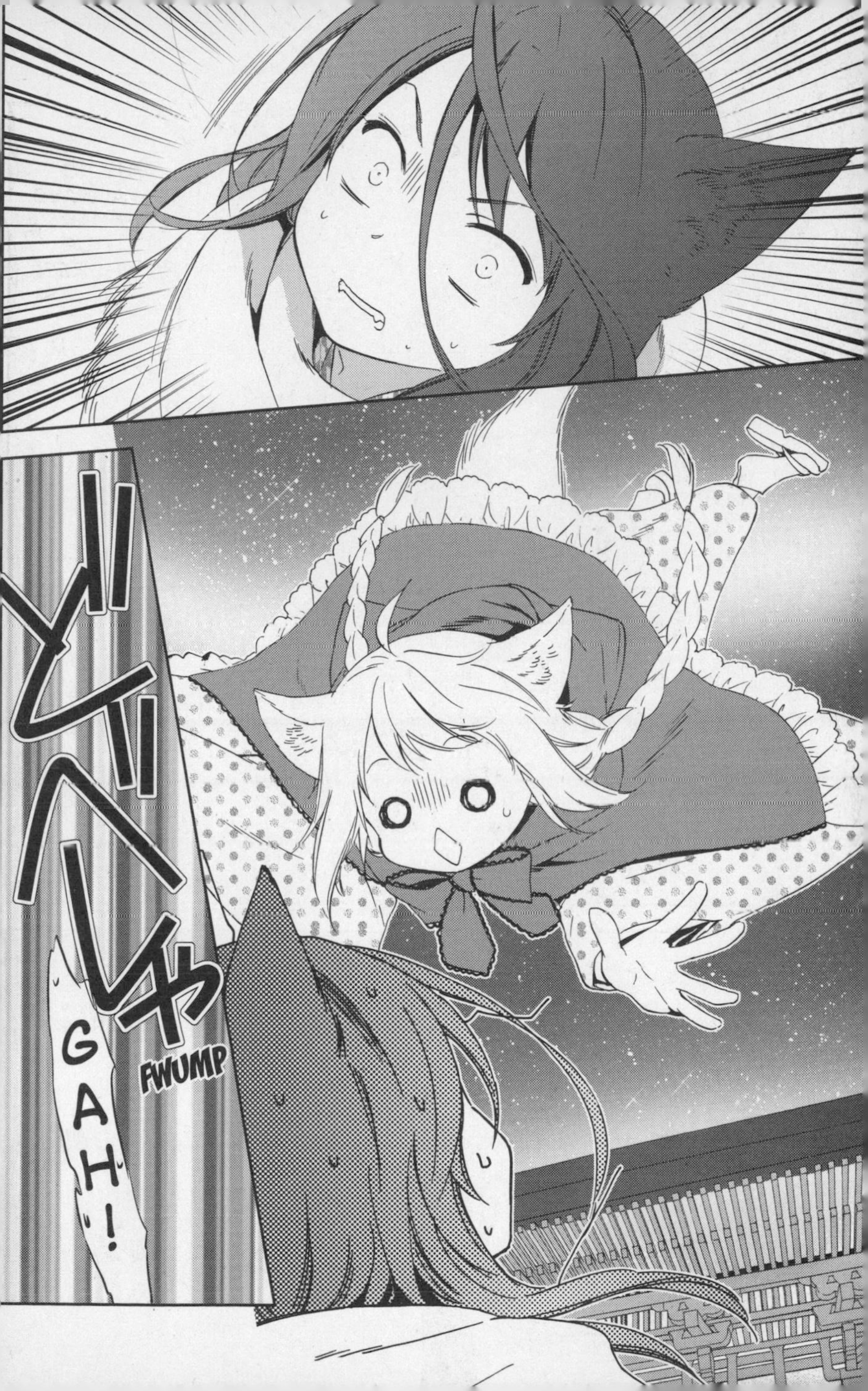
どてーんしゃ
FWUMP
GAH!

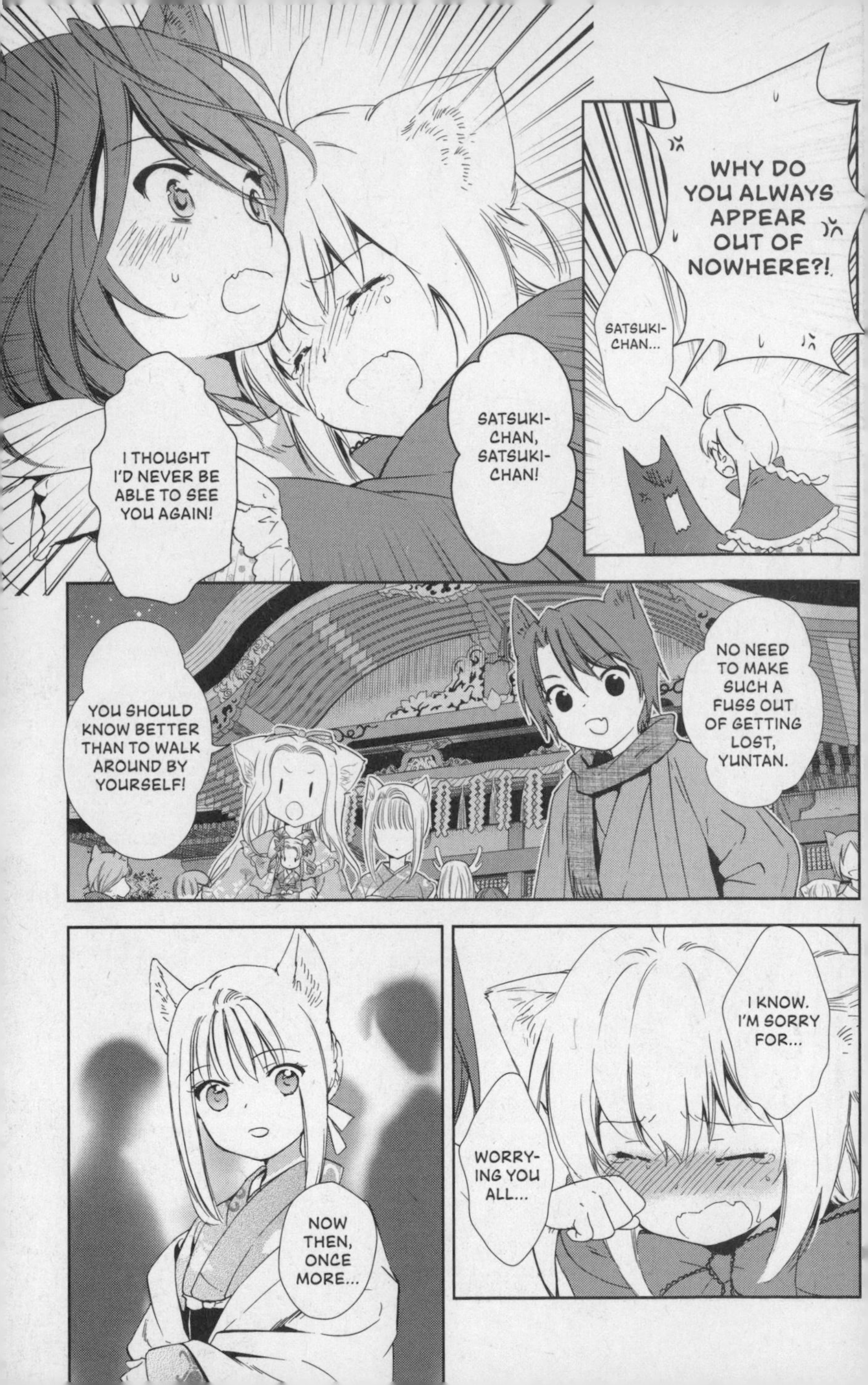
WHY DO YOU ALWAYS APPEAR OUT OF NOWHERE?!
SATSUKI-CHAN...
SATSUKI-CHAN, SATSUKI-CHAN!
I THOUGHT I'D NEVER BE ABLE TO SEE YOU AGAIN!
NO NEED TO MAKE SUCH A FUSS OUT OF GETTING LOST, YUNTAN.
YOU SHOULD KNOW BETTER THAN TO WALK AROUND BY YOURSELF!
I KNOW. I'M SORRY FOR...
WORRY-ING YOU ALL...
NOW THEN, ONCE MORE...

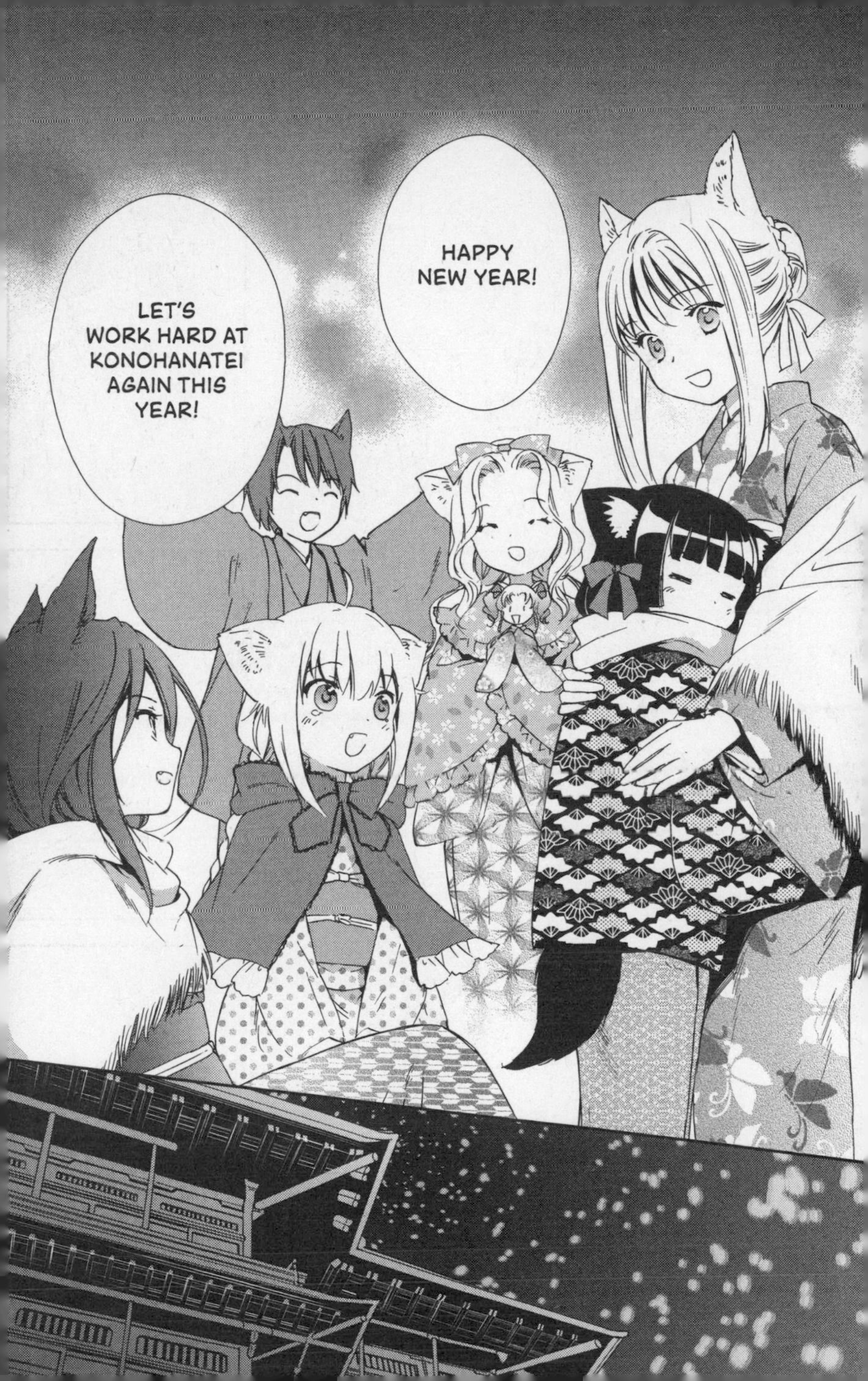
HAPPY NEW YEAR!
LET'S WORK HARD AT KONOHANATEI AGAIN THIS YEAR!

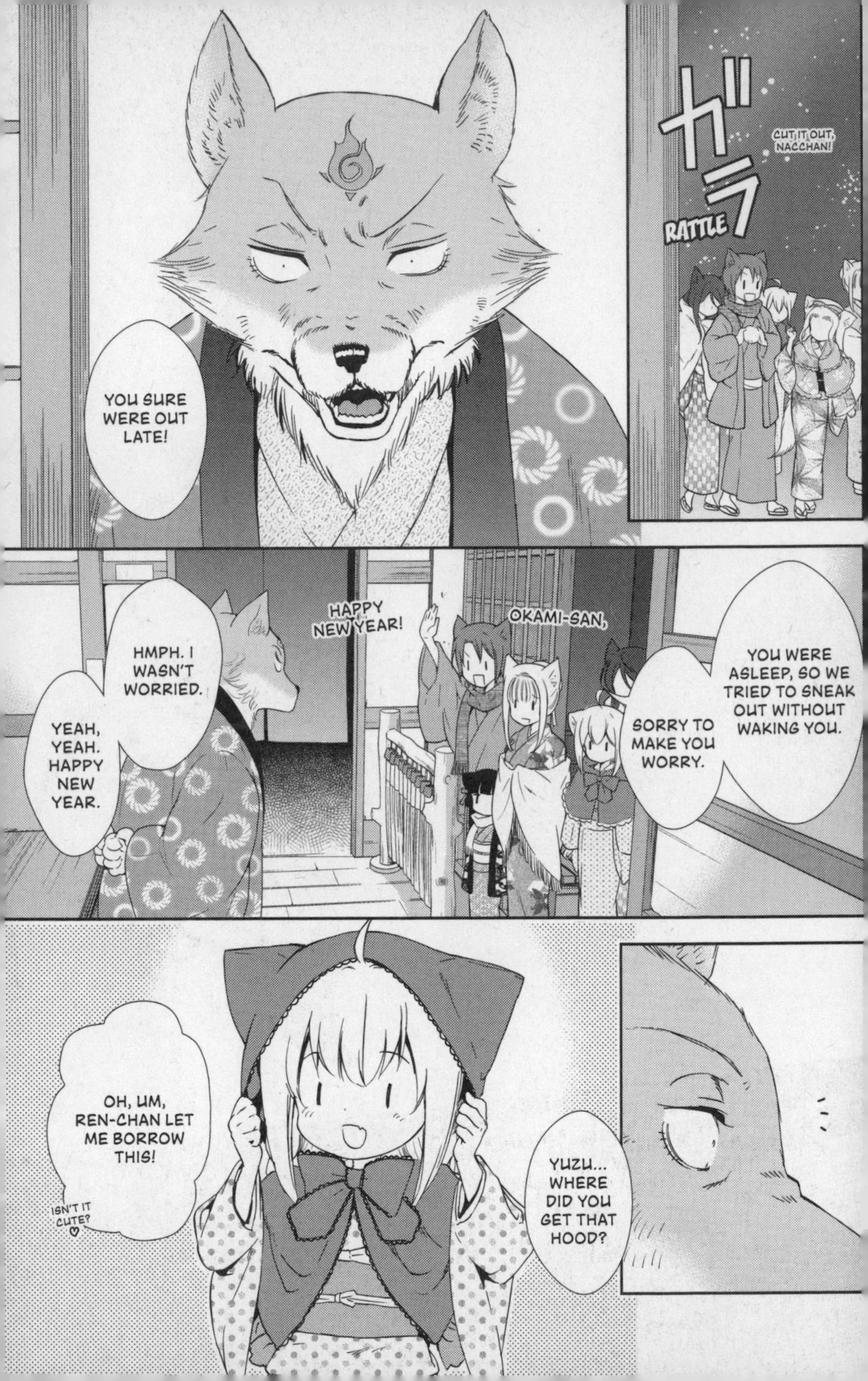
ガラ
RATTLE
CUT IT OUT, NACCHAN!
YOU SURE WERE OUT LATE!
YOU WERE ASLEEP, SO WE TRIED TO SNEAK OUT WITHOUT WAKING YOU.
SORRY TO MAKE YOU WORRY.
OKAMI-SAN,
HAPPY NEW YEAR!
HMPH. I WASN'T WORRIED.
YEAH, YEAH. HAPPY NEW YEAR.
YUZU... WHERE DID YOU GET THAT HOOD?
OH, UM, REN-CHAN LET ME BORROW THIS!
ISN'T IT CUTE? ♡

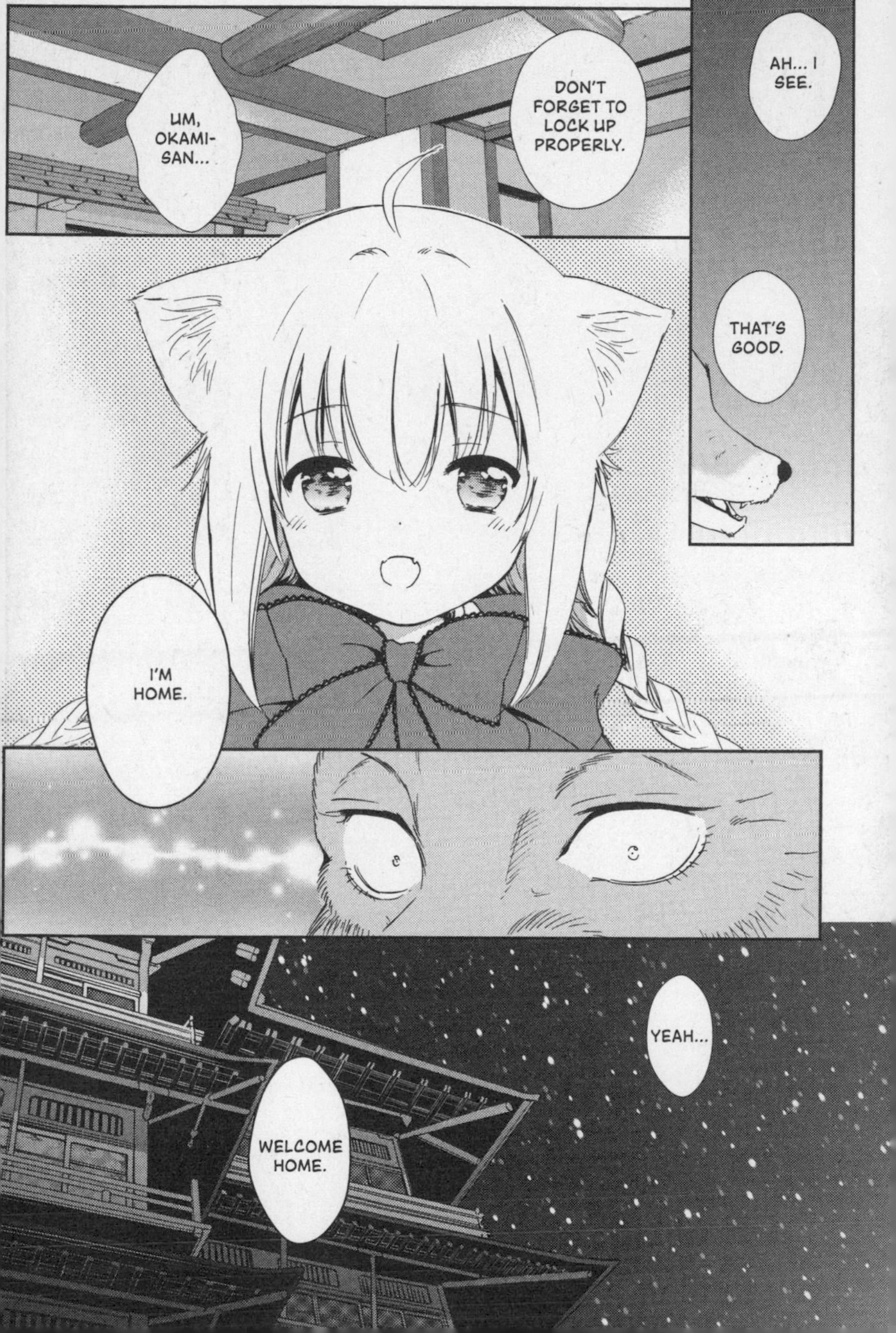
AH... I SEE.
THAT'S GOOD.
DON'T FORGET TO LOCK UP PROPERLY.
UM, OKAMI-SAN...
I'M HOME.
YEAH...
WELCOME HOME.

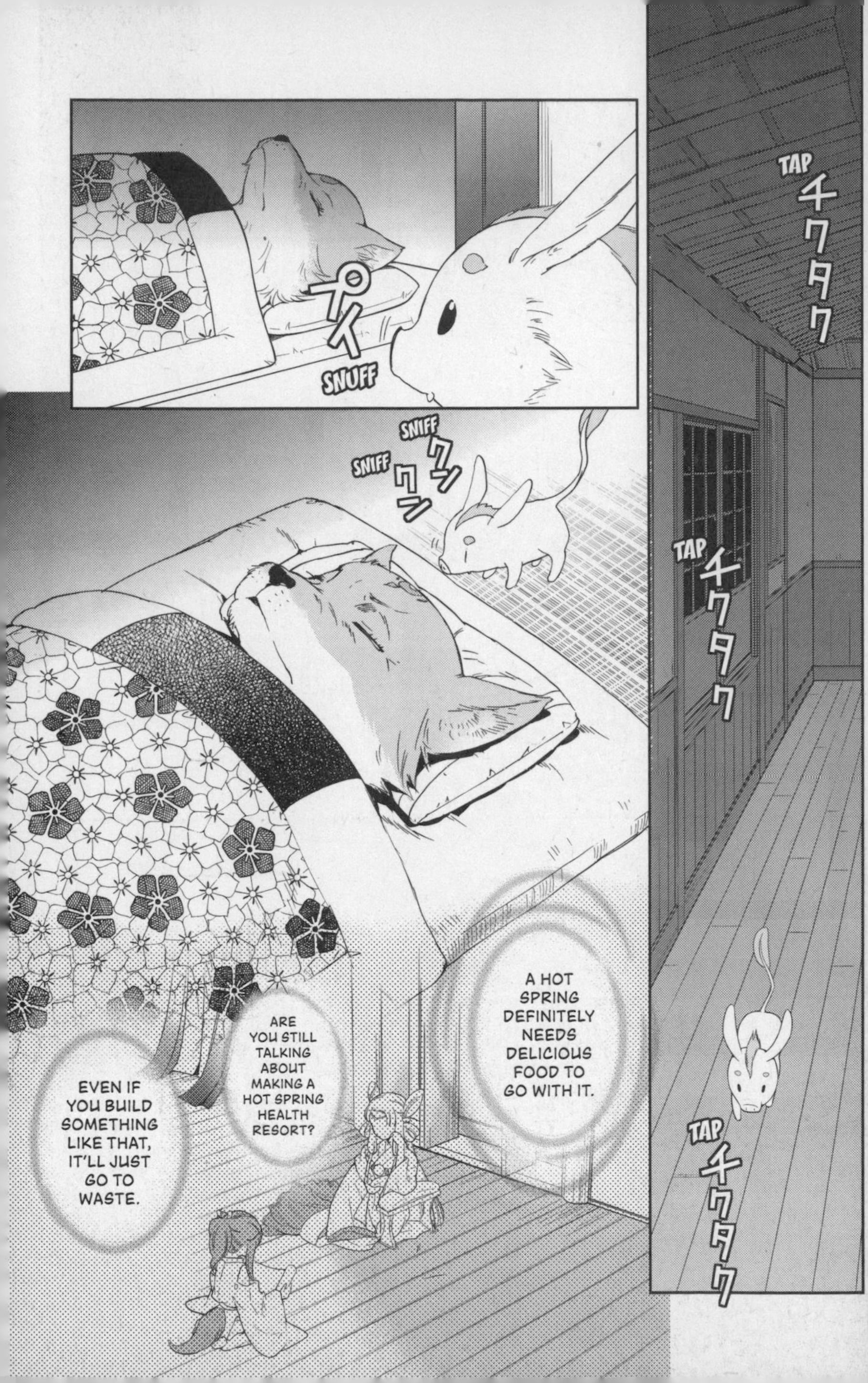
TAP
チクタク
TAP
チクタク
TAP
チクタク
プイ
SNUFF
SNIFF
クン
SNIFF
クン
A HOT SPRING DEFINITELY NEEDS DELICIOUS FOOD TO GO WITH IT.
ARE YOU STILL TALKING ABOUT MAKING A HOT SPRING HEALTH RESORT?
EVEN IF YOU BUILD SOMETHING LIKE THAT, IT'LL JUST GO TO WASTE.

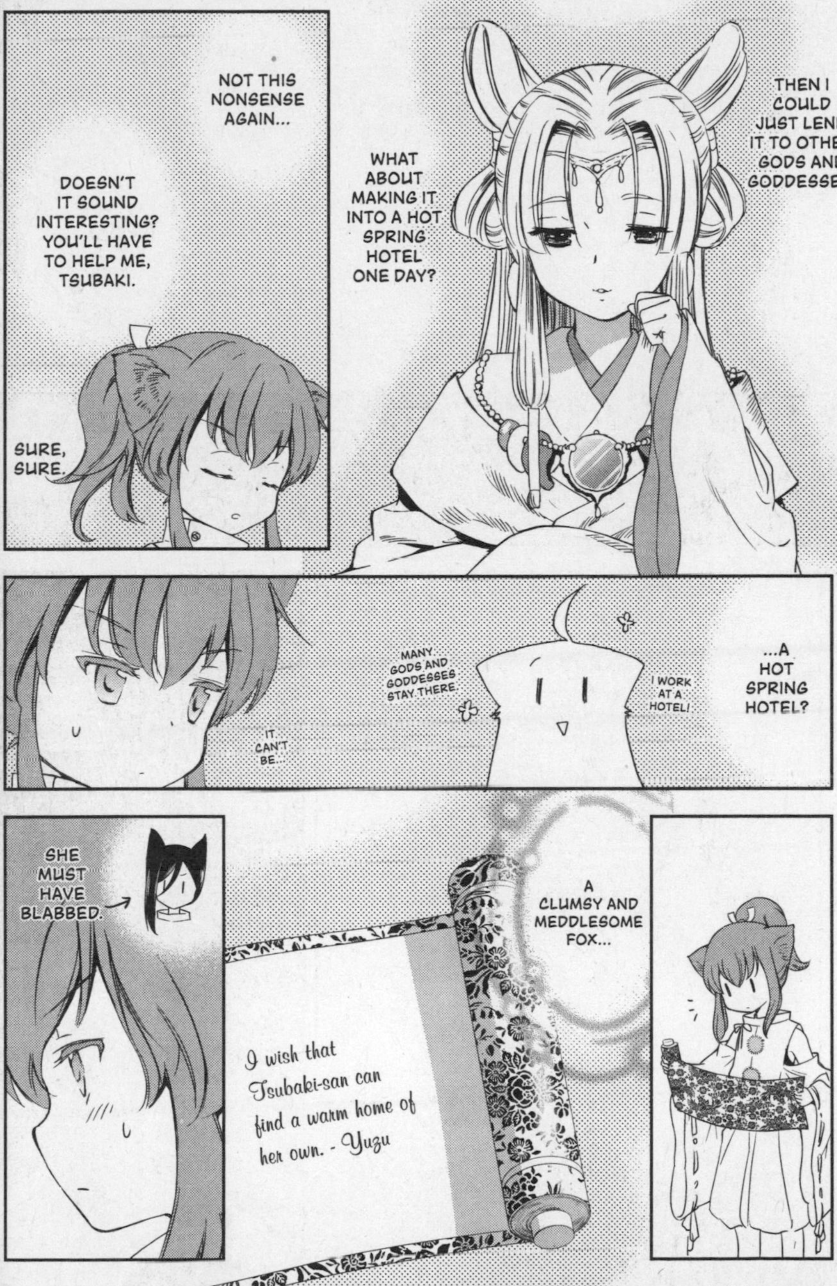
THEN I COULD JUST LEND IT TO OTHER GODS AND GODDESSES.
WHAT ABOUT MAKING IT INTO A HOT SPRING HOTEL ONE DAY?
NOT THIS NONSENSE AGAIN...
DOESN'T IT SOUND INTERESTING? YOU'LL HAVE TO HELP ME, TSUBAKI.
SURE, SURE.
...A HOT SPRING HOTEL?
I WORK AT A HOTEL!
MANY GODS AND GODDESSES STAY THERE.
IT CAN'T BE...
A CLUMSY AND MEDDLESOME FOX...
I wish that Tsubaki-san can find a warm home of her own. - Yuzu
SHE MUST HAVE BLABBED.

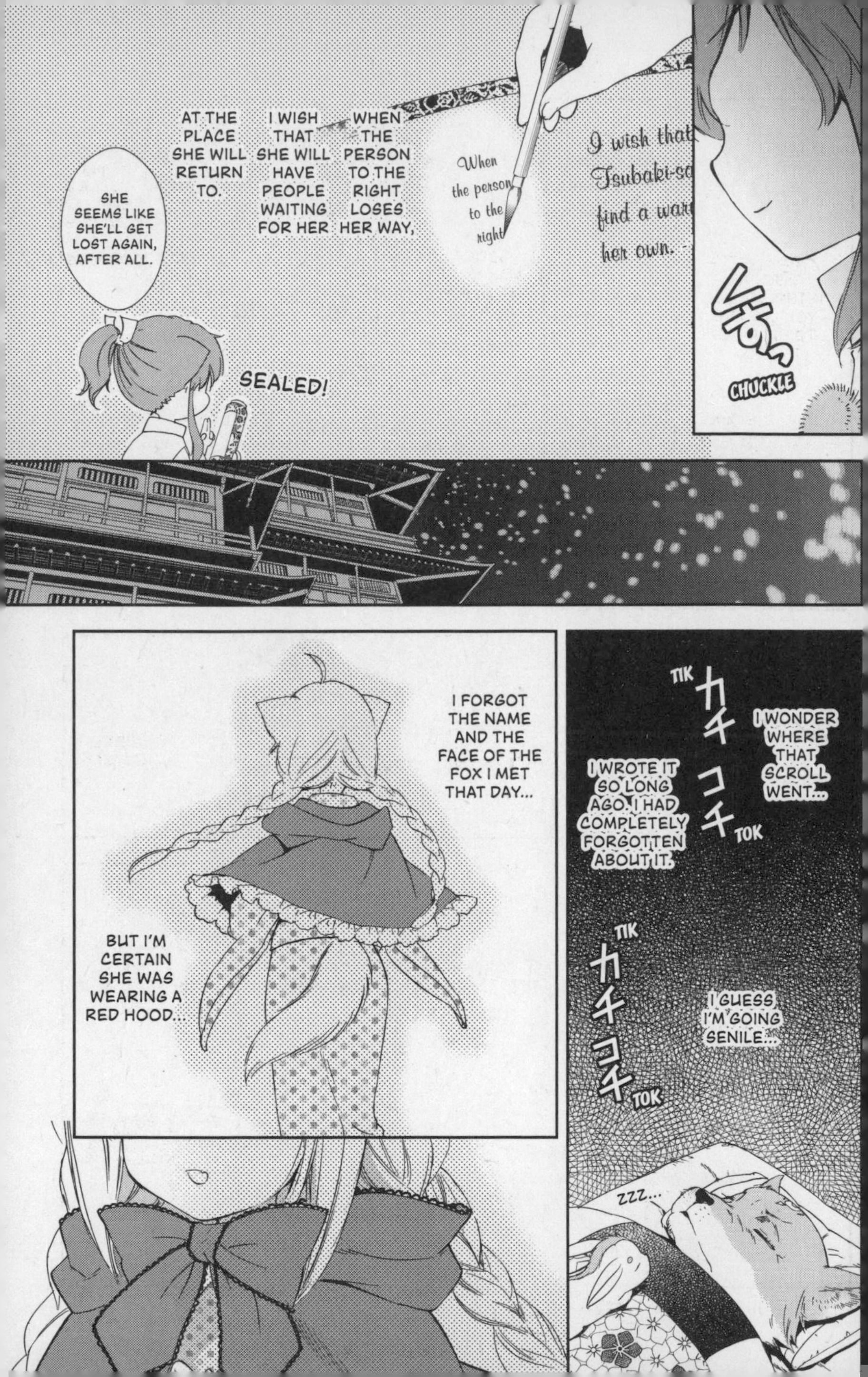
CHUCKLE
I wish that
Tsubaki-sa
find a war
her own.
When the person to the right
WHEN THE PERSON TO THE RIGHT LOSES HER WAY,
I WISH THAT SHE WILL HAVE PEOPLE WAITING FOR HER
AT THE PLACE SHE WILL RETURN TO.
SHE SEEMS LIKE SHE'LL GET LOST AGAIN, AFTER ALL.
SEALED!
TIK カチ
I WONDER WHERE THAT SCROLL WENT...
I WROTE IT SO LONG AGO, I HAD COMPLETELY FORGOTTEN ABOUT IT.
コチ TOK
TIK カチコチ TOK
I GUESS I'M GOING SENILE...
ZZZ...
I FORGOT THE NAME AND THE FACE OF THE FOX I MET THAT DAY...
BUT I'M CERTAIN SHE WAS WEARING A RED HOOD...

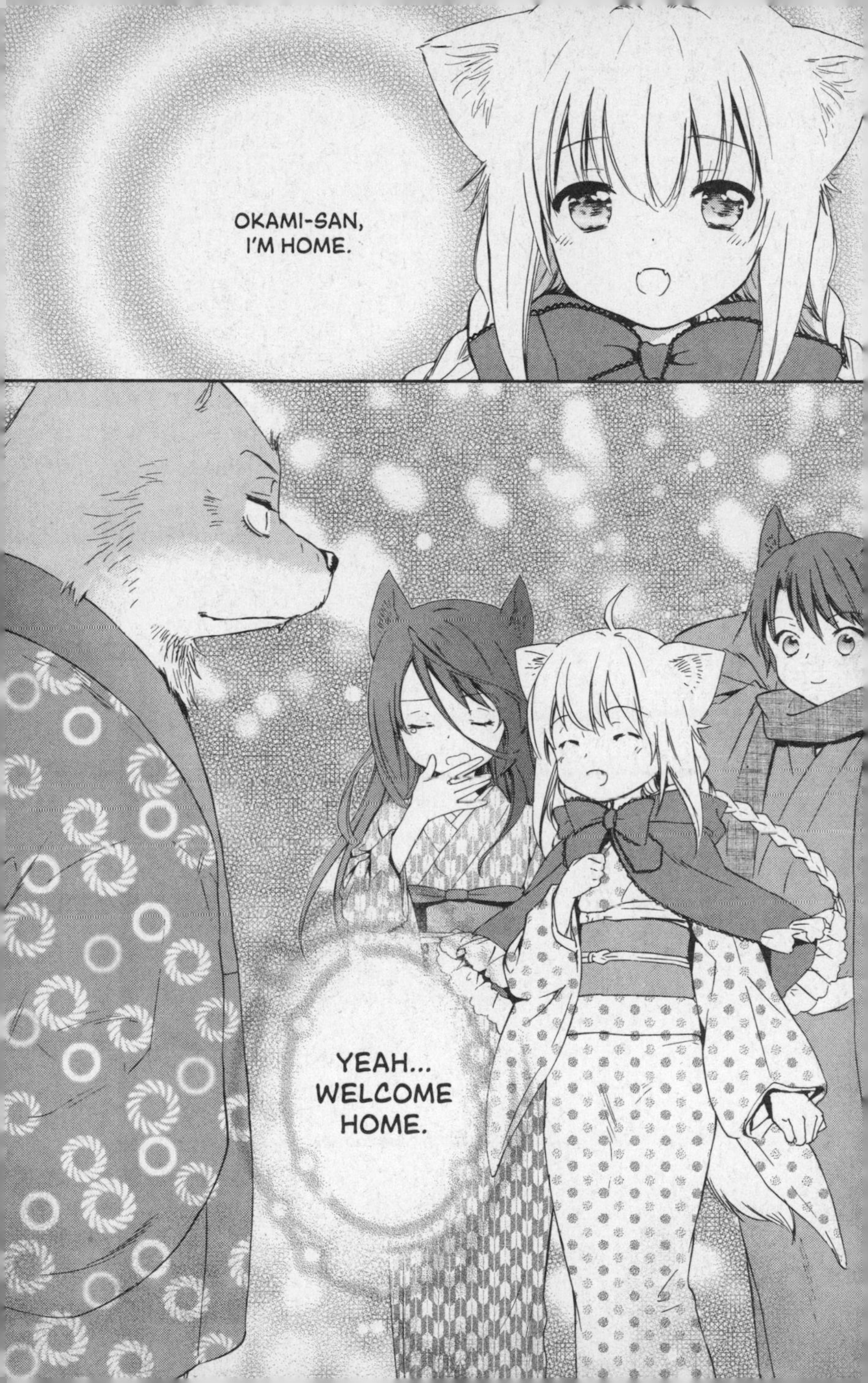
OKAMI-SAN, I'M HOME.
YEAH... WELCOME HOME.

KONOHANA KITAN

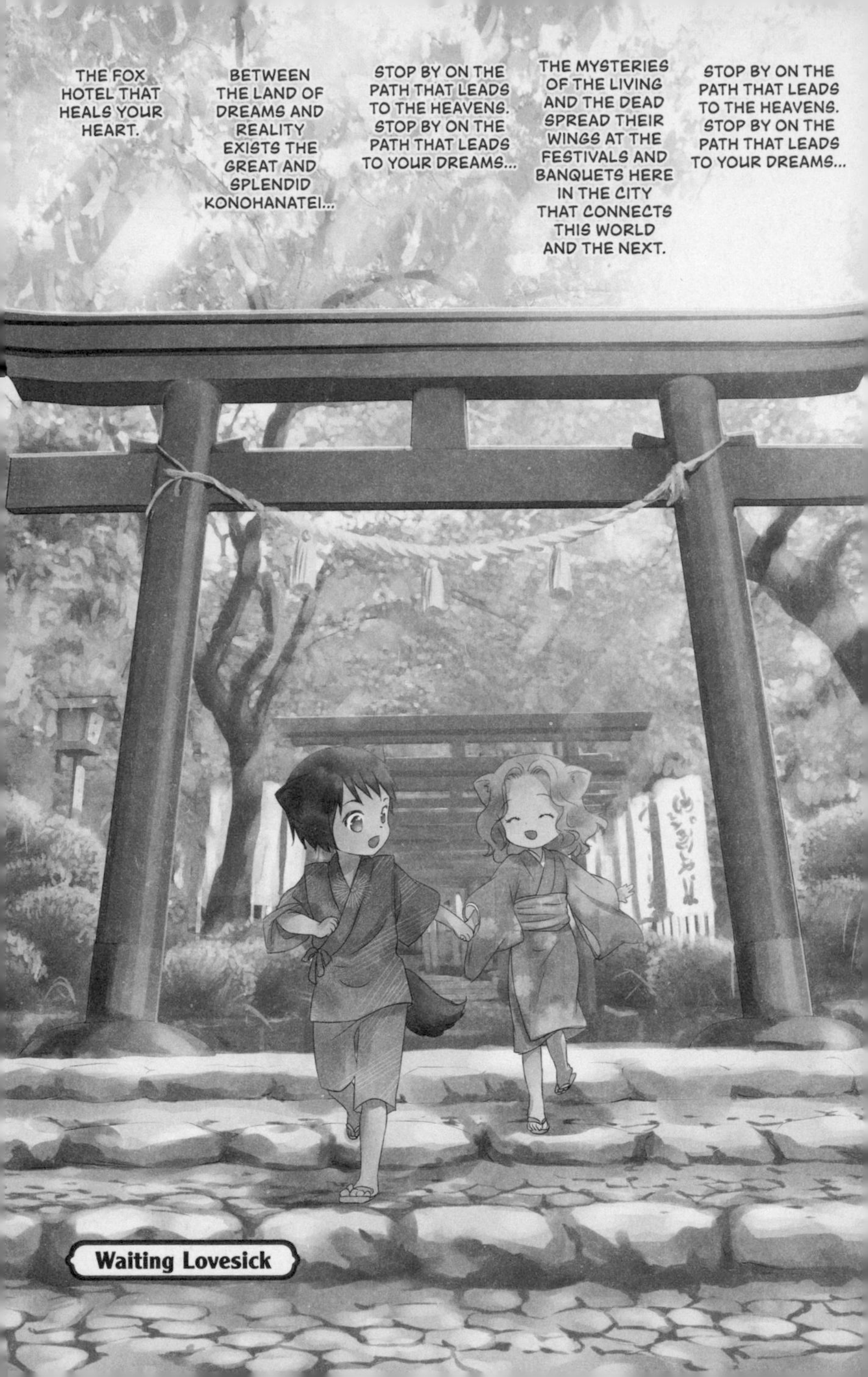
THE FOX HOTEL THAT HEALS YOUR HEART.
BETWEEN THE LAND OF DREAMS AND REALITY EXISTS THE GREAT AND SPLENDID KONOHANATEI...
STOP BY ON THE PATH THAT LEADS TO THE HEAVENS. STOP BY ON THE PATH THAT LEADS TO YOUR DREAMS...
THE MYSTERIES OF THE LIVING AND THE DEAD SPREAD THEIR WINGS AT THE FESTIVALS AND BANQUETS HERE IN THE CITY THAT CONNECTS THIS WORLD AND THE NEXT.
STOP BY ON THE PATH THAT LEADS TO THE HEAVENS. STOP BY ON THE PATH THAT LEADS TO YOUR DREAMS...
Waiting Lovesick

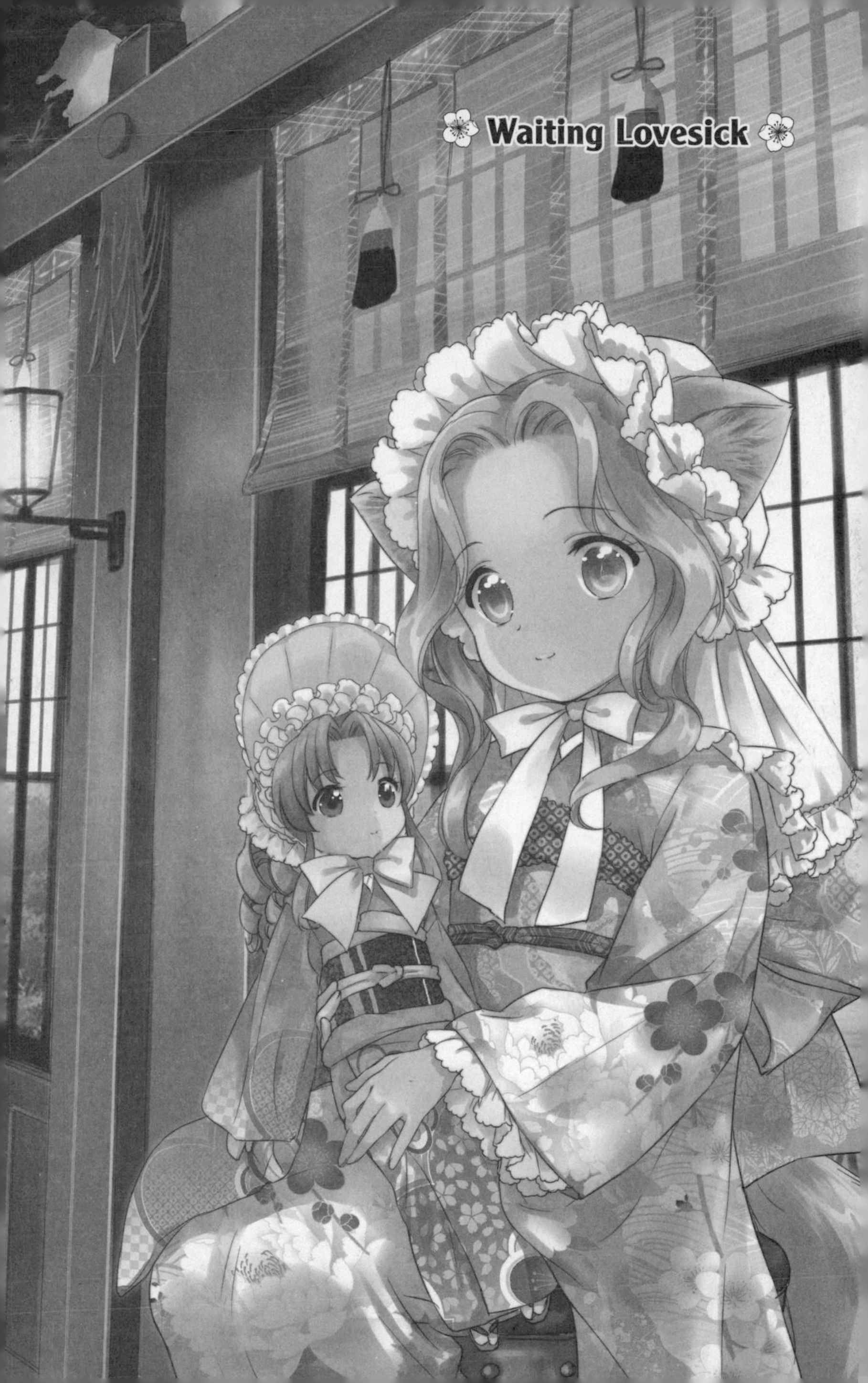
Waiting Lovesick

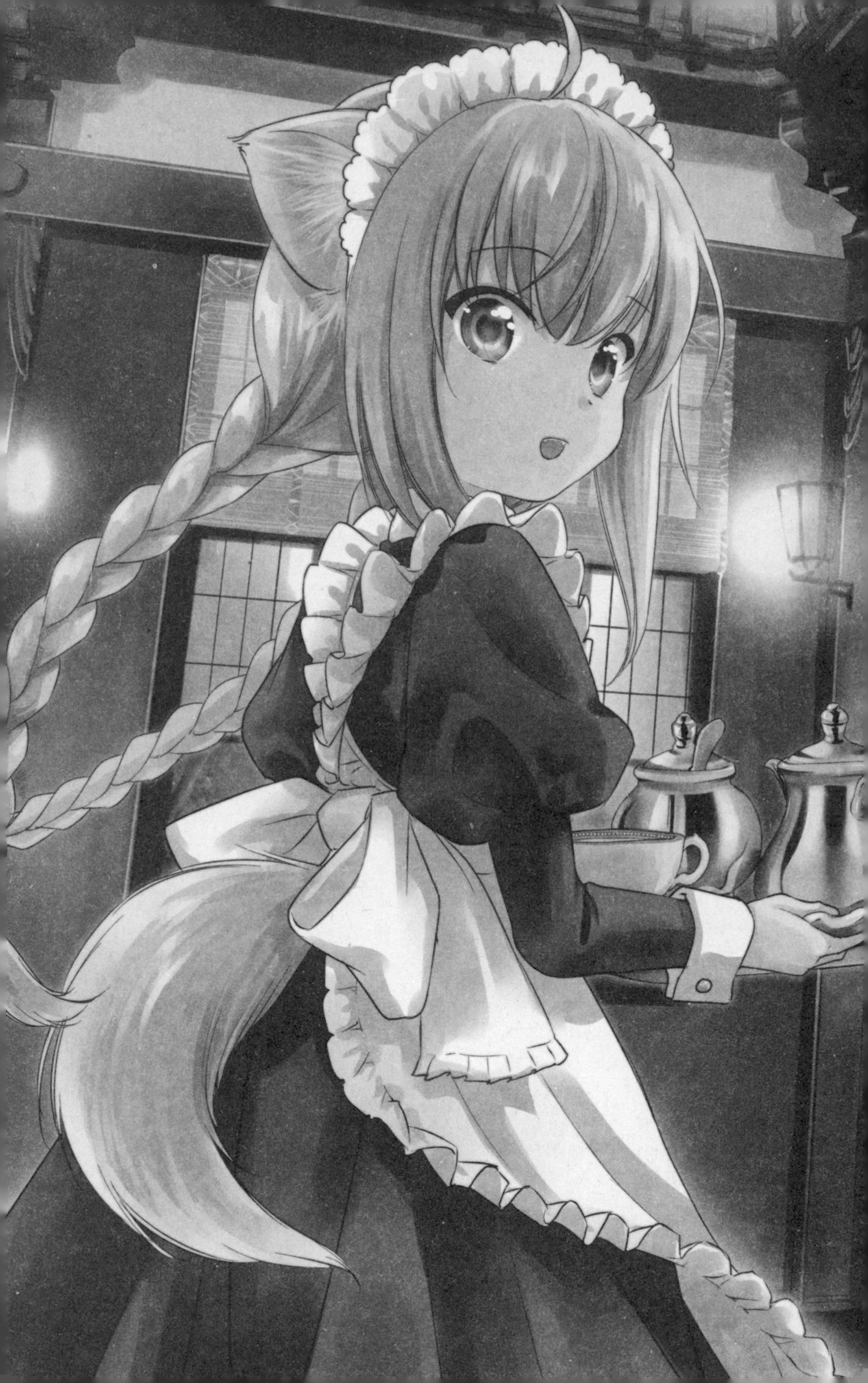

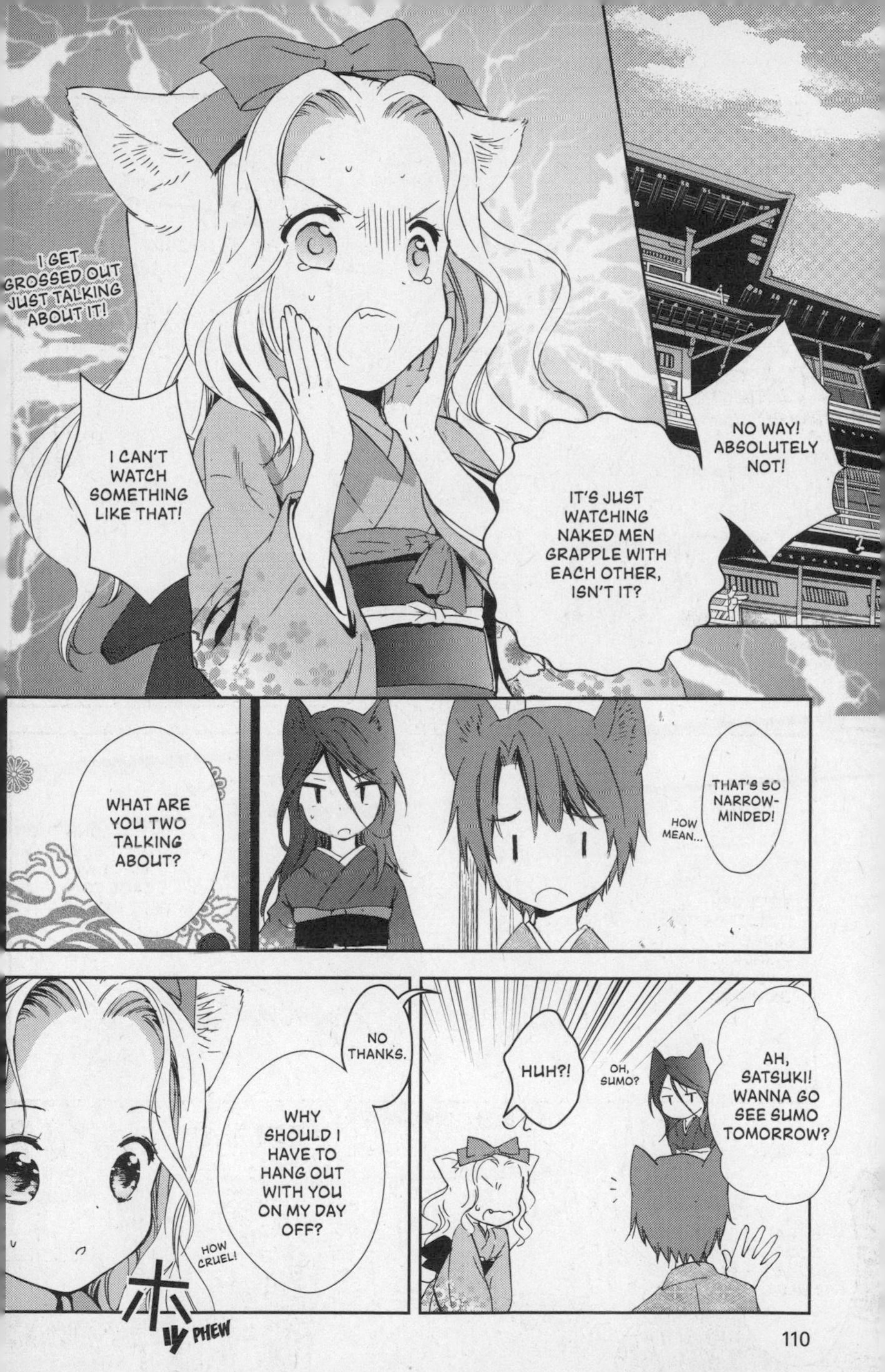
NO WAY! ABSOLUTELY NOT!
IT'S JUST WATCHING NAKED MEN GRAPPLE WITH EACH OTHER, ISN'T IT?
I CAN'T WATCH SOMETHING LIKE THAT!
I GET GROSSED OUT JUST TALKING ABOUT IT!
THAT'S SO NARROW-MINDED!
HOW MEAN...
WHAT ARE YOU TWO TALKING ABOUT?
AH, SATSUKI! WANNA GO SEE SUMO TOMORROW?
OH, SUMO?
HUH?!
NO THANKS.
WHY SHOULD I HAVE TO HANG OUT WITH YOU ON MY DAY OFF?
HOW CRUEL!
PHEW

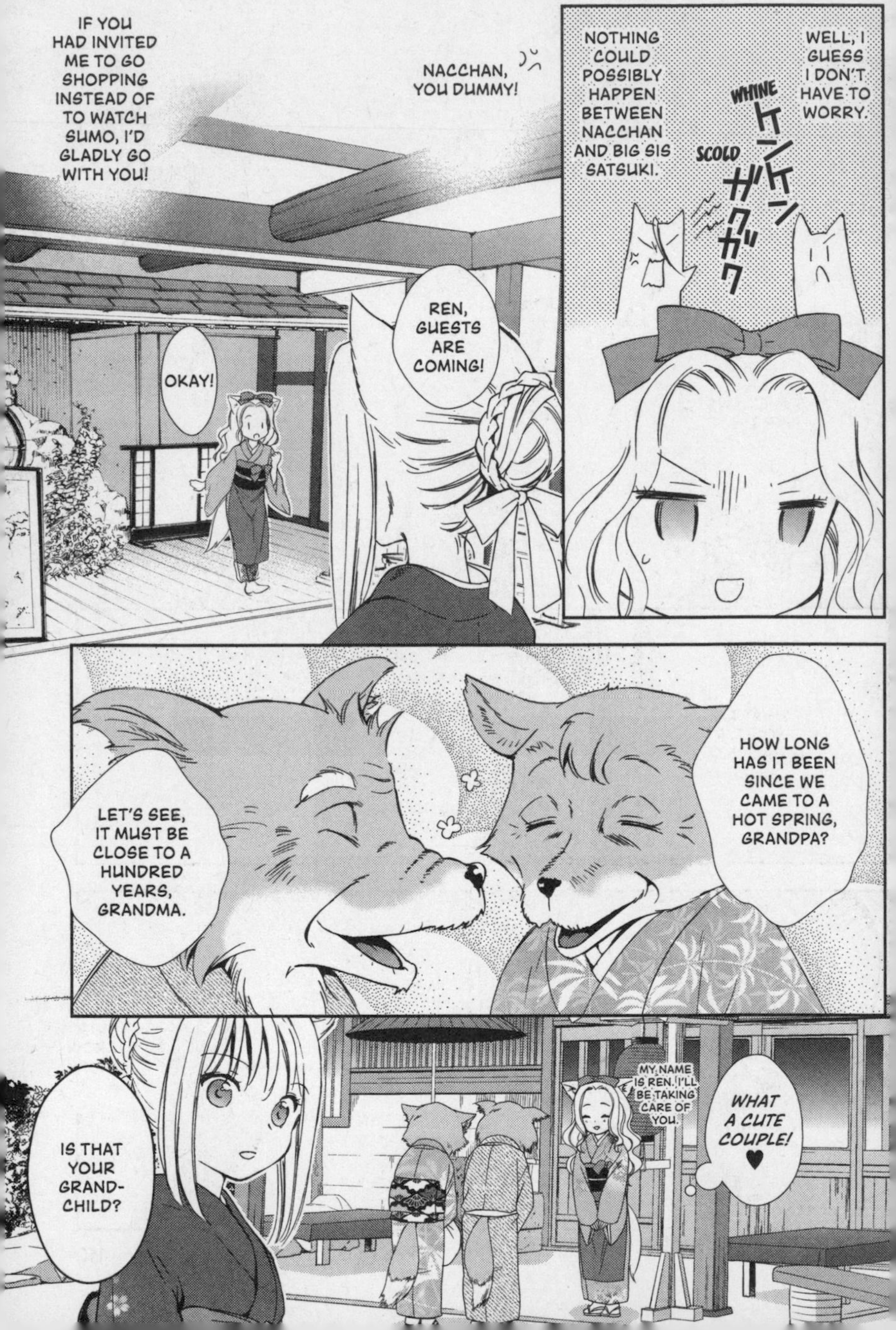
WELL, I GUESS I DON'T HAVE TO WORRY.
NOTHING COULD POSSIBLY HAPPEN BETWEEN NACCHAN AND BIG SIS SATSUKI.
WHINE ケンケン
SCOLD ガクガク
NACCHAN, YOU DUMMY!
IF YOU HAD INVITED ME TO GO SHOPPING INSTEAD OF TO WATCH SUMO, I'D GLADLY GO WITH YOU!
REN, GUESTS ARE COMING!
OKAY!
HOW LONG HAS IT BEEN SINCE WE CAME TO A HOT SPRING, GRANDPA?
LET'S SEE, IT MUST BE CLOSE TO A HUNDRED YEARS, GRANDMA.
WHAT A CUTE COUPLE! ♥
MY NAME IS REN. I'LL BE TAKING CARE OF YOU.
IS THAT YOUR GRAND-CHILD?

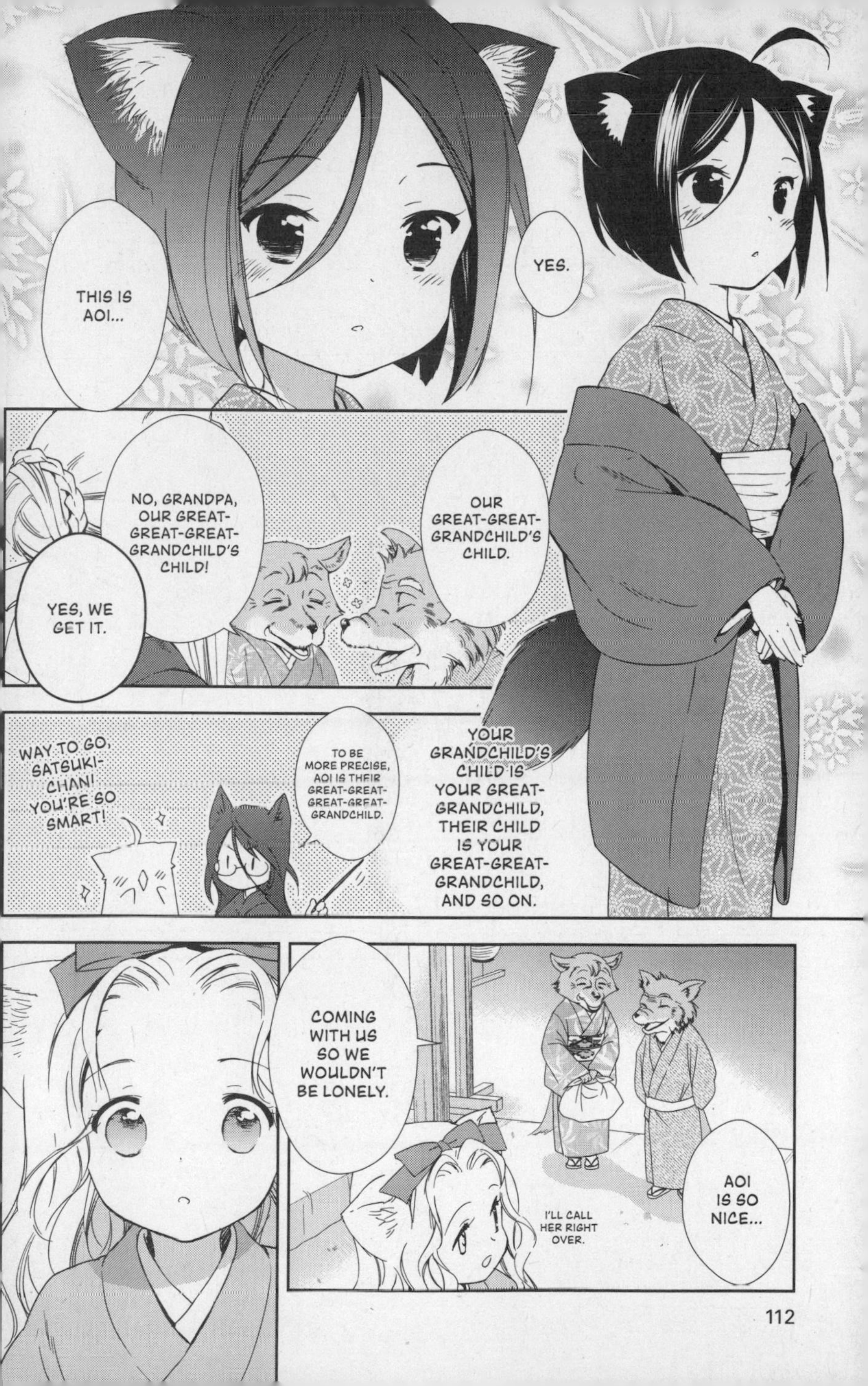
THIS IS AOI...
YES.
OUR GREAT-GREAT-GRANDCHILD'S CHILD.
NO, GRANDPA, OUR GREAT-GREAT-GREAT-GRANDCHILD'S CHILD!
YES, WE GET IT.
YOUR GRANDCHILD'S CHILD IS YOUR GREAT-GRANDCHILD, THEIR CHILD IS YOUR GREAT-GREAT-GRANDCHILD, AND SO ON.
TO BE MORE PRECISE, AOI IS THEIR GREAT-GREAT-GREAT-GREAT-GRANDCHILD.
WAY TO GO, SATSUKI-CHAN! YOU'RE SO SMART!
AOI IS SO NICE...
COMING WITH US SO WE WOULDN'T BE LONELY.
I'LL CALL HER RIGHT OVER.

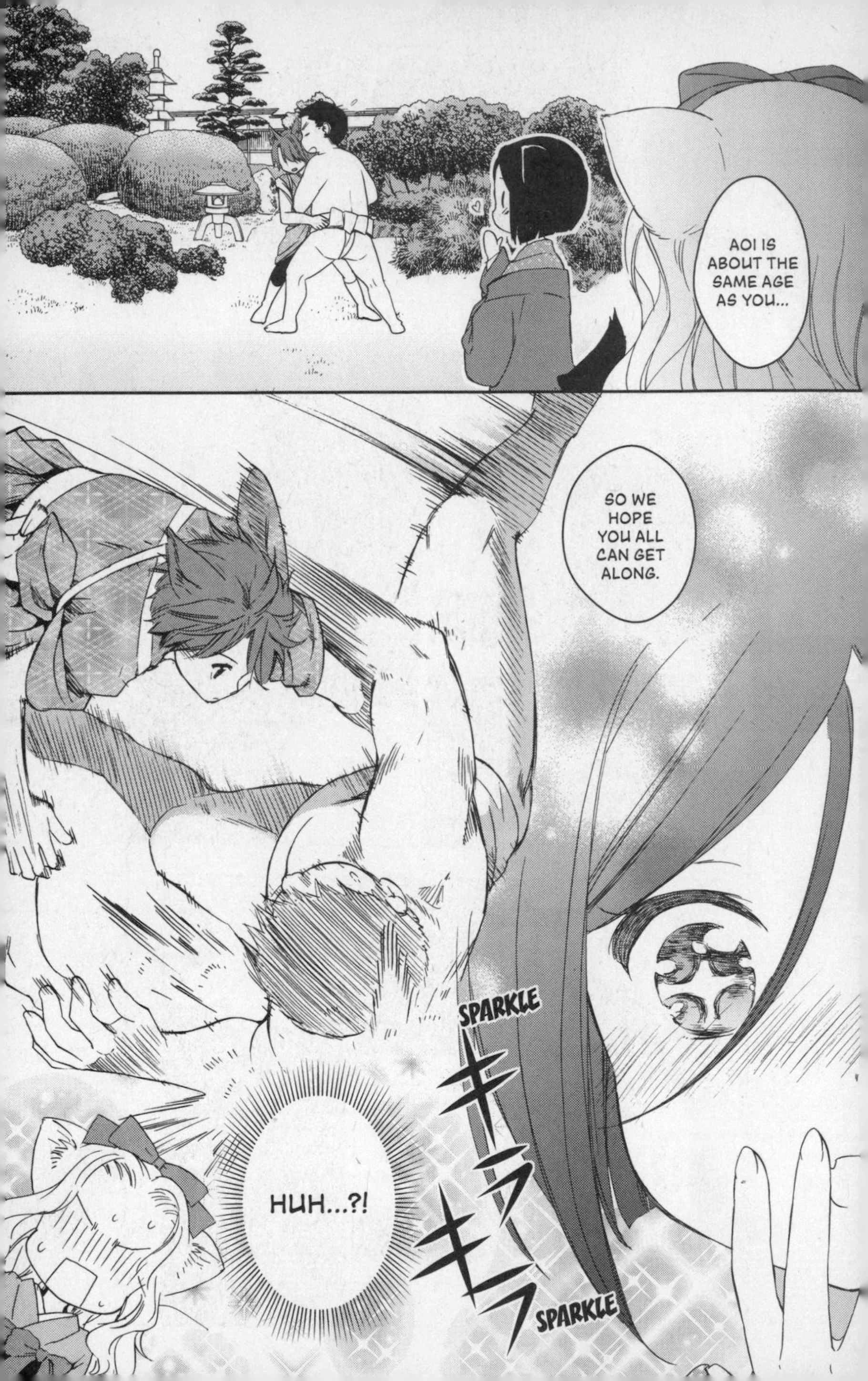
AOI IS ABOUT THE SAME AGE AS YOU...
SO WE HOPE YOU ALL CAN GET ALONG.
SPARKLE
キラキラ
SPARKLE
HUH...?!

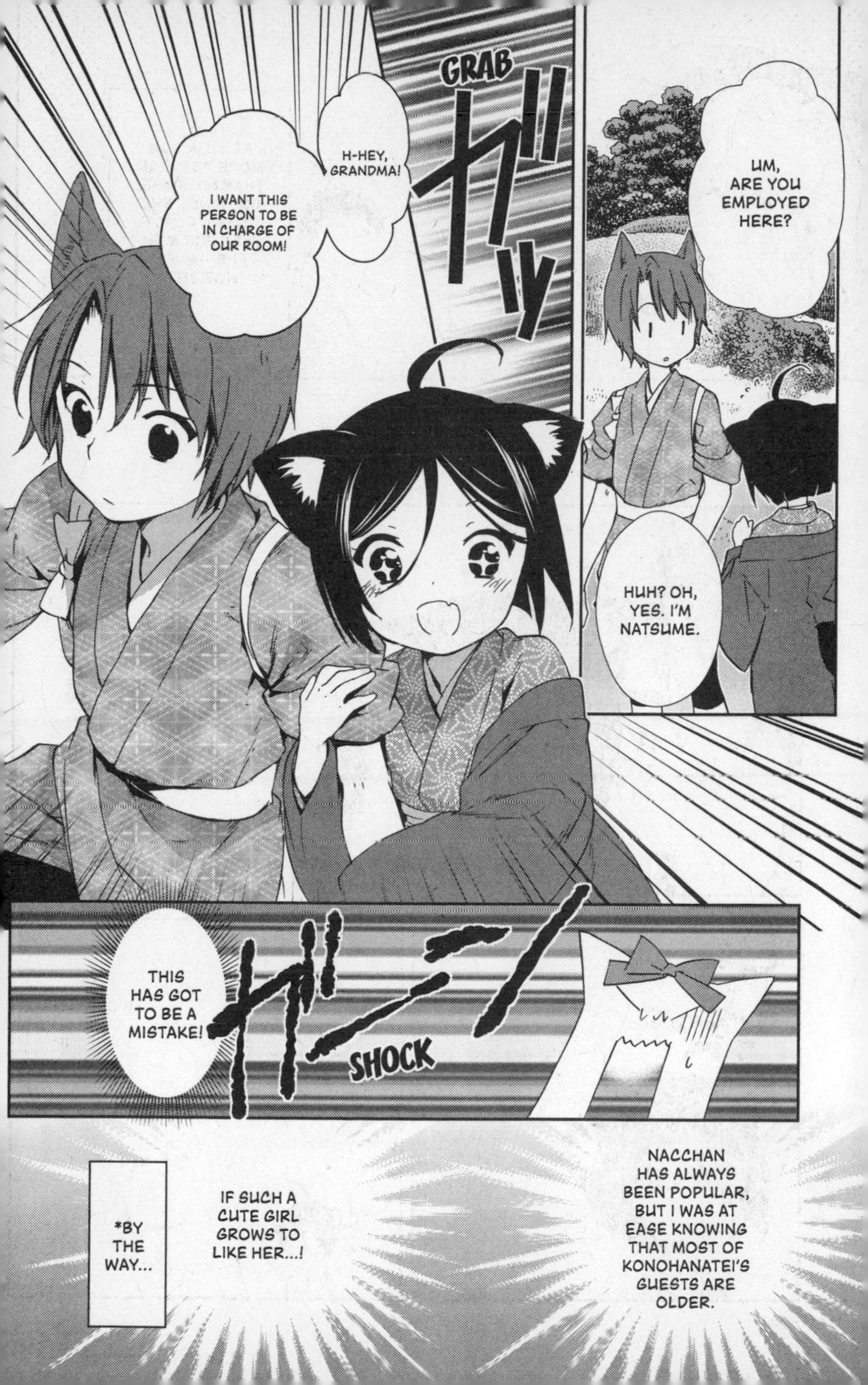
UM, ARE YOU EMPLOYED HERE?
HUH? OH, YES. I'M NATSUME.
GRAB
H-HEY, GRANDMA!
I WANT THIS PERSON TO BE IN CHARGE OF OUR ROOM!
THIS HAS GOT TO BE A MISTAKE!
SHOCK
NACCHAN HAS ALWAYS BEEN POPULAR, BUT I WAS AT EASE KNOWING THAT MOST OF KONOHANATEI'S GUESTS ARE OLDER.
IF SUCH A CUTE GIRL GROWS TO LIKE HER...!
*BY THE WAY...

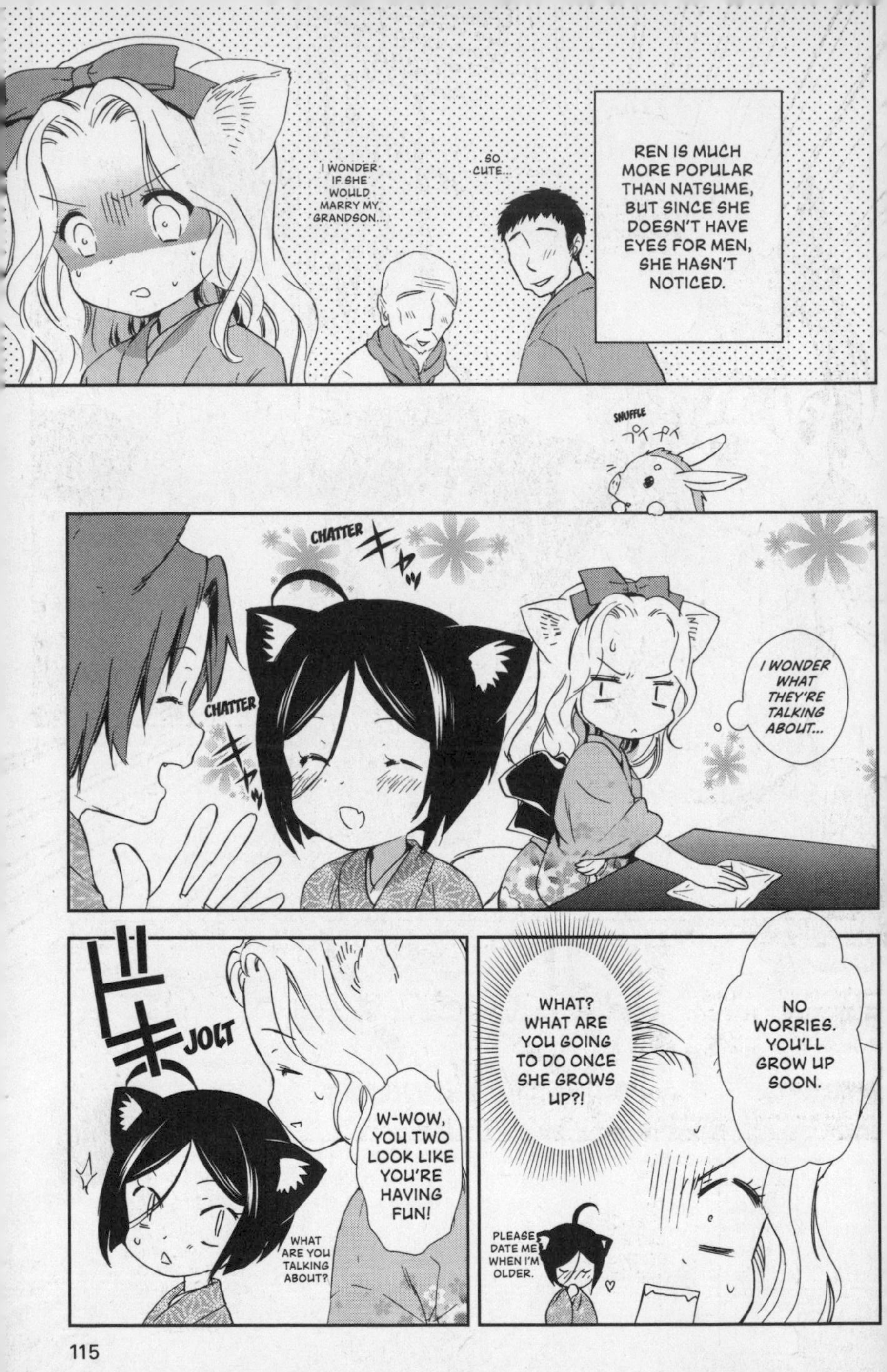
REN IS MUCH MORE POPULAR THAN NATSUME, BUT SINCE SHE DOESN'T HAVE EYES FOR MEN, SHE HASN'T NOTICED.
SO CUTE...
I WONDER IF SHE WOULD MARRY MY GRANDSON...
SNUFFLE
I WONDER WHAT THEY'RE TALKING ABOUT...
CHATTER
CHATTER
NO WORRIES. YOU'LL GROW UP SOON.
WHAT? WHAT ARE YOU GOING TO DO ONCE SHE GROWS UP?!
PLEASE DATE ME WHEN I'M OLDER.
JOLT
W-WOW, YOU TWO LOOK LIKE YOU'RE HAVING FUN!
WHAT ARE YOU TALKING ABOUT?

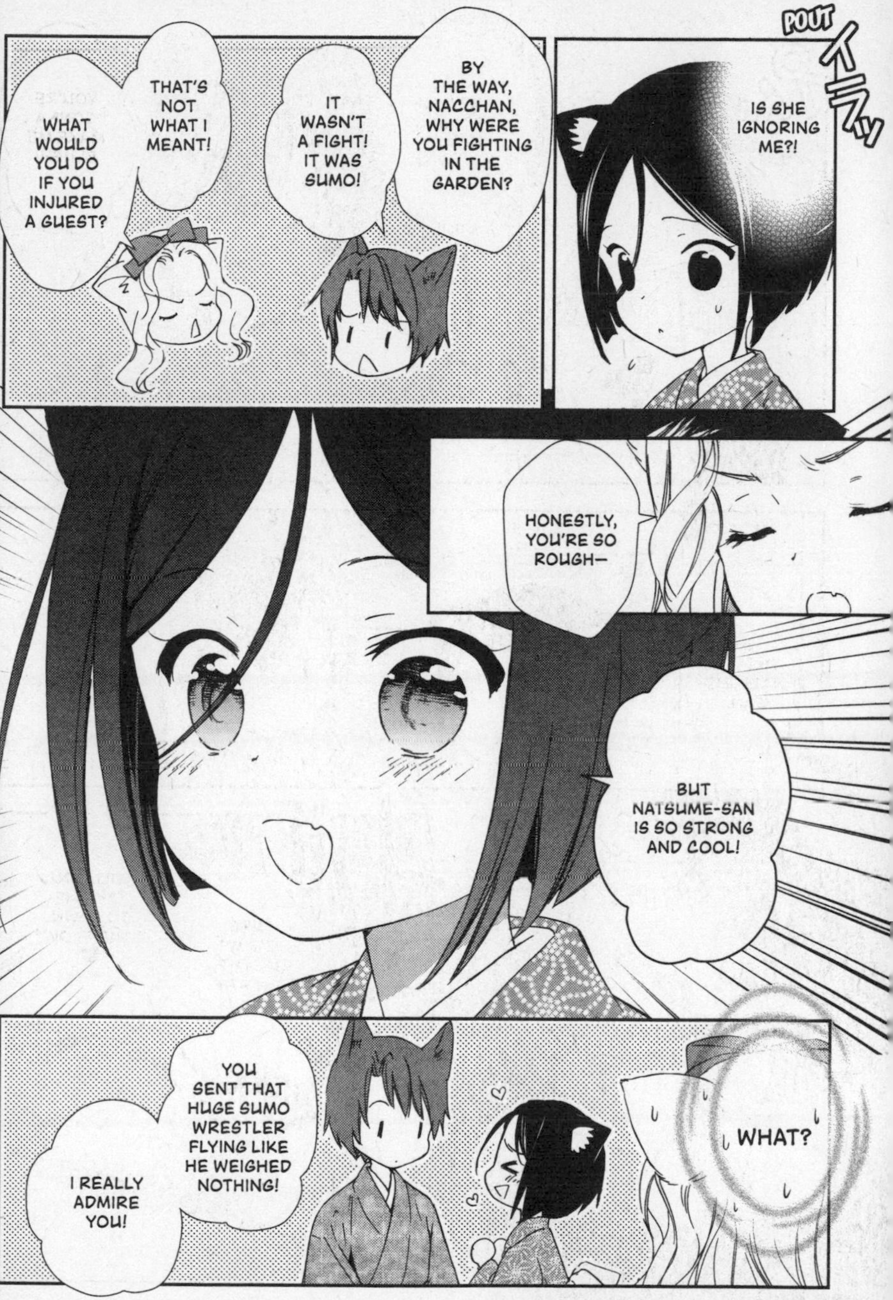
POUT
IS SHE IGNORING ME?!
BY THE WAY, NACCHAN, WHY WERE YOU FIGHTING IN THE GARDEN?
IT WASN'T A FIGHT! IT WAS SUMO!
THAT'S NOT WHAT I MEANT!
WHAT WOULD YOU DO IF YOU INJURED A GUEST?
HONESTLY, YOU'RE SO ROUGH—
BUT NATSUME-SAN IS SO STRONG AND COOL!
WHAT?
YOU SENT THAT HUGE SUMO WRESTLER FLYING LIKE HE WEIGHED NOTHING!
I REALLY ADMIRE YOU!

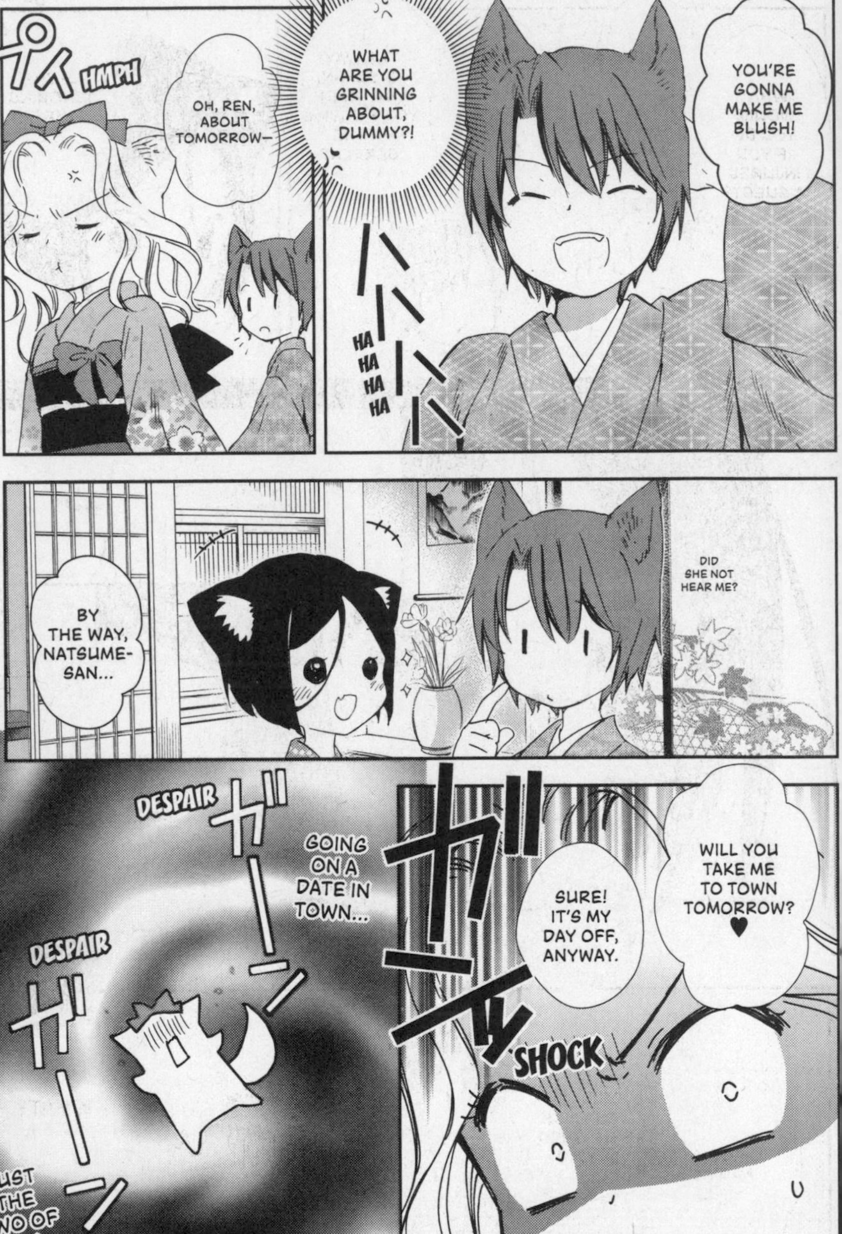
YOU'RE GONNA MAKE ME BLUSH!
HA HA HA HA
WHAT ARE YOU GRINNING ABOUT, DUMMY?!
OH, REN, ABOUT TOMORROW—
HMPH
DID SHE NOT HEAR ME?
BY THE WAY, NATSUME-SAN...
WILL YOU TAKE ME TO TOWN TOMORROW? ♥
SURE! IT'S MY DAY OFF, ANYWAY.
SHOCK
DESPAIR
GOING ON A DATE IN TOWN...
DESPAIR
JUST THE TWO OF THEM...

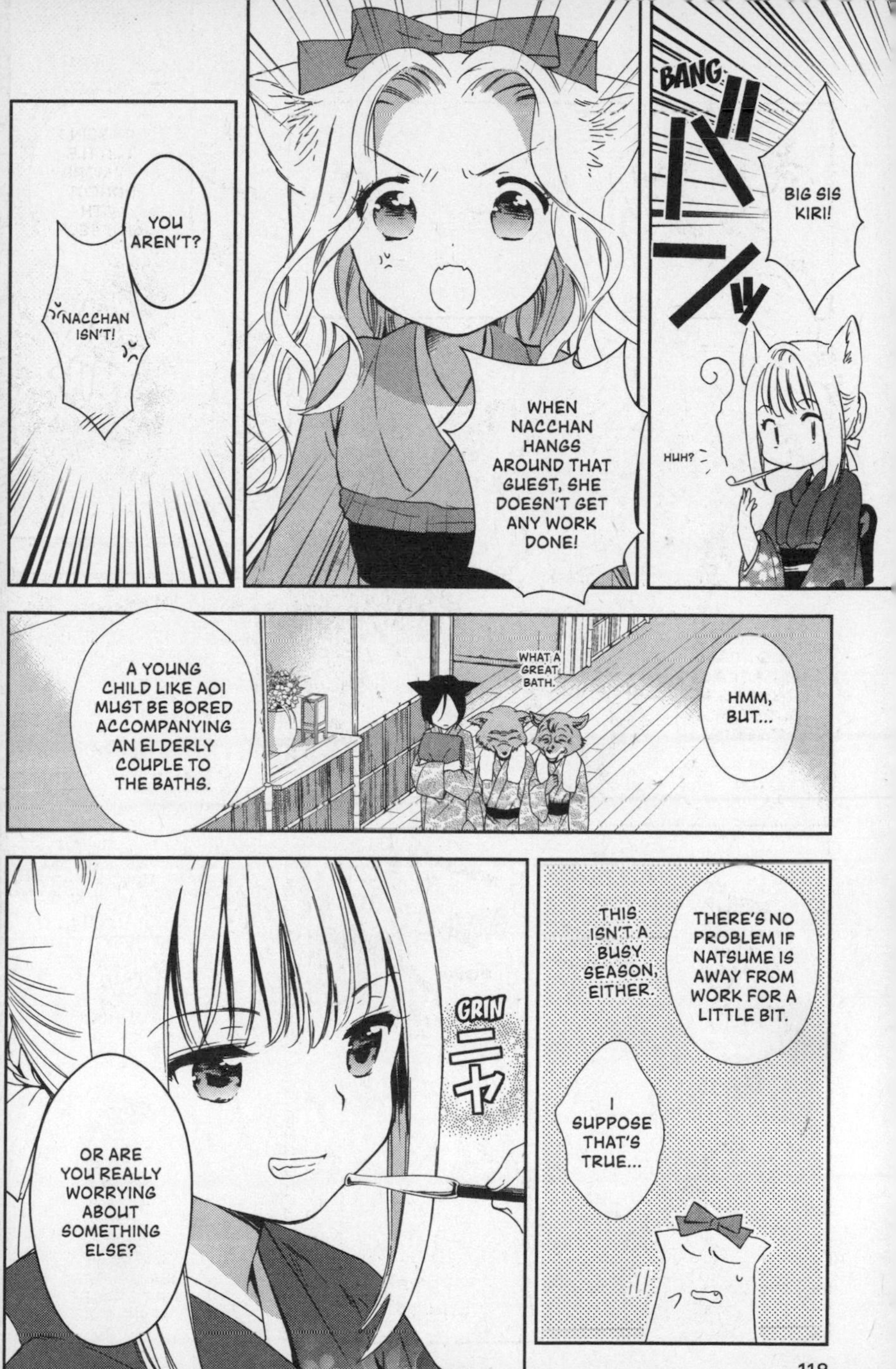
BANG
BIG SIS KIRI!
HUH?
WHEN NACCHAN HANGS AROUND THAT GUEST, SHE DOESN'T GET ANY WORK DONE!
YOU AREN'T?
NACCHAN ISN'T!
HMM, BUT...
WHAT A GREAT BATH.
A YOUNG CHILD LIKE AOI MUST BE BORED ACCOMPANYING AN ELDERLY COUPLE TO THE BATHS.
THERE'S NO PROBLEM IF NATSUME IS AWAY FROM WORK FOR A LITTLE BIT.
THIS ISN'T A BUSY SEASON, EITHER.
I SUPPOSE THAT'S TRUE...
GRIN
OR ARE YOU REALLY WORRYING ABOUT SOMETHING ELSE?

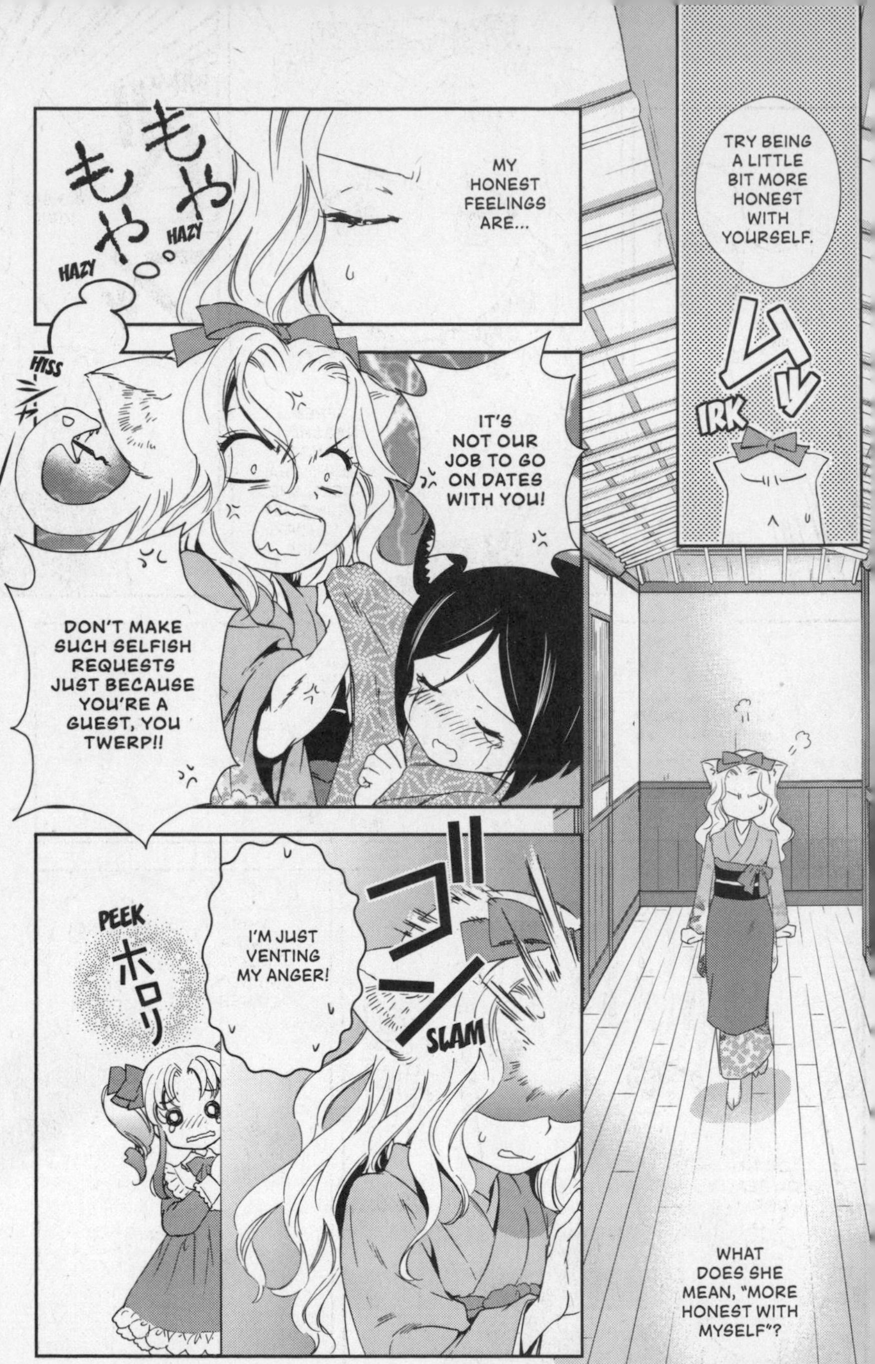
TRY BEING A LITTLE BIT MORE HONEST WITH YOURSELF.
IRK
WHAT DOES SHE MEAN, "MORE HONEST WITH MYSELF"?
MY HONEST FEELINGS ARE...
HAZY
HAZY
HISS
IT'S NOT OUR JOB TO GO ON DATES WITH YOU!
DON'T MAKE SUCH SELFISH REQUESTS JUST BECAUSE YOU'RE A GUEST, YOU TWERP!!
SLAM
I'M JUST VENTING MY ANGER!
PEEK

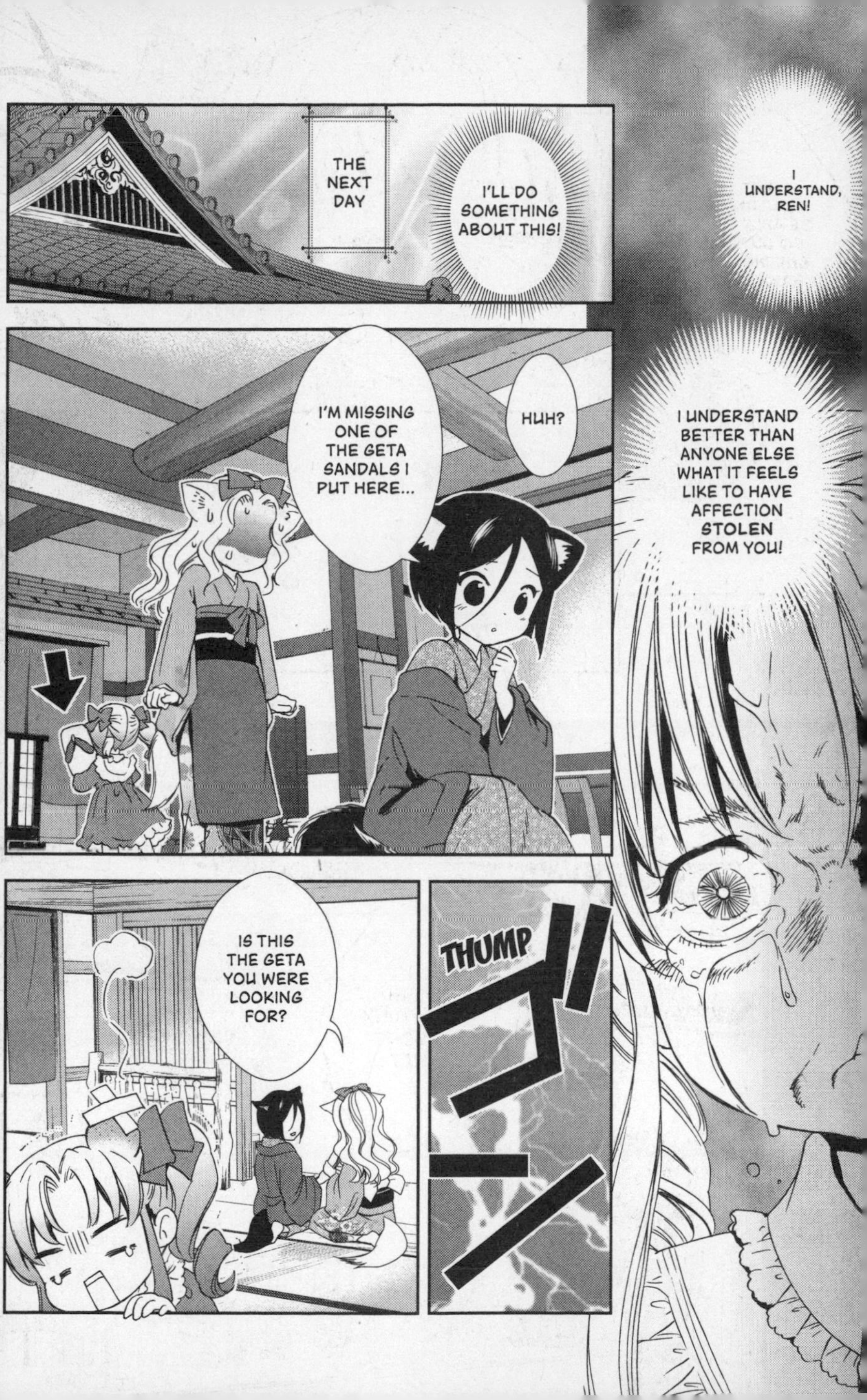
I UNDERSTAND, REN!
I UNDERSTAND BETTER THAN ANYONE ELSE WHAT IT FEELS LIKE TO HAVE AFFECTION STOLEN FROM YOU!
I'LL DO SOMETHING ABOUT THIS!
THE NEXT DAY
HUH?
I'M MISSING ONE OF THE GETA SANDALS I PUT HERE...
THUMP
IS THIS THE GETA YOU WERE LOOKING FOR?

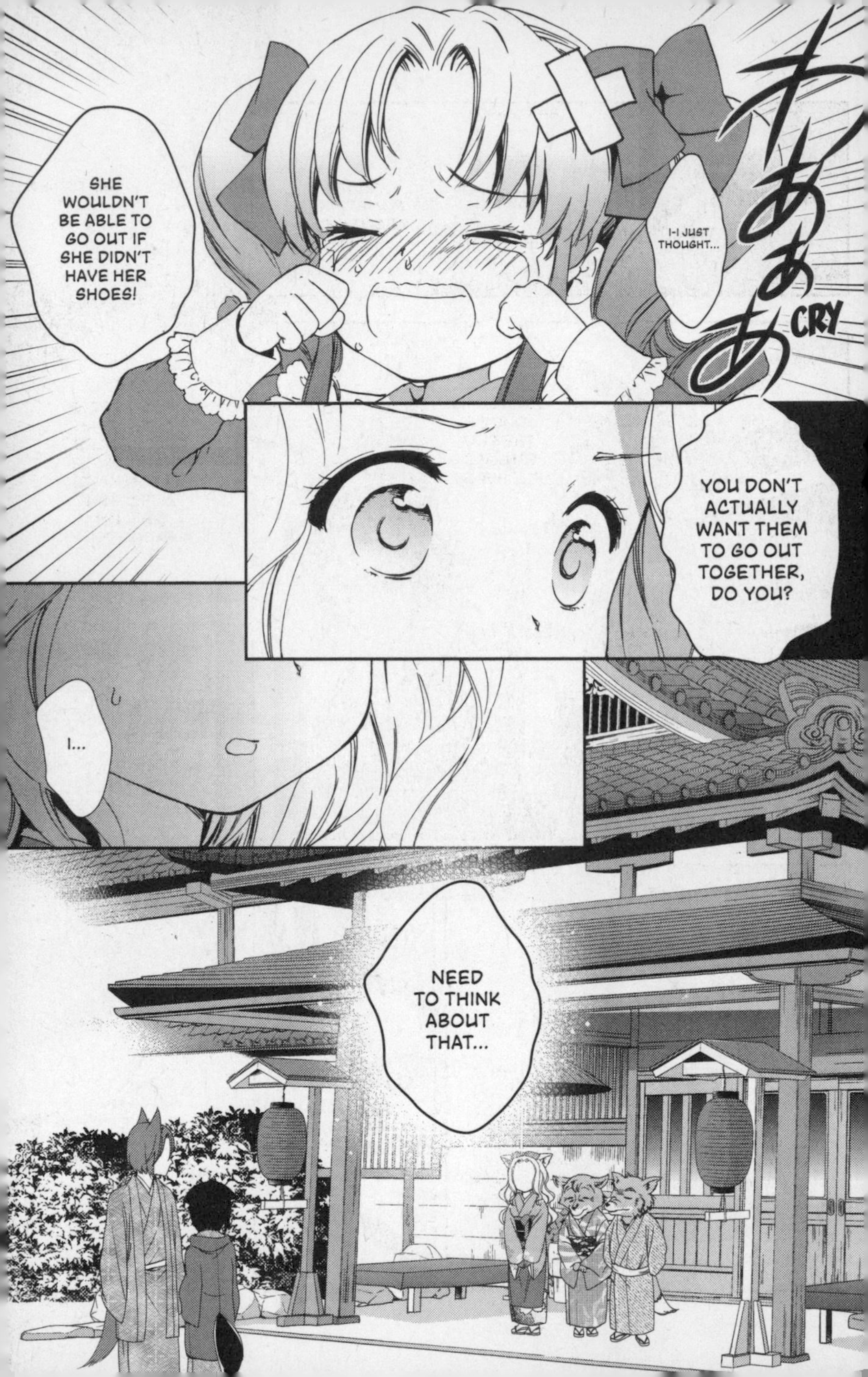
CRY
I-I JUST THOUGHT...
SHE WOULDN'T BE ABLE TO GO OUT IF SHE DIDN'T HAVE HER SHOES!
YOU DON'T ACTUALLY WANT THEM TO GO OUT TOGETHER, DO YOU?
I...
NEED TO THINK ABOUT THAT...

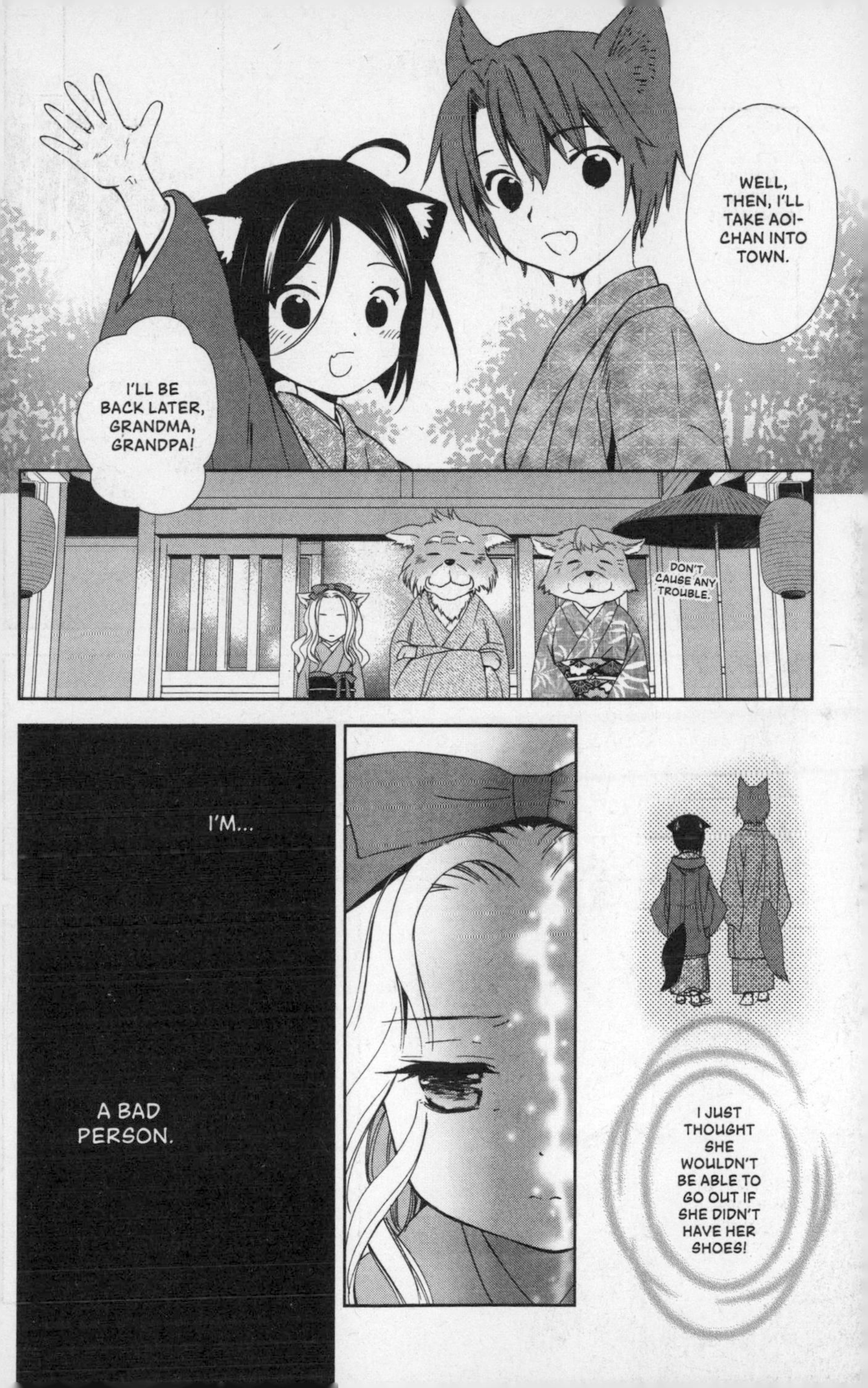
WELL, THEN, I'LL TAKE AOI-CHAN INTO TOWN.
I'LL BE BACK LATER, GRANDMA, GRANDPA!
DON'T CAUSE ANY TROUBLE.
I JUST THOUGHT SHE WOULDN'T BE ABLE TO GO OUT IF SHE DIDN'T HAVE HER SHOES!
I'M...
A BAD PERSON.

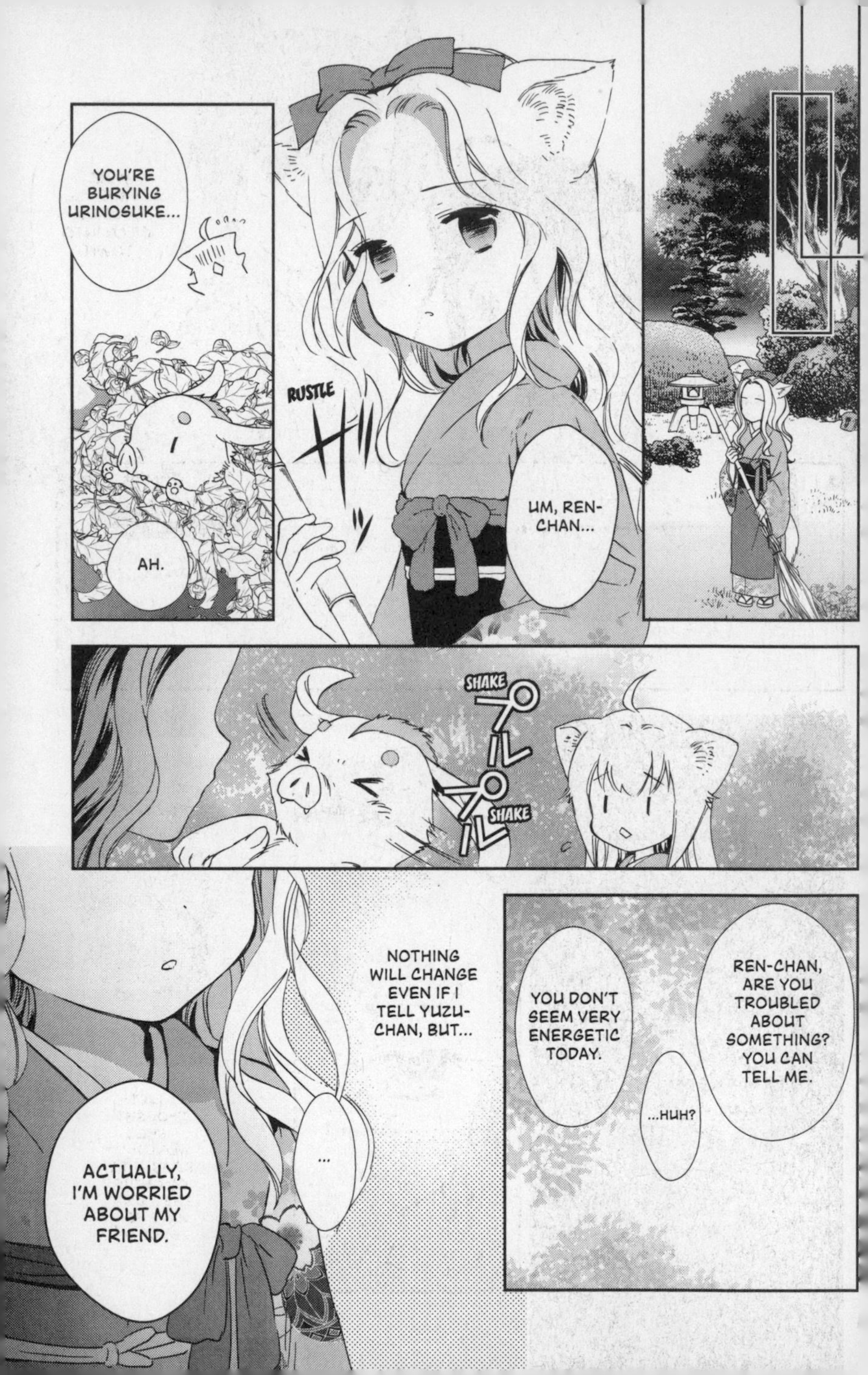
UM, REN-CHAN...
RUSTLE
YOU'RE BURYING URINOSUKE...
AH.
SHAKE
SHAKE
REN-CHAN, ARE YOU TROUBLED ABOUT SOMETHING? YOU CAN TELL ME.
YOU DON'T SEEM VERY ENERGETIC TODAY.
...HUH?
NOTHING WILL CHANGE EVEN IF I TELL YUZU-CHAN, BUT...
...
ACTUALLY, I'M WORRIED ABOUT MY FRIEND.

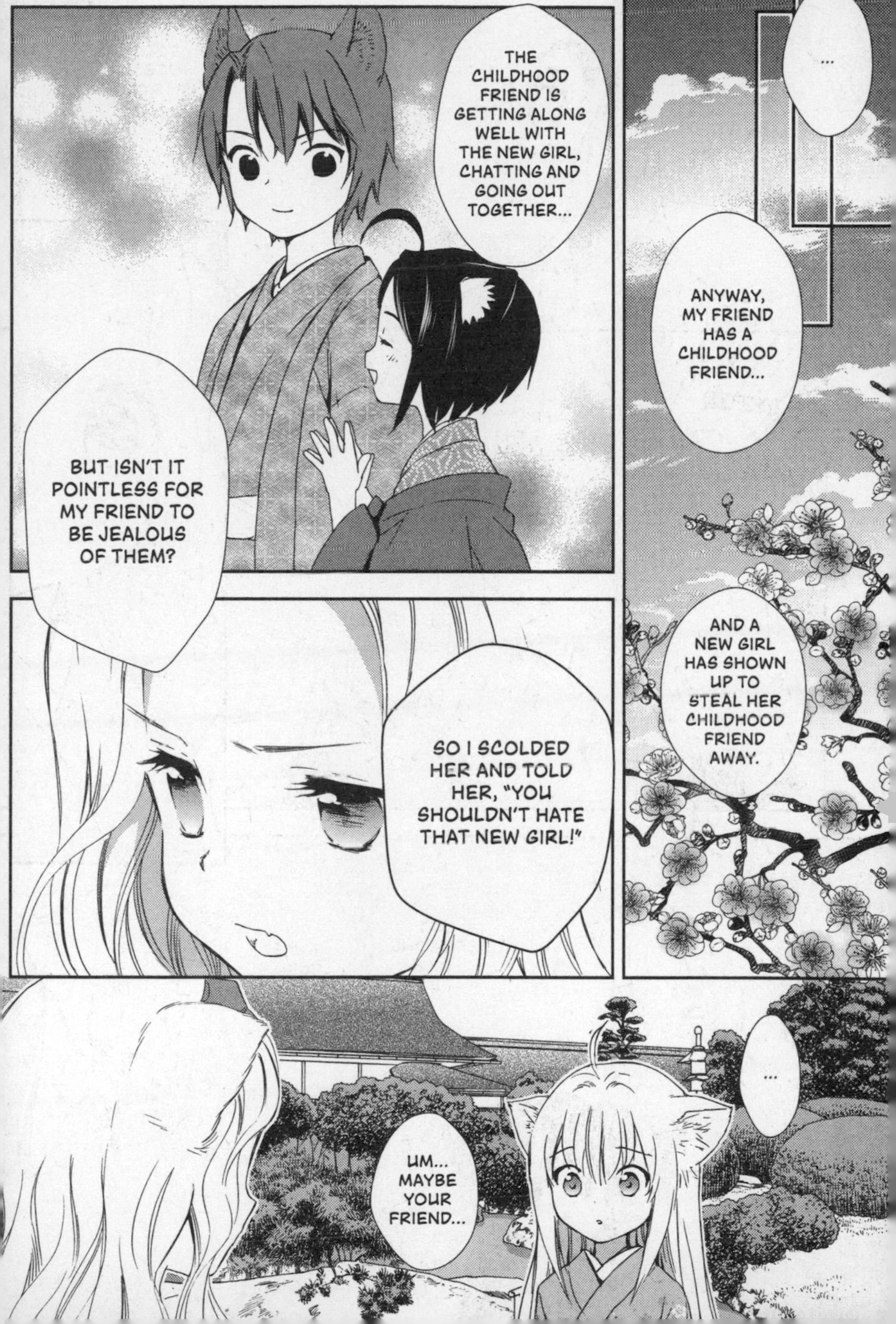
...
ANYWAY, MY FRIEND HAS A CHILDHOOD FRIEND...
AND A NEW GIRL HAS SHOWN UP TO STEAL HER CHILDHOOD FRIEND AWAY.
THE CHILDHOOD FRIEND IS GETTING ALONG WELL WITH THE NEW GIRL, CHATTING AND GOING OUT TOGETHER...
BUT ISN'T IT POINTLESS FOR MY FRIEND TO BE JEALOUS OF THEM?
SO I SCOLDED HER AND TOLD HER, "YOU SHOULDN'T HATE THAT NEW GIRL!"
...
UM... MAYBE YOUR FRIEND...

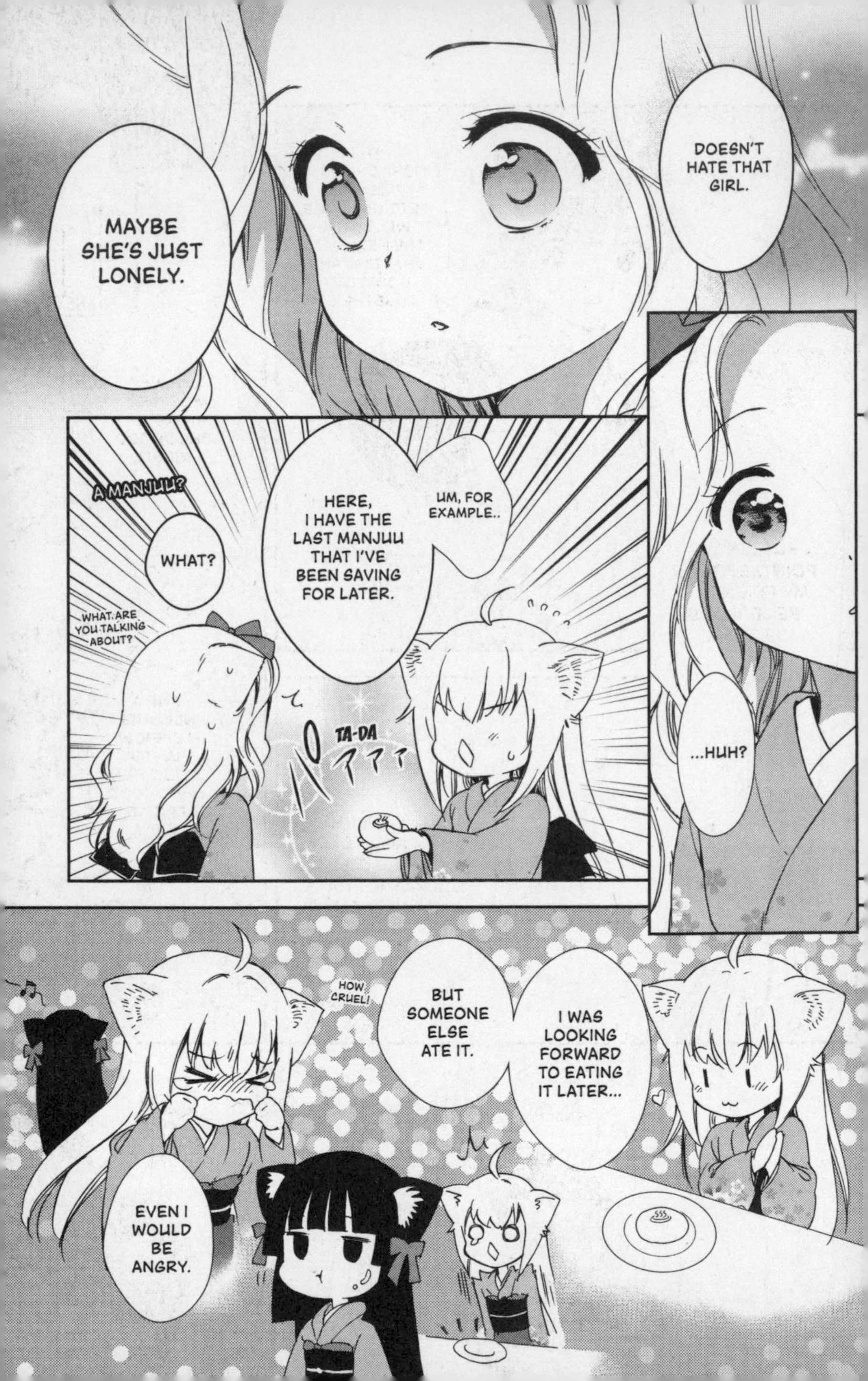
DOESN'T HATE THAT GIRL.
MAYBE SHE'S JUST LONELY.
...HUH?
UM, FOR EXAMPLE..
HERE, I HAVE THE LAST MANJUU THAT I'VE BEEN SAVING FOR LATER.
TA-DA
A MANJUU?
WHAT?
WHAT ARE YOU TALKING ABOUT?
I WAS LOOKING FORWARD TO EATING IT LATER...
BUT SOMEONE ELSE ATE IT.
HOW CRUEL!
EVEN I WOULD BE ANGRY.

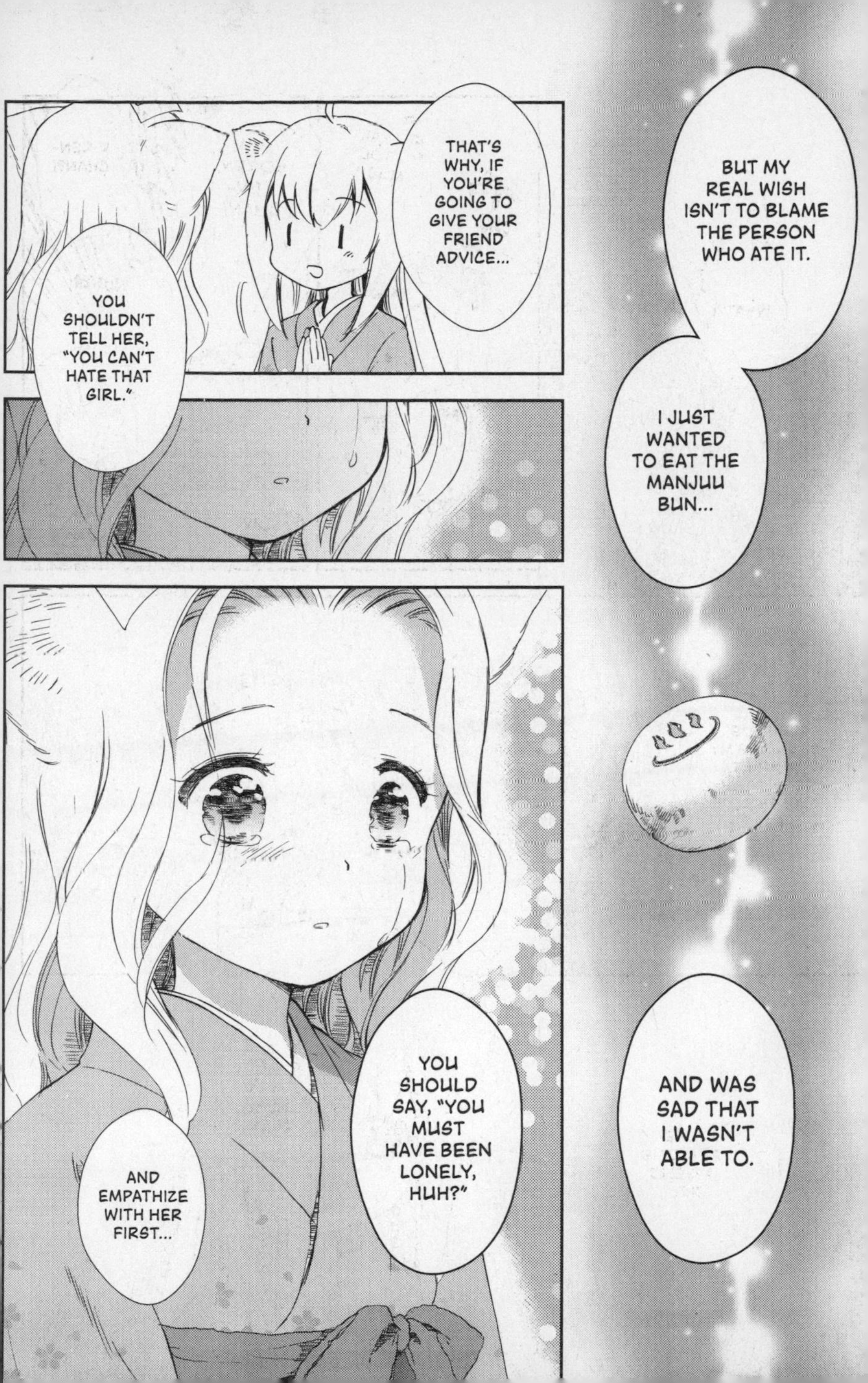
BUT MY REAL WISH ISN'T TO BLAME THE PERSON WHO ATE IT.
I JUST WANTED TO EAT THE MANJUU BUN...
AND WAS SAD THAT I WASN'T ABLE TO.
THAT'S WHY, IF YOU'RE GOING TO GIVE YOUR FRIEND ADVICE...
YOU SHOULDN'T TELL HER, "YOU CAN'T HATE THAT GIRL."
YOU SHOULD SAY, "YOU MUST HAVE BEEN LONELY, HUH?"
AND EMPATHIZE WITH HER FIRST...

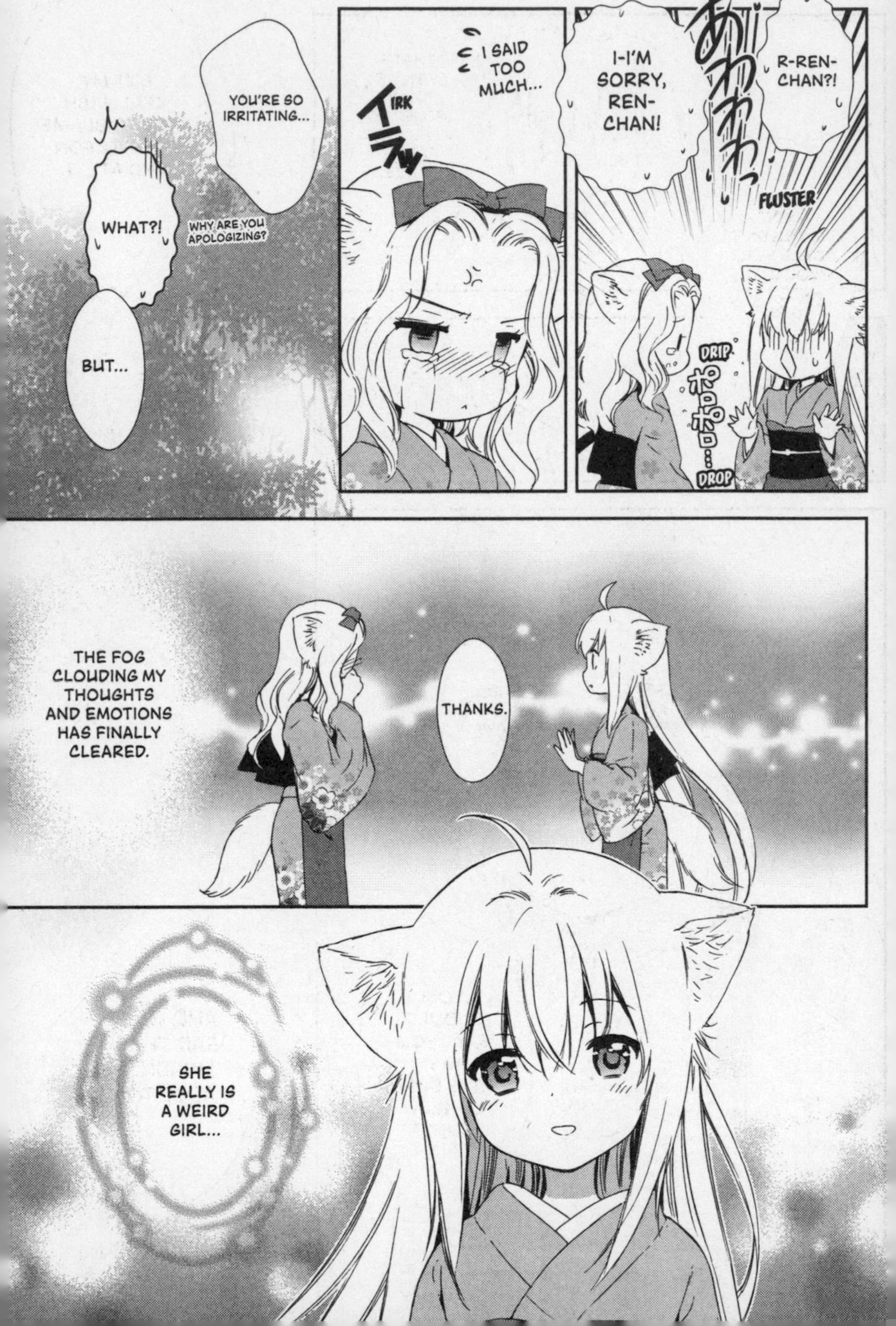
R-REN-CHAN?!
あわわわっ
FLUSTER
I-I'M SORRY, REN-CHAN!
DRIP
ポロポロ…
DROP
I SAID TOO MUCH...
イラッ
IRK
YOU'RE SO IRRITATING...
WHAT?!
WHY ARE YOU APOLOGIZING?
BUT...
THANKS.
THE FOG CLOUDING MY THOUGHTS AND EMOTIONS HAS FINALLY CLEARED.
SHE REALLY IS A WEIRD GIRL...

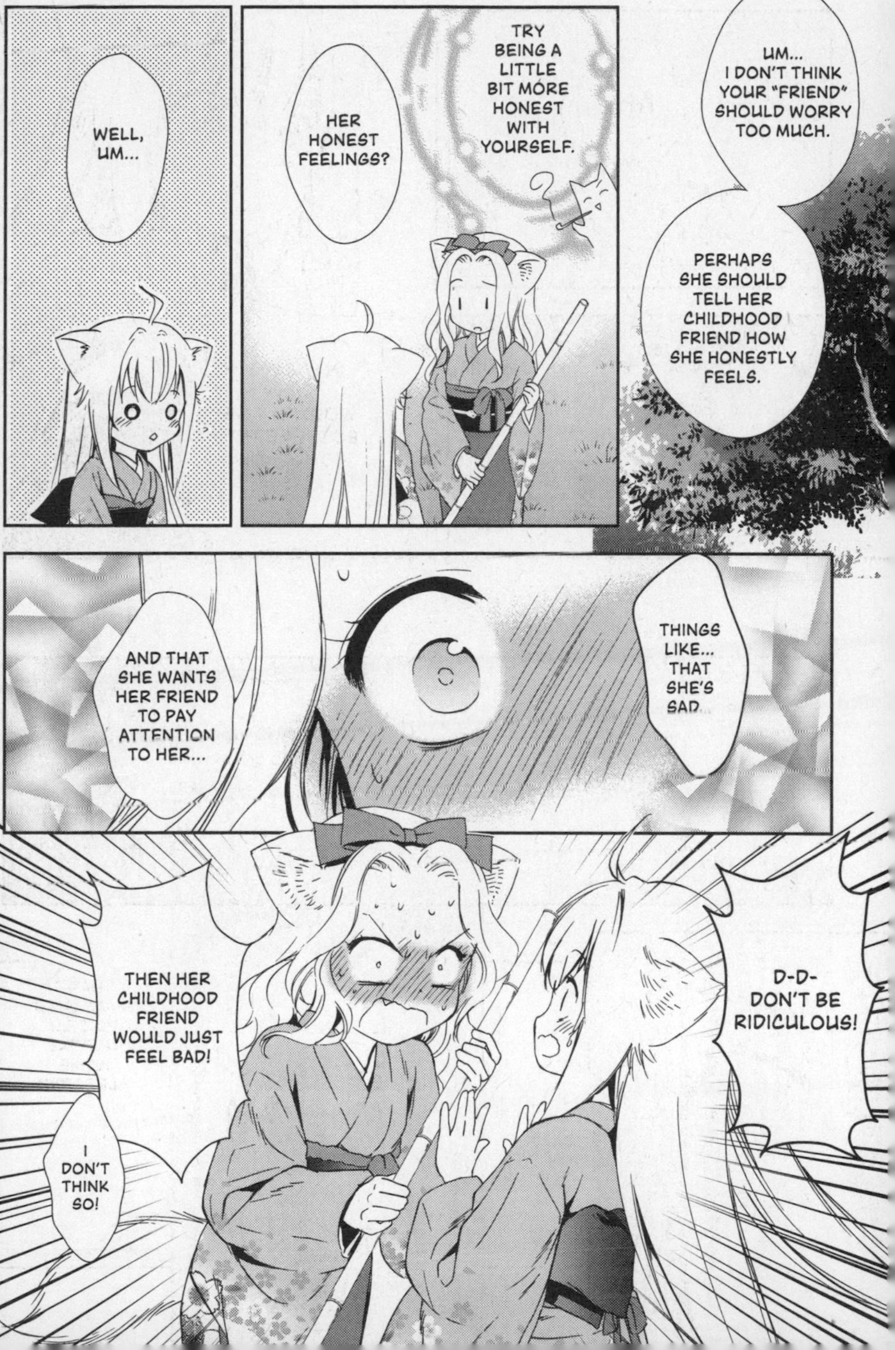
UM... I DON'T THINK YOUR "FRIEND" SHOULD WORRY TOO MUCH.
PERHAPS SHE SHOULD TELL HER CHILDHOOD FRIEND HOW SHE HONESTLY FEELS.
TRY BEING A LITTLE BIT MORE HONEST WITH YOURSELF.
HER HONEST FEELINGS?
WELL, UM...
THINGS LIKE... THAT SHE'S SAD.
AND THAT SHE WANTS HER FRIEND TO PAY ATTENTION TO HER...
D-D-DON'T BE RIDICULOUS!
THEN HER CHILDHOOD FRIEND WOULD JUST FEEL BAD!
I DON'T THINK SO!

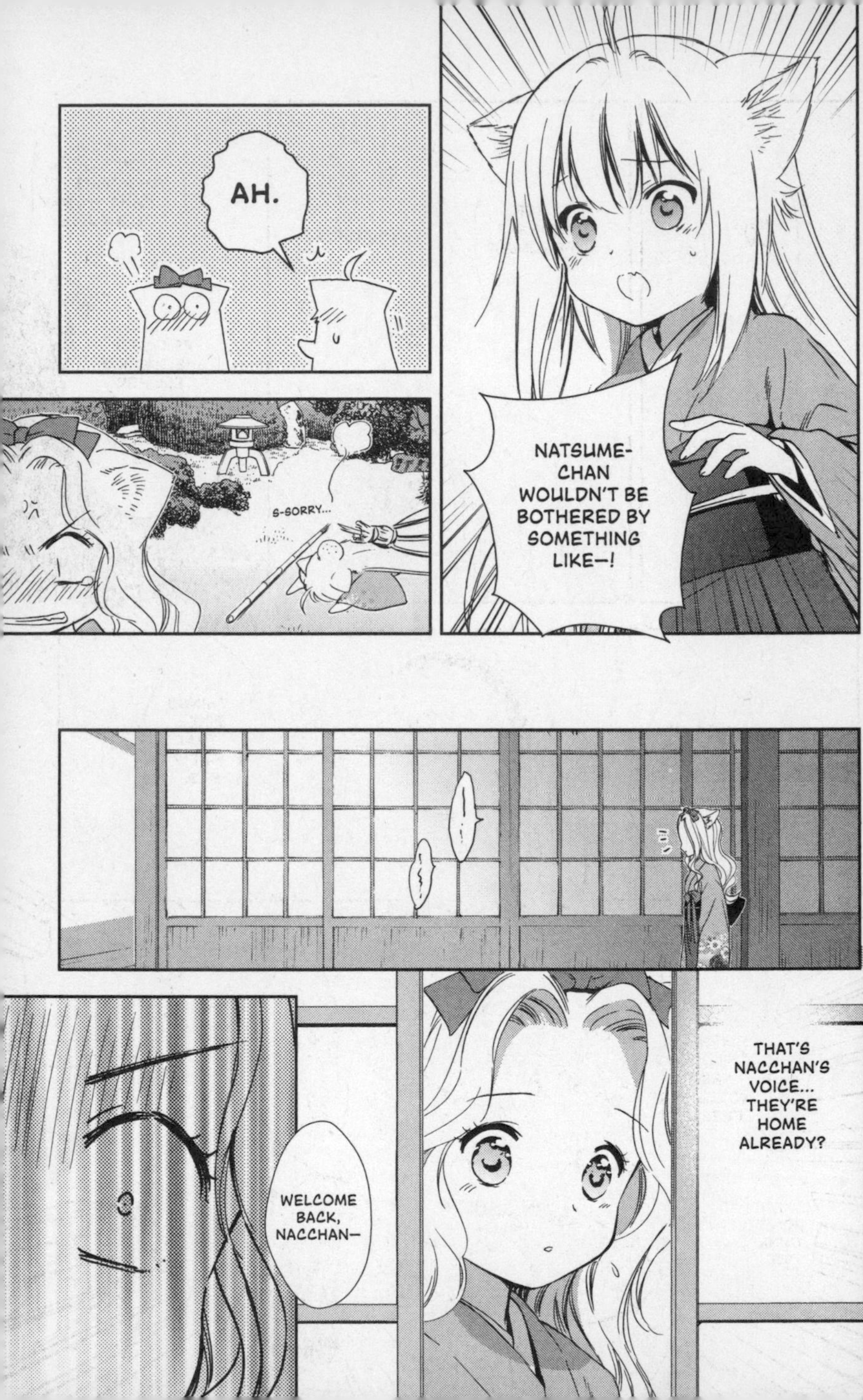
NATSUME-CHAN WOULDN'T BE BOTHERED BY SOMETHING LIKE—!
AH.
S-SORRY...
THAT'S NACCHAN'S VOICE... THEY'RE HOME ALREADY?
WELCOME BACK, NACCHAN—

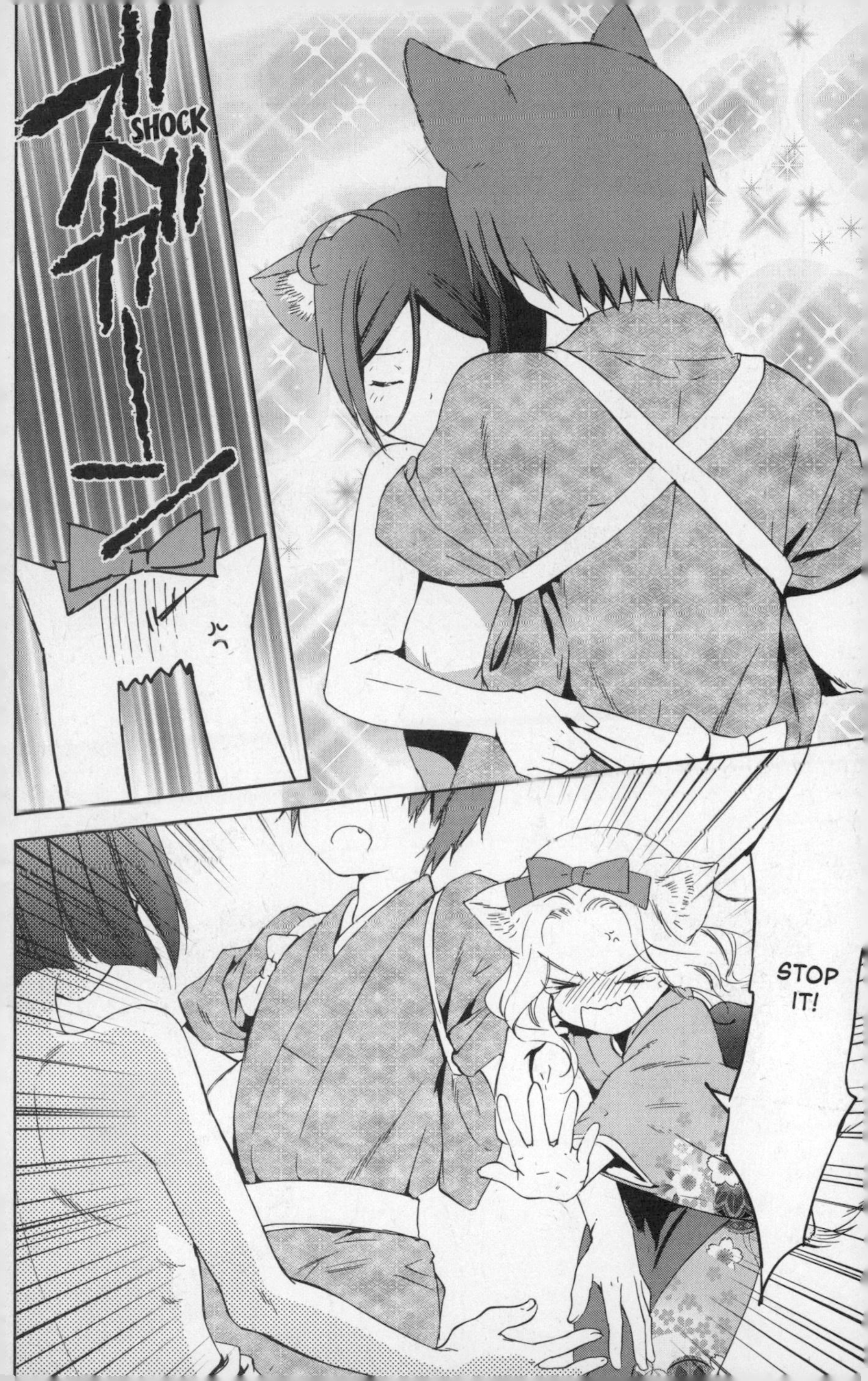
SHOCK
STOP IT!

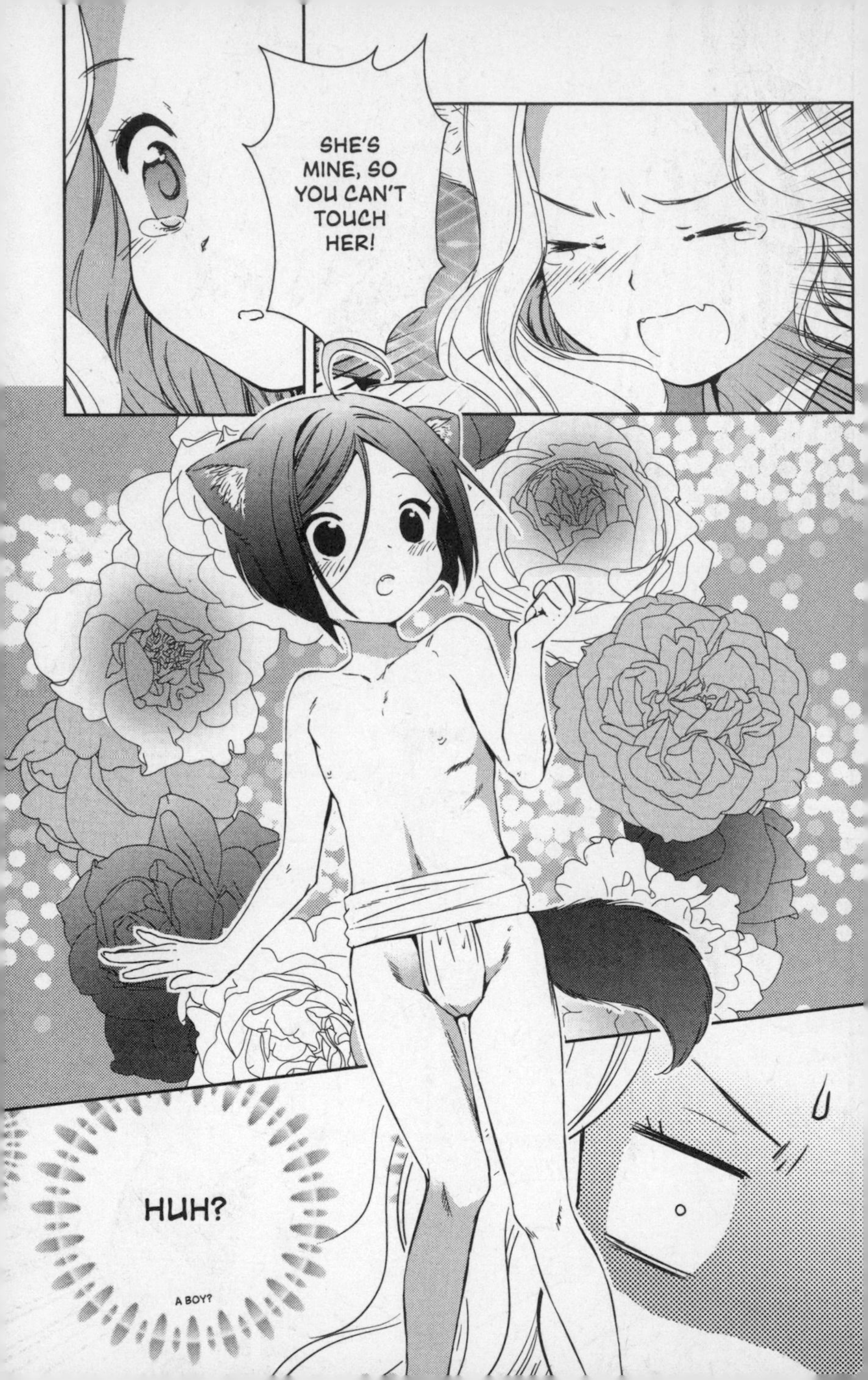
SHE'S MINE, SO YOU CAN'T TOUCH HER!
HUH?
A BOY?

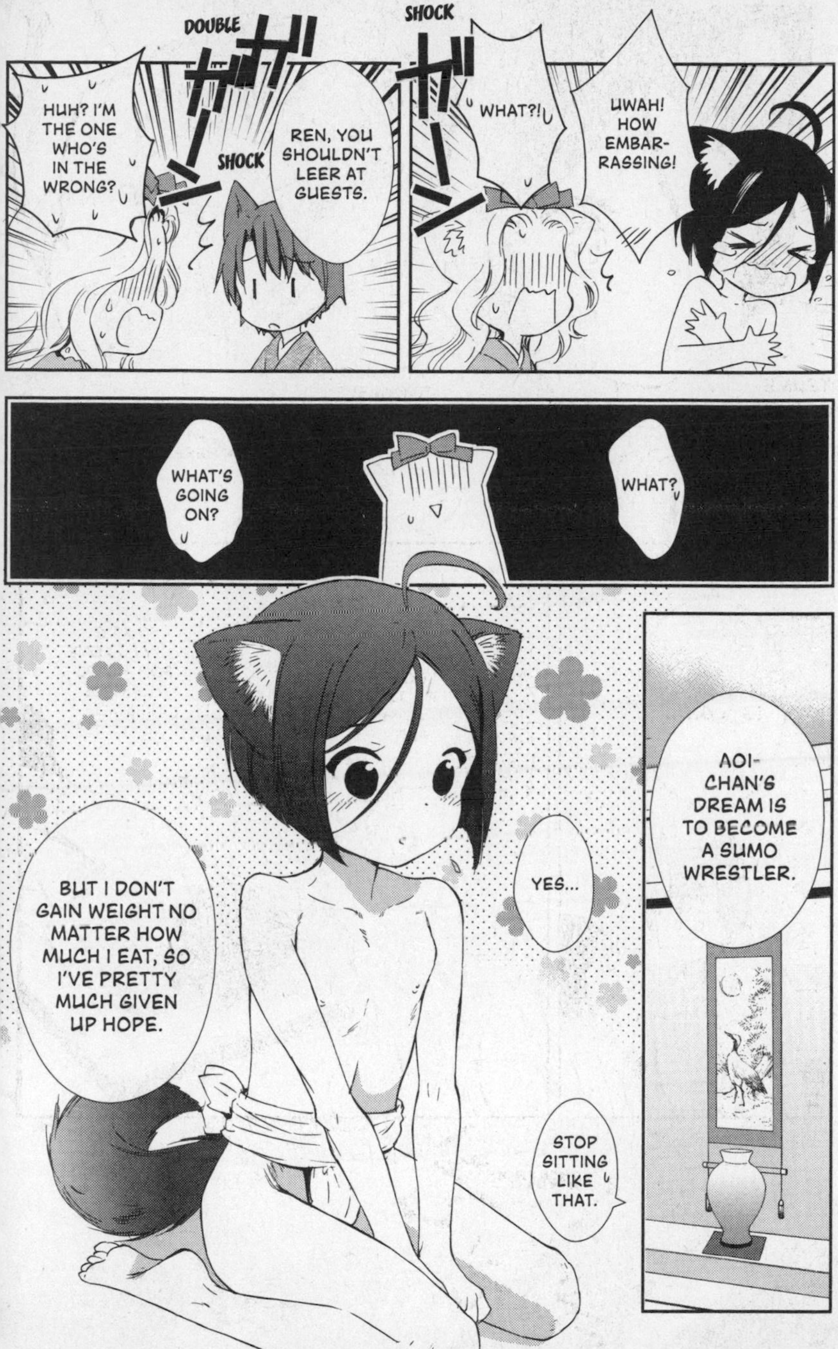
SHOCK
UWAH! HOW EMBARRASSING!
WHAT?!
DOUBLE
SHOCK
REN, YOU SHOULDN'T LEER AT GUESTS.
HUH? I'M THE ONE WHO'S IN THE WRONG?
WHAT?
WHAT'S GOING ON?
AOI-CHAN'S DREAM IS TO BECOME A SUMO WRESTLER.
YES...
BUT I DON'T GAIN WEIGHT NO MATTER HOW MUCH I EAT, SO I'VE PRETTY MUCH GIVEN UP HOPE.
STOP SITTING LIKE THAT.

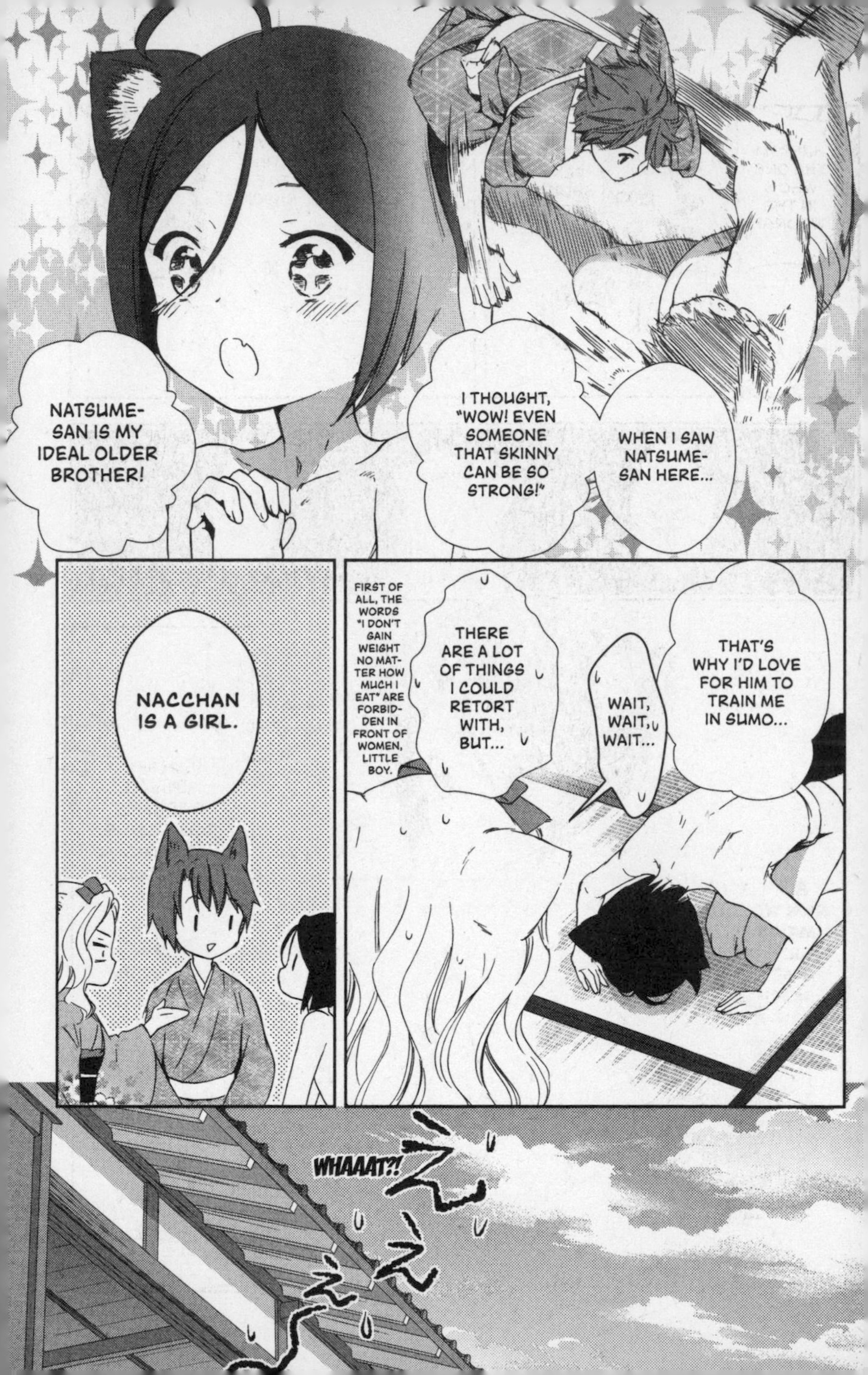
WHEN I SAW NATSUME-SAN HERE...
I THOUGHT, "WOW! EVEN SOMEONE THAT SKINNY CAN BE SO STRONG!"
NATSUME-SAN IS MY IDEAL OLDER BROTHER!
THAT'S WHY I'D LOVE FOR HIM TO TRAIN ME IN SUMO...
WAIT, WAIT, WAIT...
THERE ARE A LOT OF THINGS I COULD RETORT WITH, BUT...
FIRST OF ALL, THE WORDS "I DON'T GAIN WEIGHT NO MATTER HOW MUCH I EAT" ARE FORBIDDEN IN FRONT OF WOMEN, LITTLE BOY.
NACCHAN IS A GIRL.
WHAAAT?!

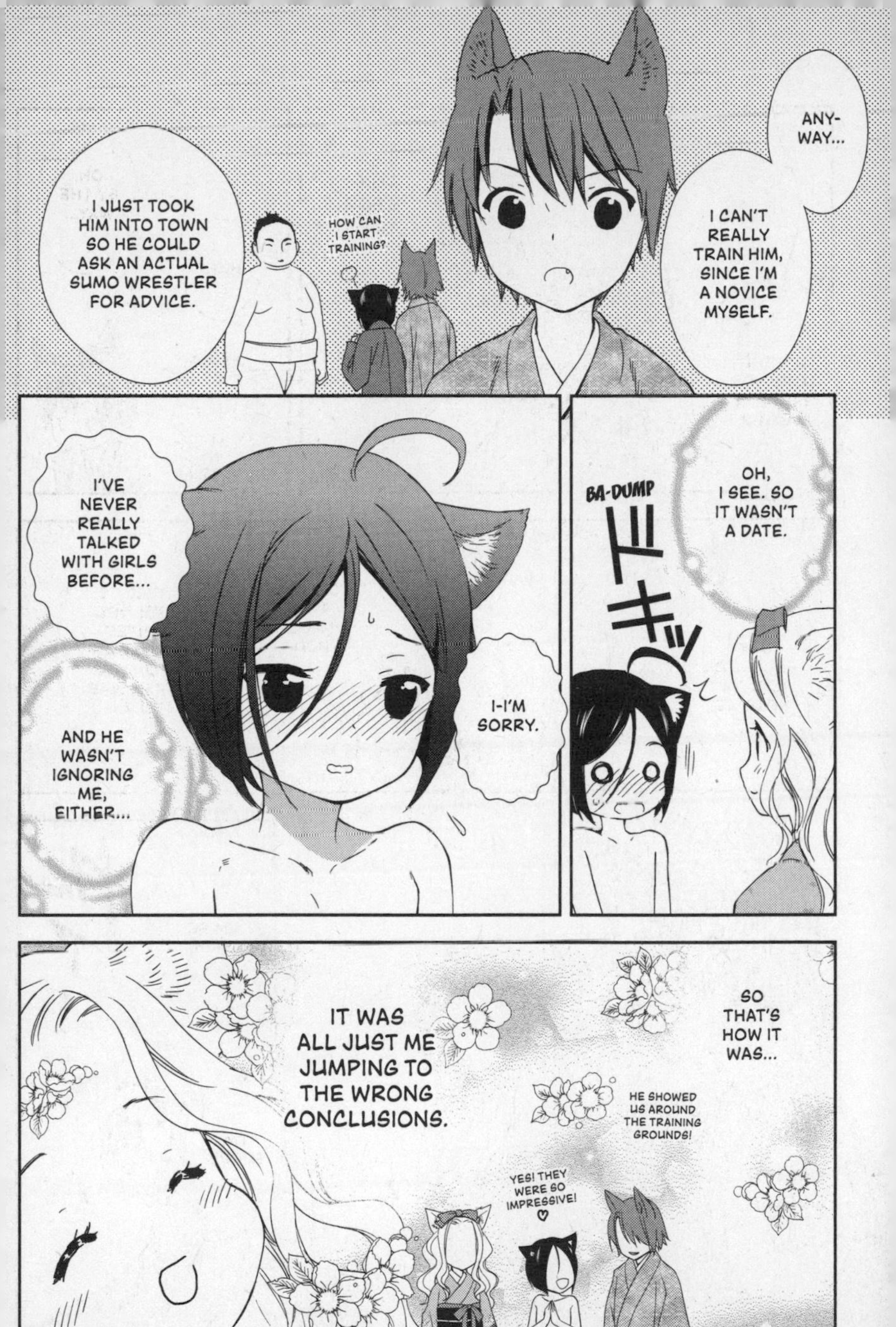
ANY-WAY...
I CAN'T REALLY TRAIN HIM, SINCE I'M A NOVICE MYSELF.
HOW CAN I START TRAINING?
I JUST TOOK HIM INTO TOWN SO HE COULD ASK AN ACTUAL SUMO WRESTLER FOR ADVICE.
OH, I SEE. SO IT WASN'T A DATE.
BA-DUMP
ドキッ
I-I'M SORRY.
I'VE NEVER REALLY TALKED WITH GIRLS BEFORE...
AND HE WASN'T IGNORING ME, EITHER...
SO THAT'S HOW IT WAS...
HE SHOWED US AROUND THE TRAINING GROUNDS!
YES! THEY WERE SO IMPRESSIVE! ♡
IT WAS ALL JUST ME JUMPING TO THE WRONG CONCLUSIONS.

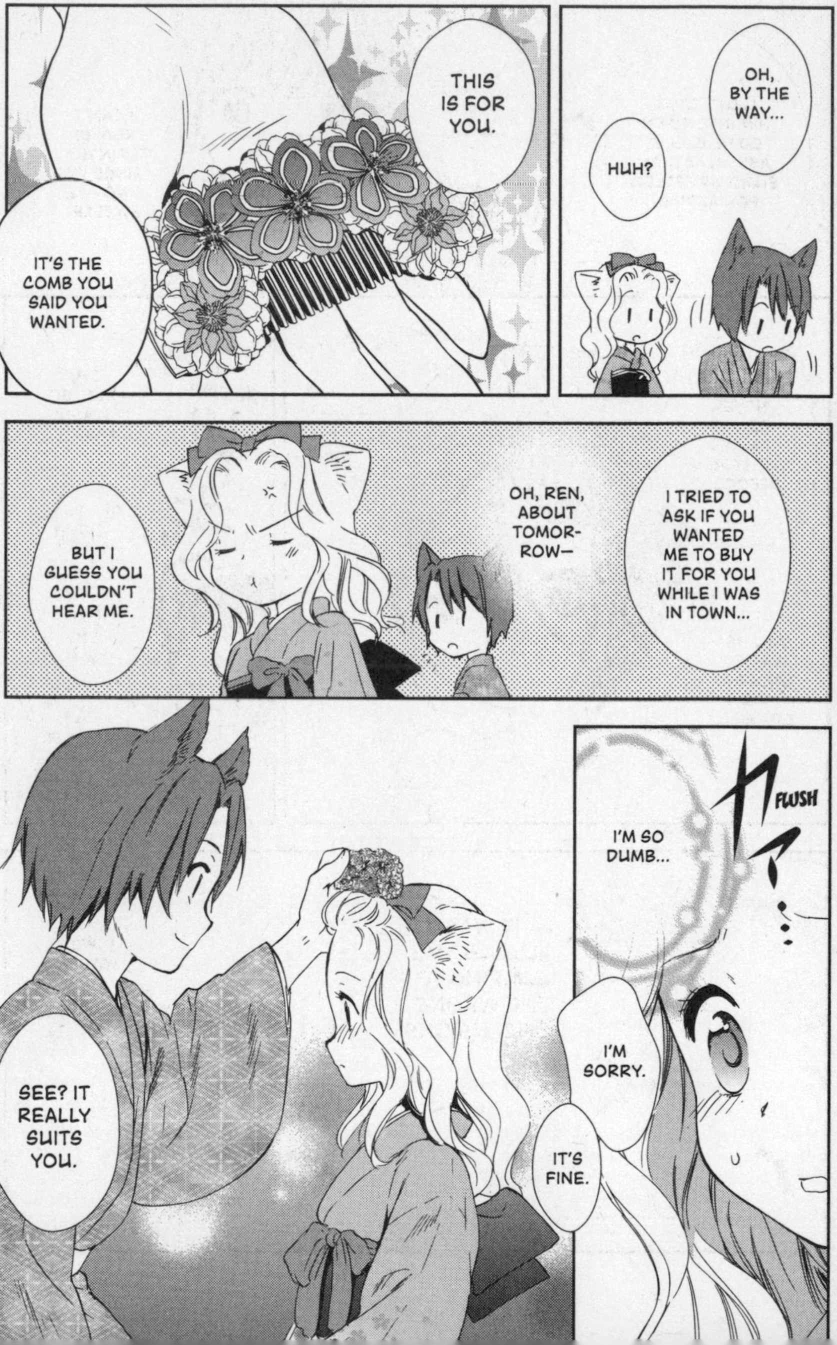
OH, BY THE WAY...
HUH?
THIS IS FOR YOU.
IT'S THE COMB YOU SAID YOU WANTED.
I TRIED TO ASK IF YOU WANTED ME TO BUY IT FOR YOU WHILE I WAS IN TOWN...
OH, REN, ABOUT TOMOR-ROW—
BUT I GUESS YOU COULDN'T HEAR ME.
FLUSH
I'M SO DUMB...
I'M SORRY.
IT'S FINE.
SEE? IT REALLY SUITS YOU.

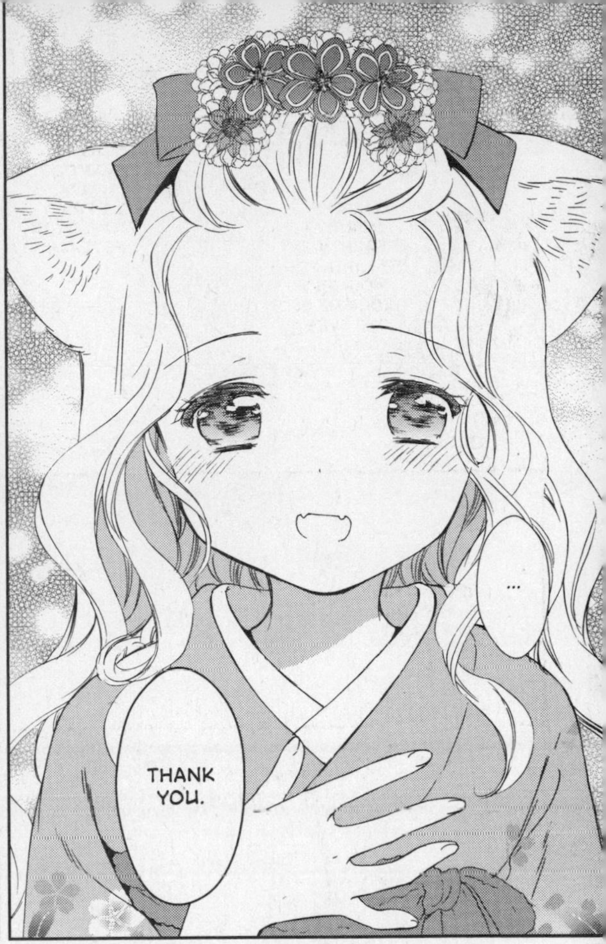
...
THANK YOU.

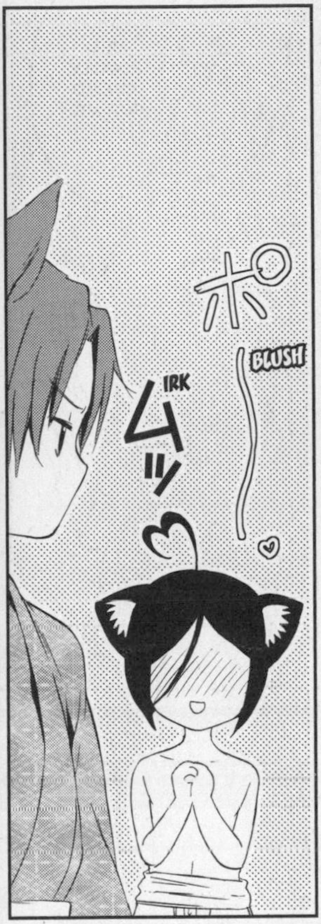
ポ—
BLUSH
ムッ
IRK

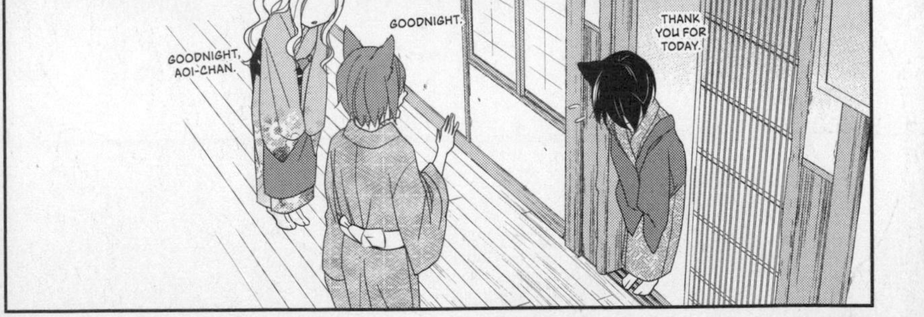
THANK YOU FOR TODAY.
GOODNIGHT.
GOODNIGHT, AOI-CHAN.

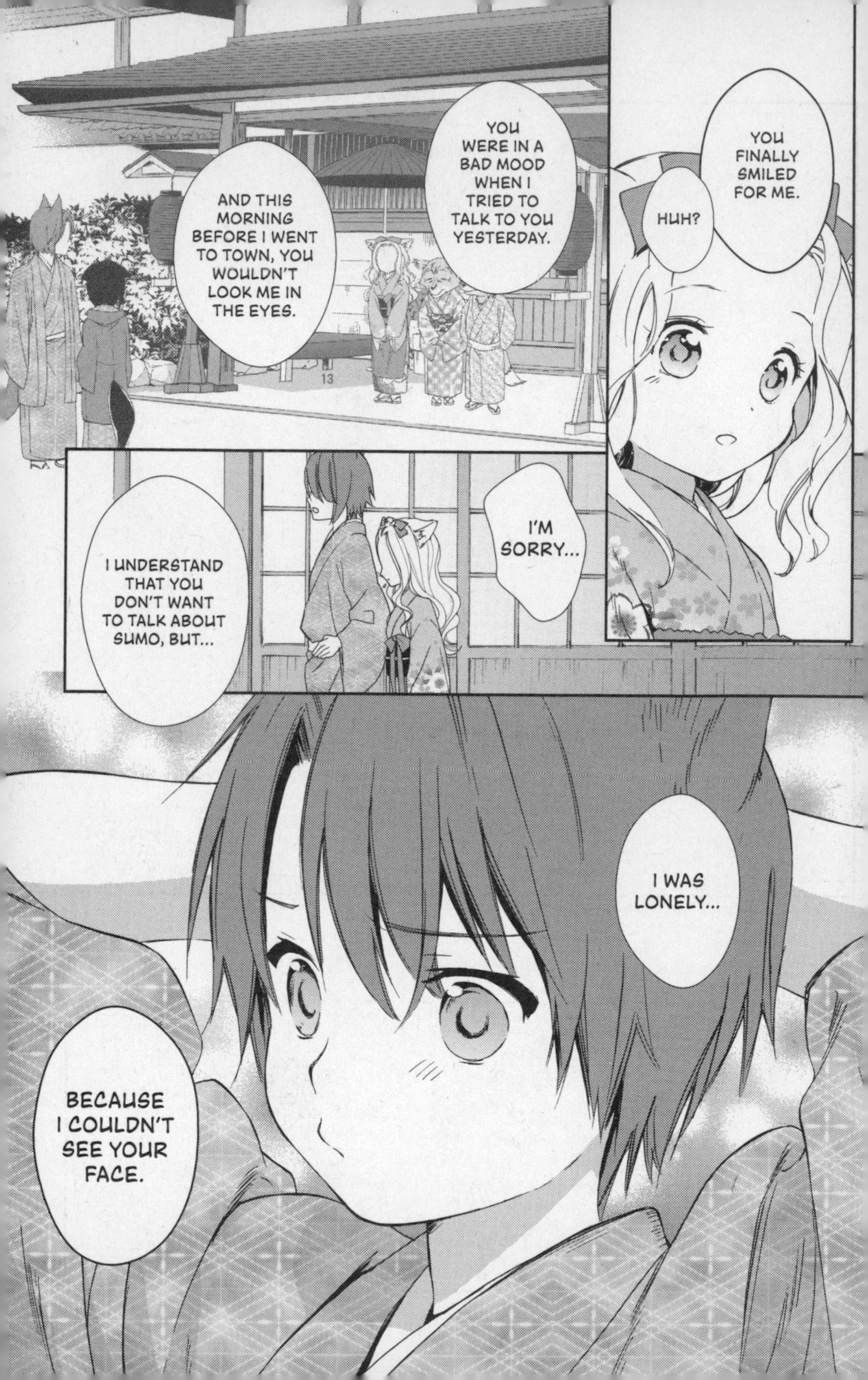
YOU FINALLY SMILED FOR ME.
HUH?
YOU WERE IN A BAD MOOD WHEN I TRIED TO TALK TO YOU YESTERDAY.
AND THIS MORNING BEFORE I WENT TO TOWN, YOU WOULDN'T LOOK ME IN THE EYES.
I'M SORRY...
I UNDERSTAND THAT YOU DON'T WANT TO TALK ABOUT SUMO, BUT...
I WAS LONELY...
BECAUSE I COULDN'T SEE YOUR FACE.

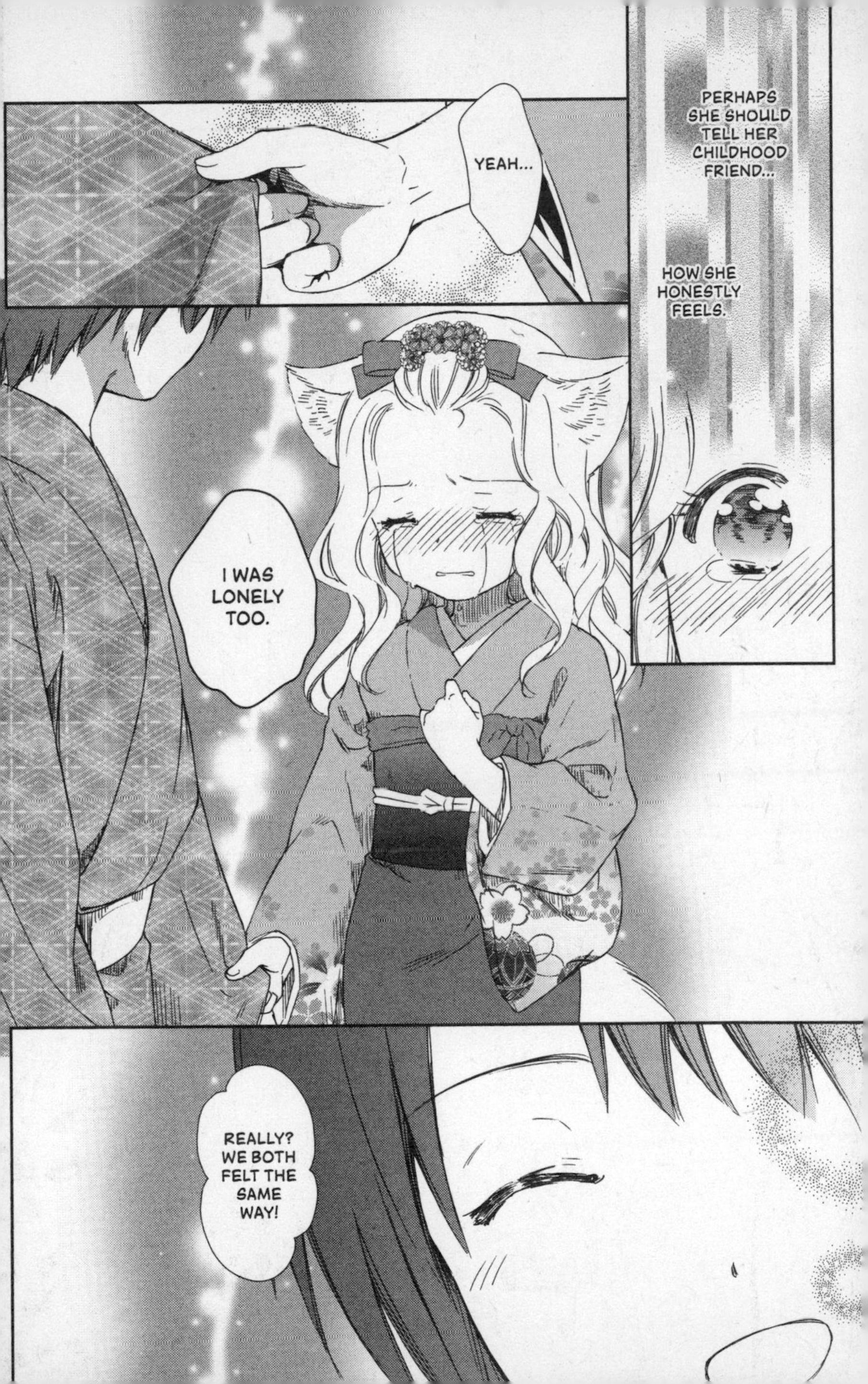
PERHAPS SHE SHOULD TELL HER CHILDHOOD FRIEND...
HOW SHE HONESTLY FEELS.
YEAH...
I WAS LONELY TOO.
REALLY? WE BOTH FELT THE SAME WAY!

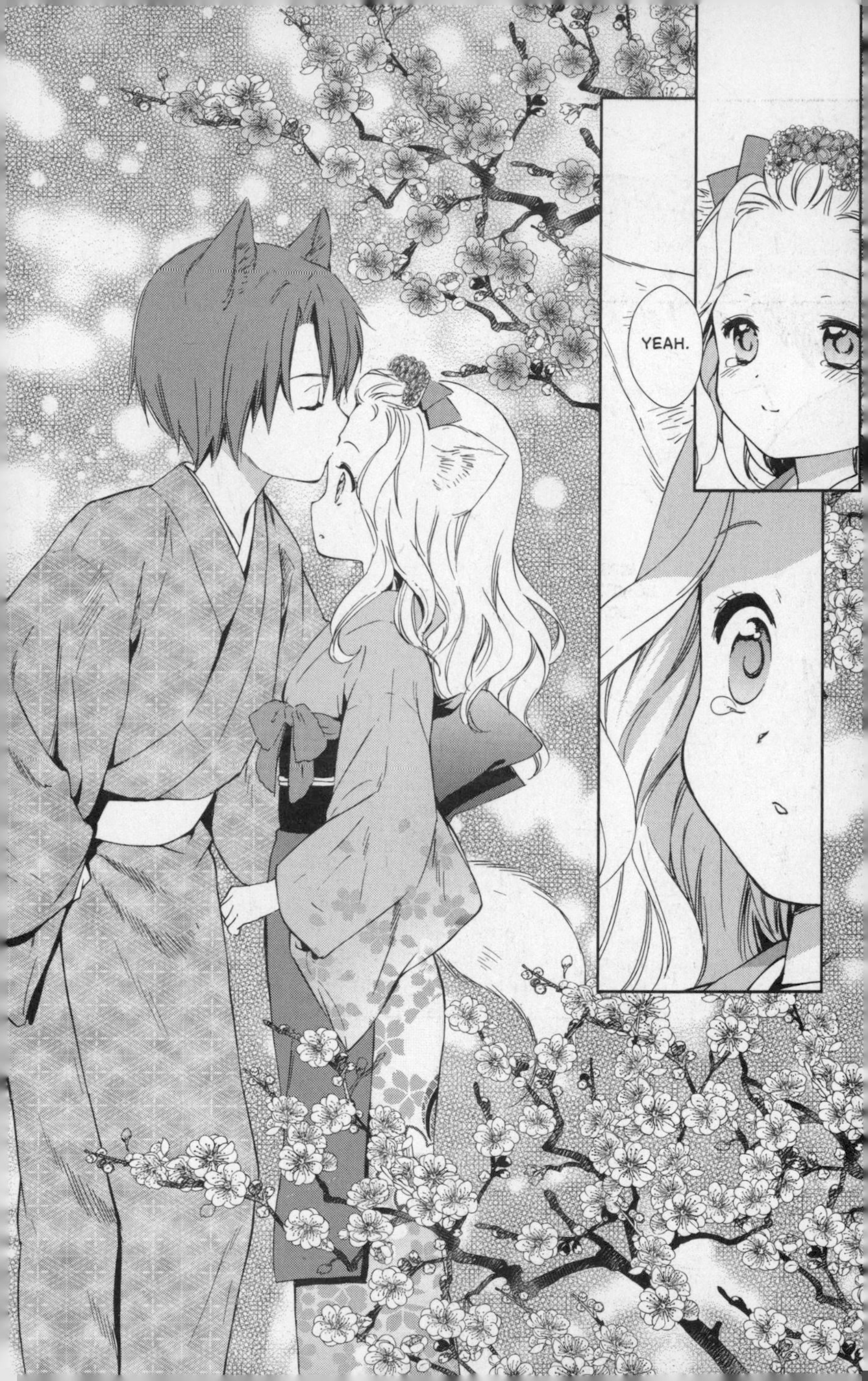
YEAH.

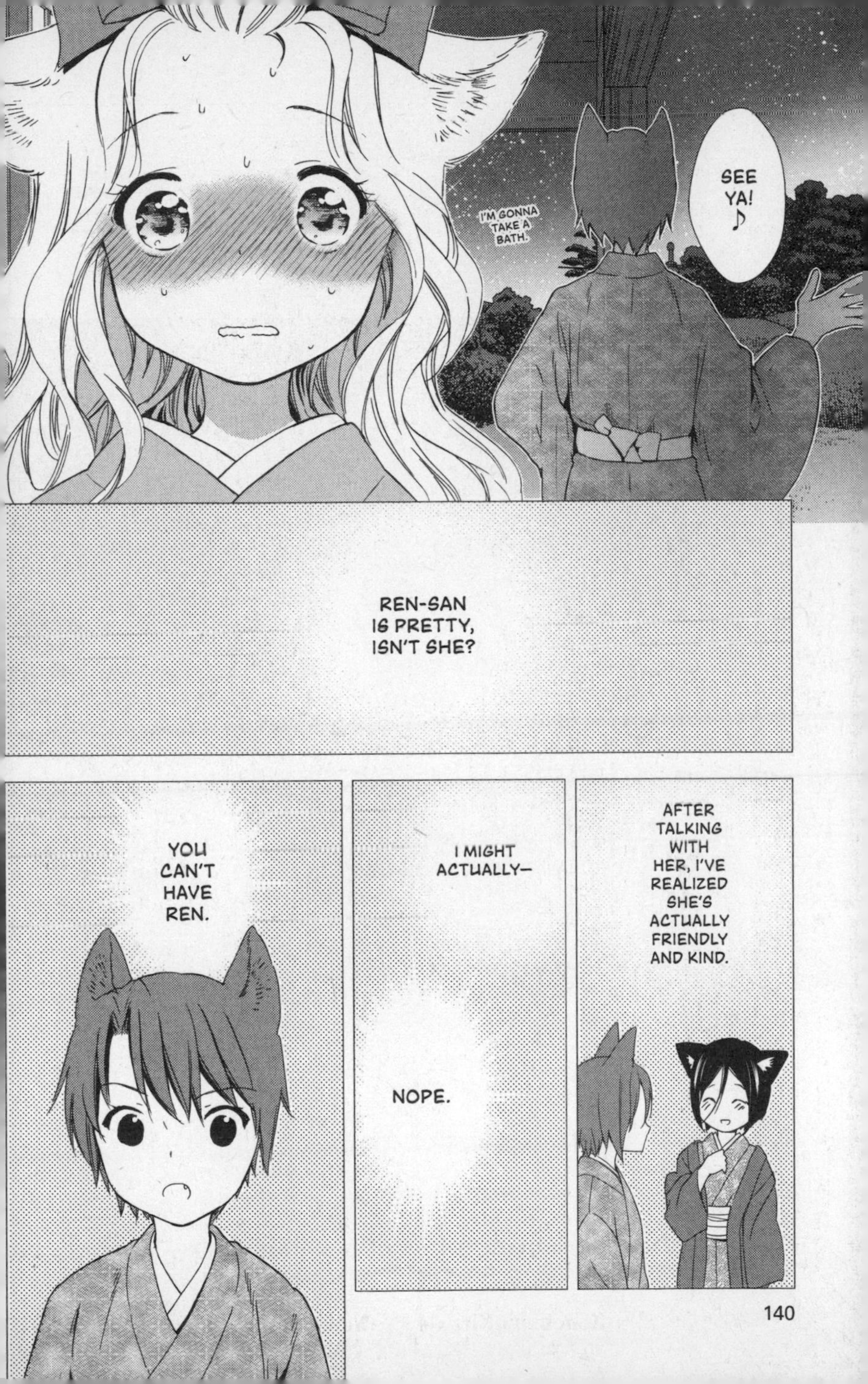
SEE YA! ♪
I'M GONNA TAKE A BATH.
REN-SAN IS PRETTY, ISN'T SHE?
AFTER TALKING WITH HER, I'VE REALIZED SHE'S ACTUALLY FRIENDLY AND KIND.
I MIGHT ACTUALLY—
NOPE.
YOU CAN'T HAVE REN.

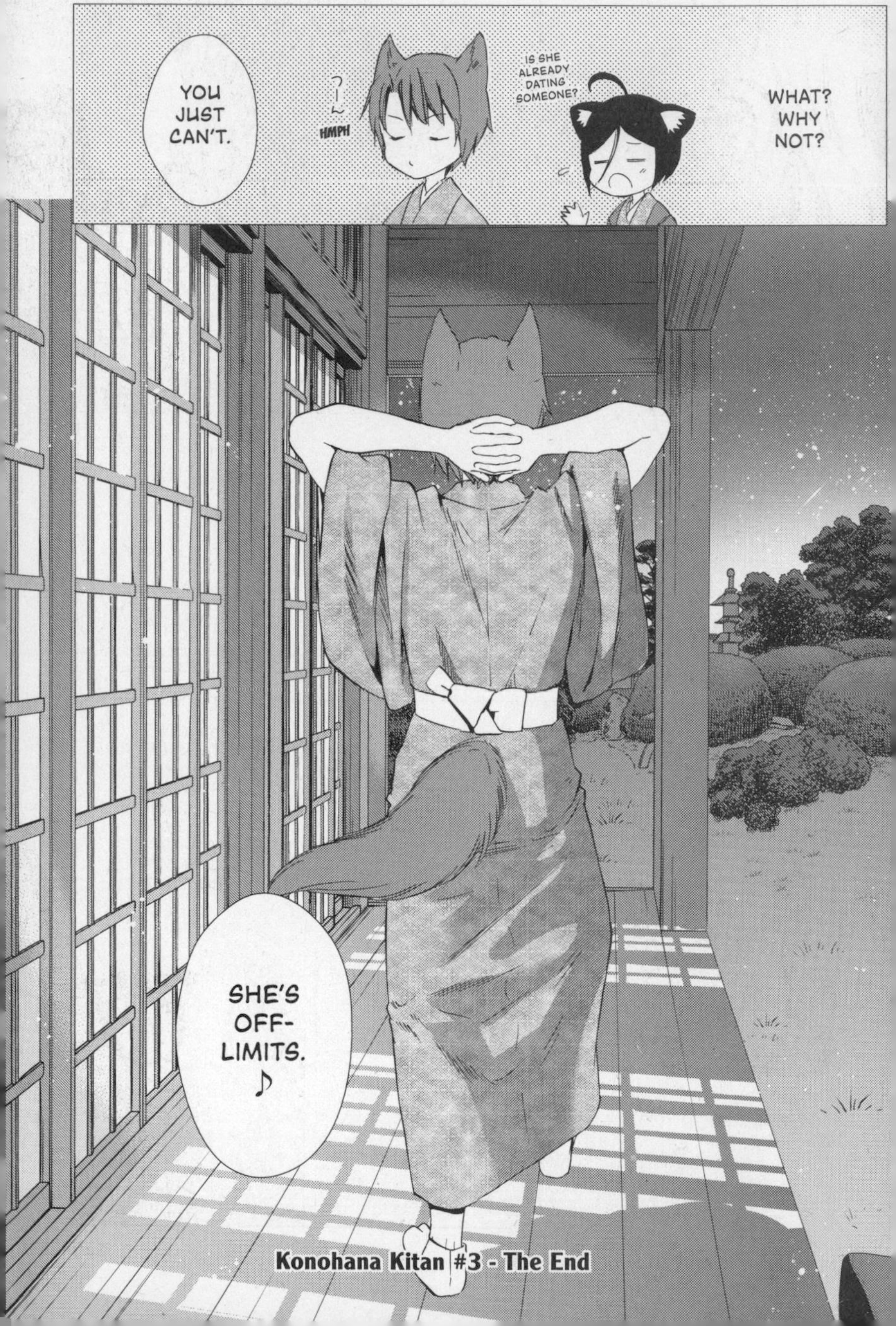
WHAT? WHY NOT?
IS SHE ALREADY DATING SOMEONE?
HMPH
YOU JUST CAN'T.
SHE'S OFF-LIMITS. ♪
Konohana Kitan #3 - The End

KONOHANA KITAN

IN THE NEXT VOLUME OF

KONOHANA KITAN

Every day, the foxes who staff Konohanatei work hard to make sure each of their guests is taken care of, accommodated and comfortable. After all, at Konohanatei, every guest is a god! But the healing power of the legendary fox inn that sits between worlds affects not only its guests but its workers as well. Each of them has been drawn to the inn from their various personal experiences, and each chooses to stay for her own reason.

In the next volume of *Konohana Kitan*, take a stroll down memory lane with Kiri, one of the foxes who has been working there as an attendant since she was young, and who currently acts as a supervisor and mentor to Yuzu, Satsuki, Natsume, Ren, and Sakura. A glimpse of Kiri's past reveals what her first days at Konohanatei were like, and how working at the inn changed her destiny— and brought her together with one very special person.

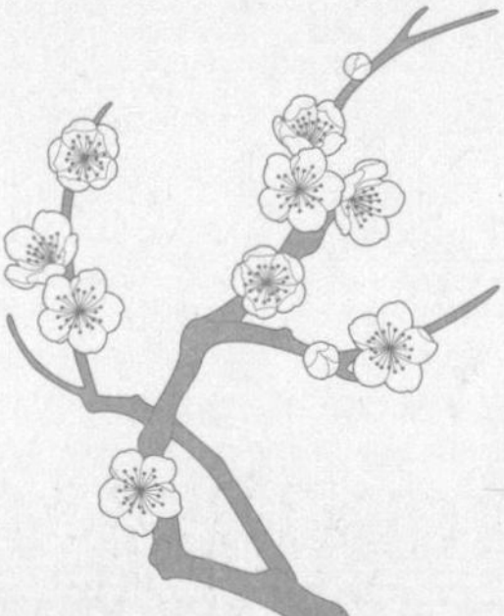

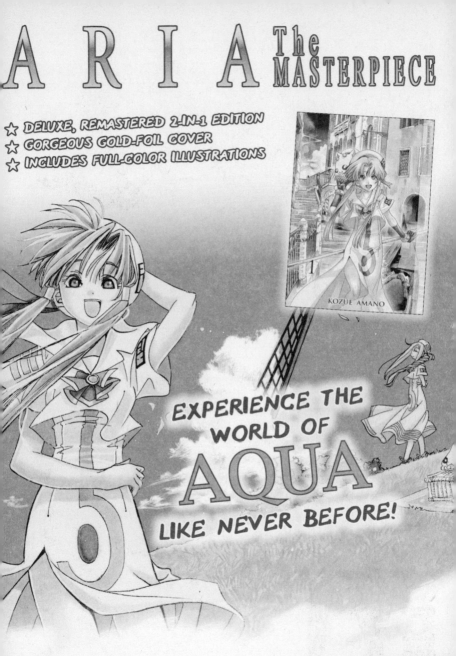

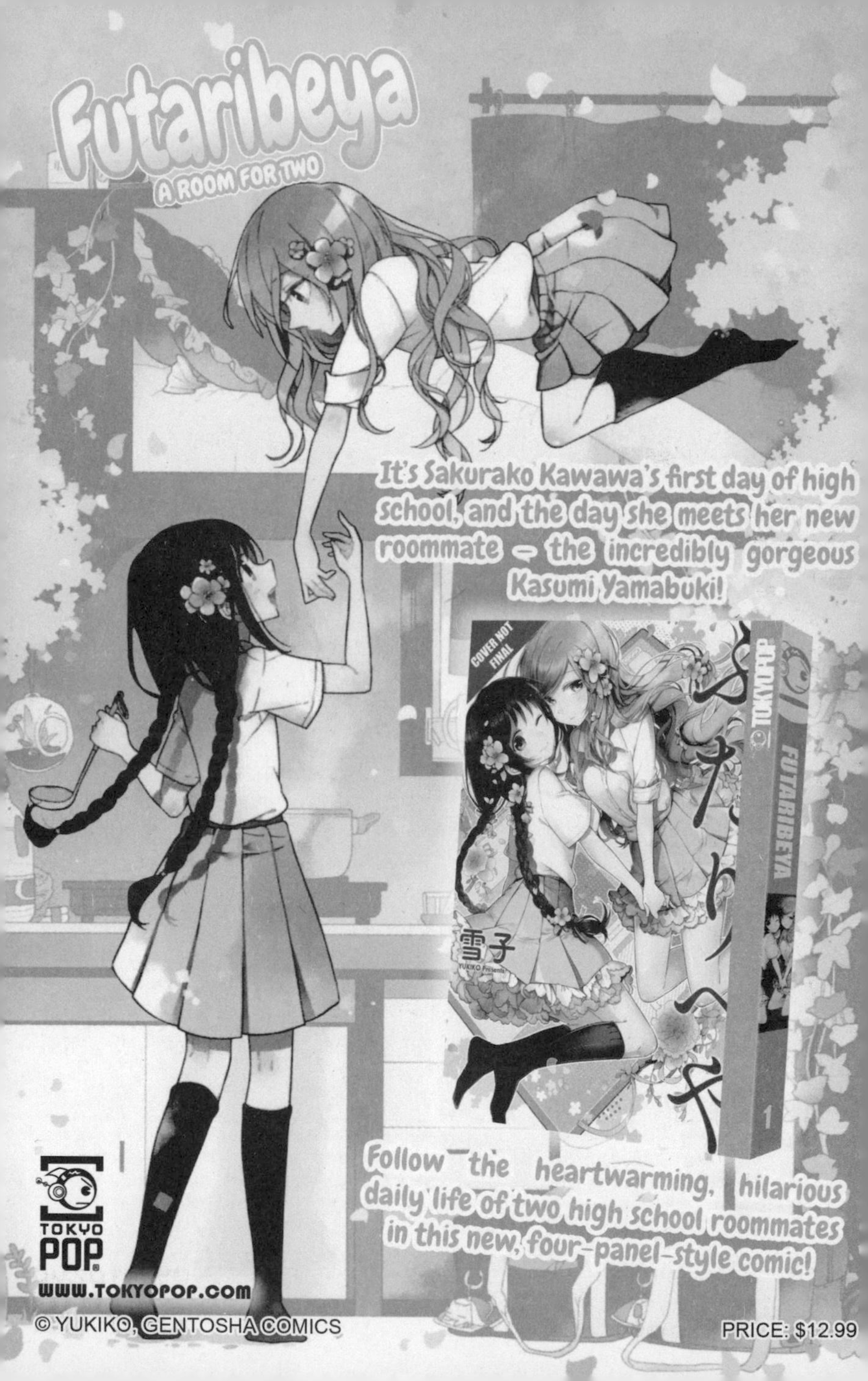
Futaribeya
A ROOM FOR TWO
It's Sakurako Kawawa's first day of high school, and the day she meets her new roommate – the incredibly gorgeous Kasumi Yamabuki!
COVER NOT FINAL
TOKYOPOP
FUTARIBEYA
雪子
YUKIKO Presents
1
Follow the heartwarming, hilarious daily life of two high school roommates in this new, four-panel-style comic!
TOKYO POP
WWW.TOKYOPOP.COM
© YUKIKO, GENTOSHA COMICS
PRICE: $12.99

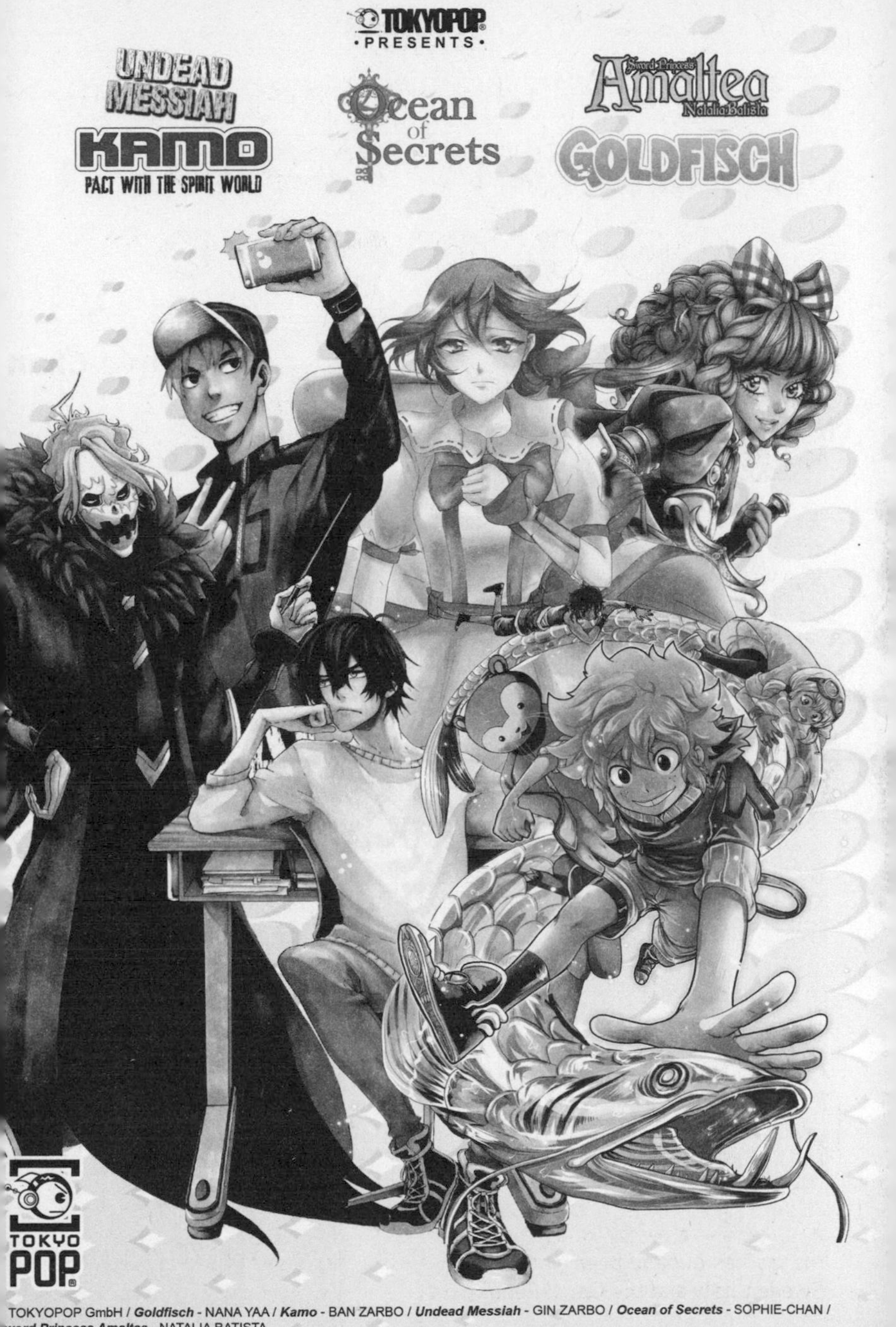
TOKYOPOP
PRESENTS
UNDEAD MESSIAH
Ocean of Secrets
Sword Princess Amaltea
Natalia Batista
KAMO
PACT WITH THE SPIRIT WORLD
GOLDFISCH
TOKYO POP

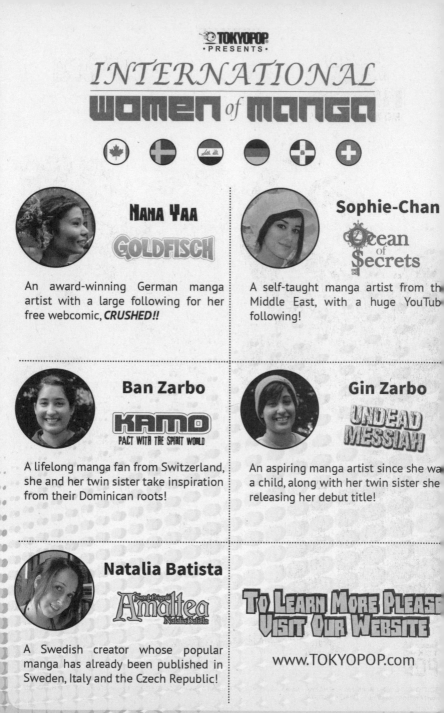

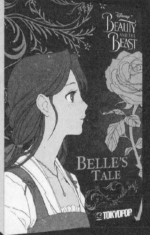

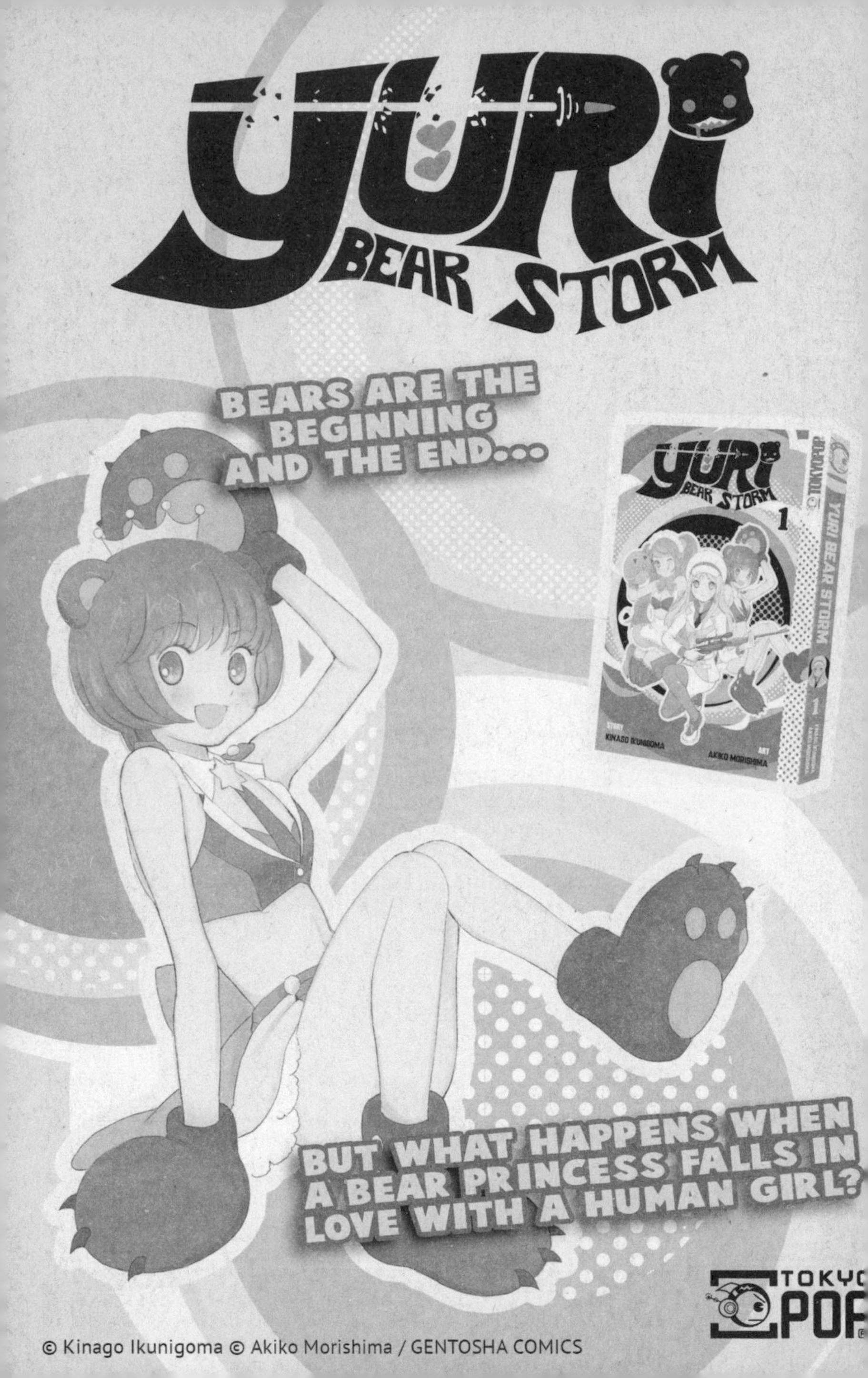

YURI BEAR STORM
BEARS ARE THE BEGINNING AND THE END...
YURI BEAR STORM 1
STORY KINAGO IKUNIGOMA
ART AKIKO MORISHIMA
TOKYOPOP
BUT WHAT HAPPENS WHEN A BEAR PRINCESS FALLS IN LOVE WITH A HUMAN GIRL?
TOKYO POP
© Kinago Ikunigoma © Akiko Morishima / GENTOSHA COMICS

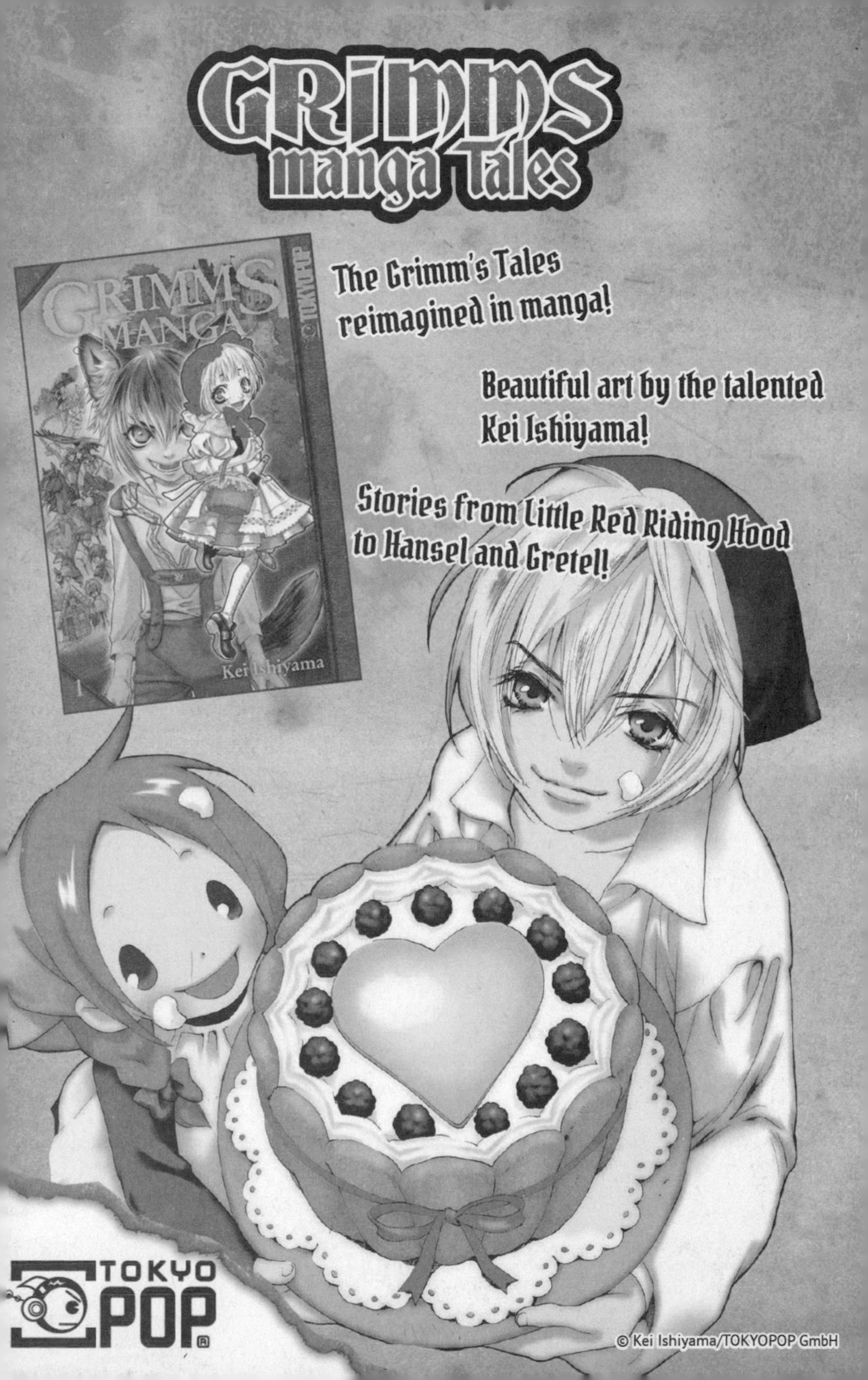
Grimms manga Tales
GRIMMS MANGA
TOKYOPOP
Kei Ishiyama
1
The Grimm's Tales reimagined in manga!
Beautiful art by the talented Kei Ishiyama!
Stories from Little Red Riding Hood to Hansel and Gretel!
TOKYO POP
© Kei Ishiyama/TOKYOPOP GmbH

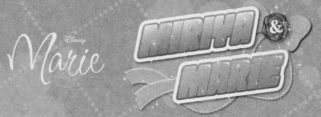

Disney **Marie** MIRIYA & MARIE

☆ **Inspired by the characters from Disney's The Aristocats**

☆ **Learn facts about Paris and Japan!**

☆ **Adorable original shojo story**

☆ **Full color manga**

Even though the wealthy young girl Miriya has almost everything she could ever need, what she really wants is the one thing money can't buy: her missing parents. But this year, she gets an extra special birthday gift when Marie, a magical white kitten, appears and whisks her away to Paris! Learning the art of magic is one thing, but getting to eat the tastiest French pastries and wear the most beautiful fashion takes Miriya and Marie's journey to a whole new level!

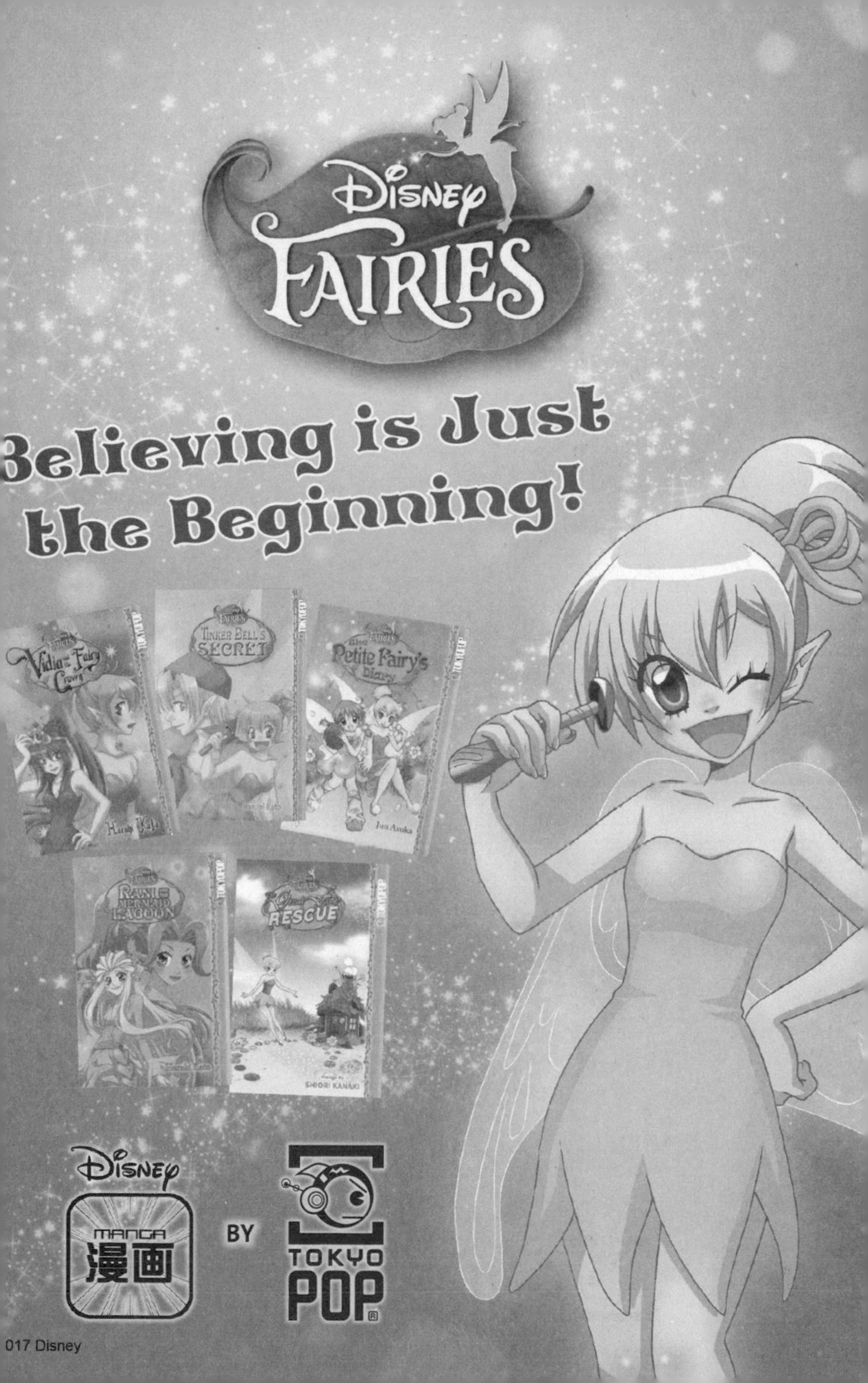

Disney
FAIRIES
Believing is Just the Beginning!
Vidia and the Fairy Crown
TINKER BELL'S SECRET
The Petite Fairy's Diary
Rani in the Mermaid Lagoon
RESCUE
SHIORI KANAKI
Disney
MANGA
漫画
BY
TOKYOPOP

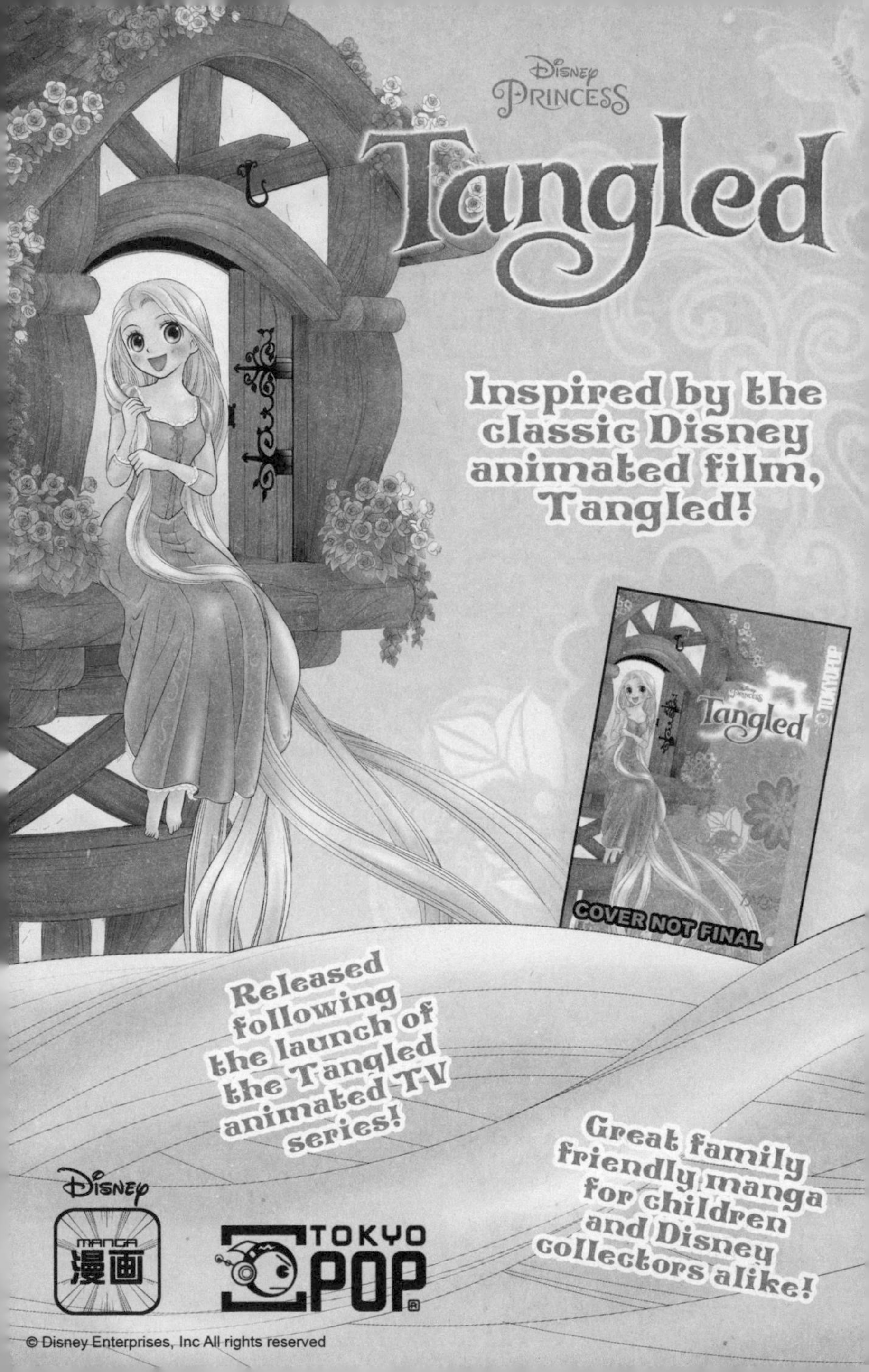
Disney
Princess
Tangled
Inspired by the classic Disney animated film, Tangled!
Disney Princess
Tangled
TOKYOPOP
COVER NOT FINAL
Released following the launch of the Tangled the Tangled animated TV series!
Great family friendly manga for children and Disney collectors alike!
Disney
MANGA
漫画
TOKYO POP
© Disney Enterprises, Inc All rights reserved

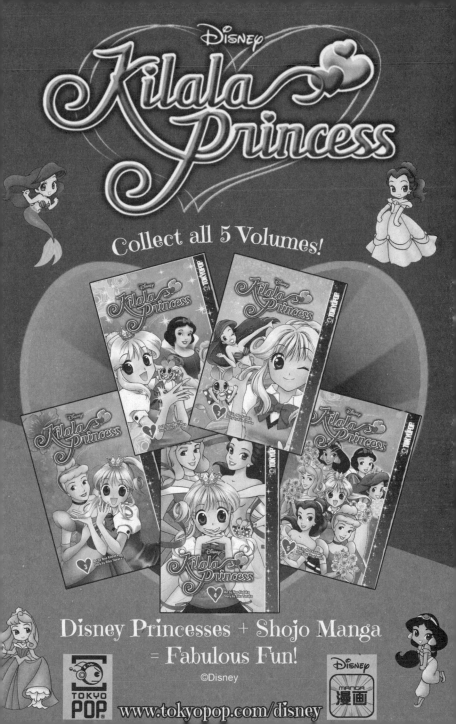

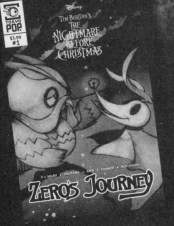

ZERO IS LOST...
CAN HE FIND HIS
WAY HOME?

DISNEY

TIM BURTON'S
THE
NIGHTMARE
BEFORE
CHRISTMAS

ZERO'S JOURNEY

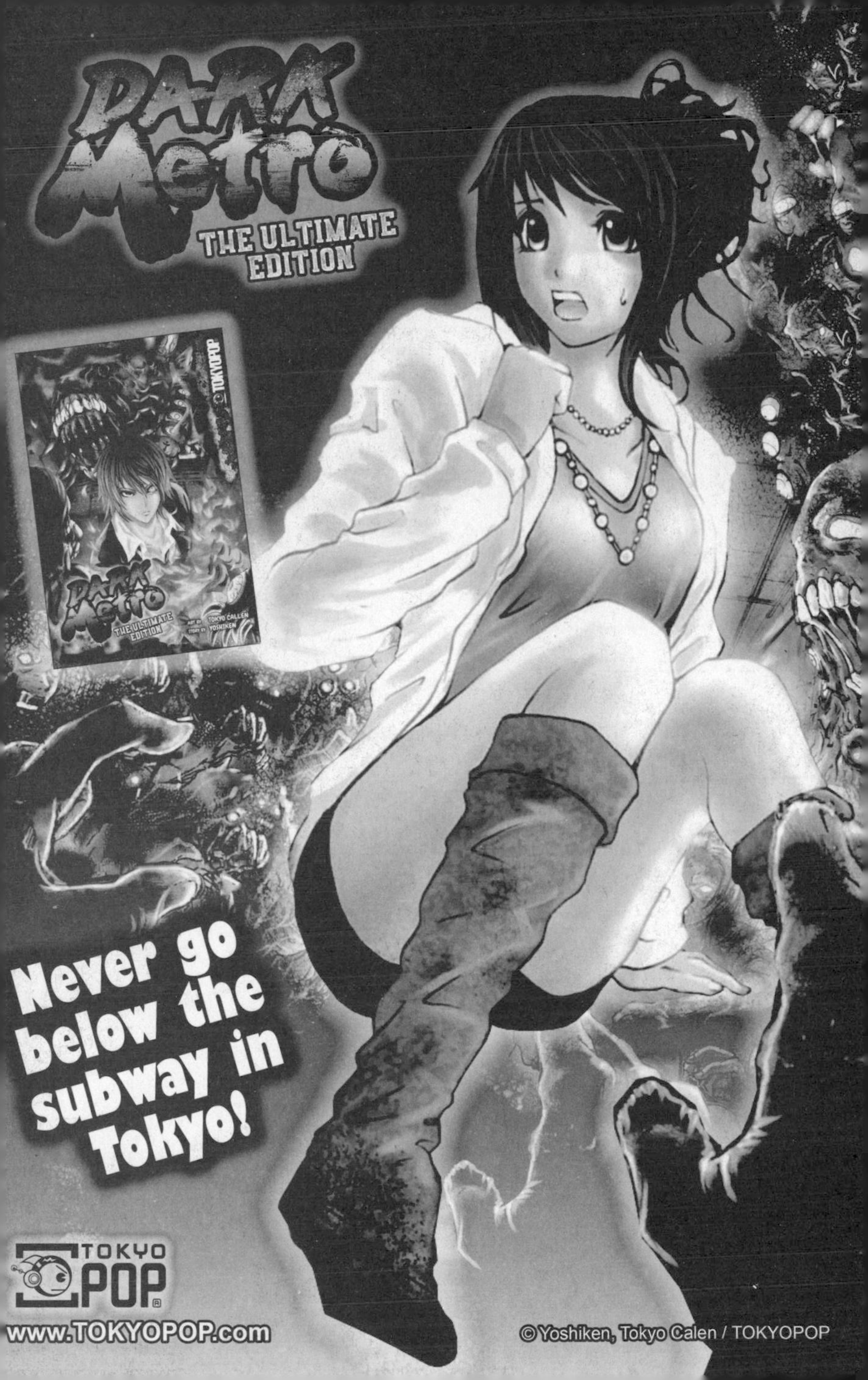
DARK Metro
THE ULTIMATE EDITION
Never go below the subway in Tokyo!
TOKYOPOP
www.TOKYOPOP.com
© Yoshiken, Tokyo Calen / TOKYOPOP

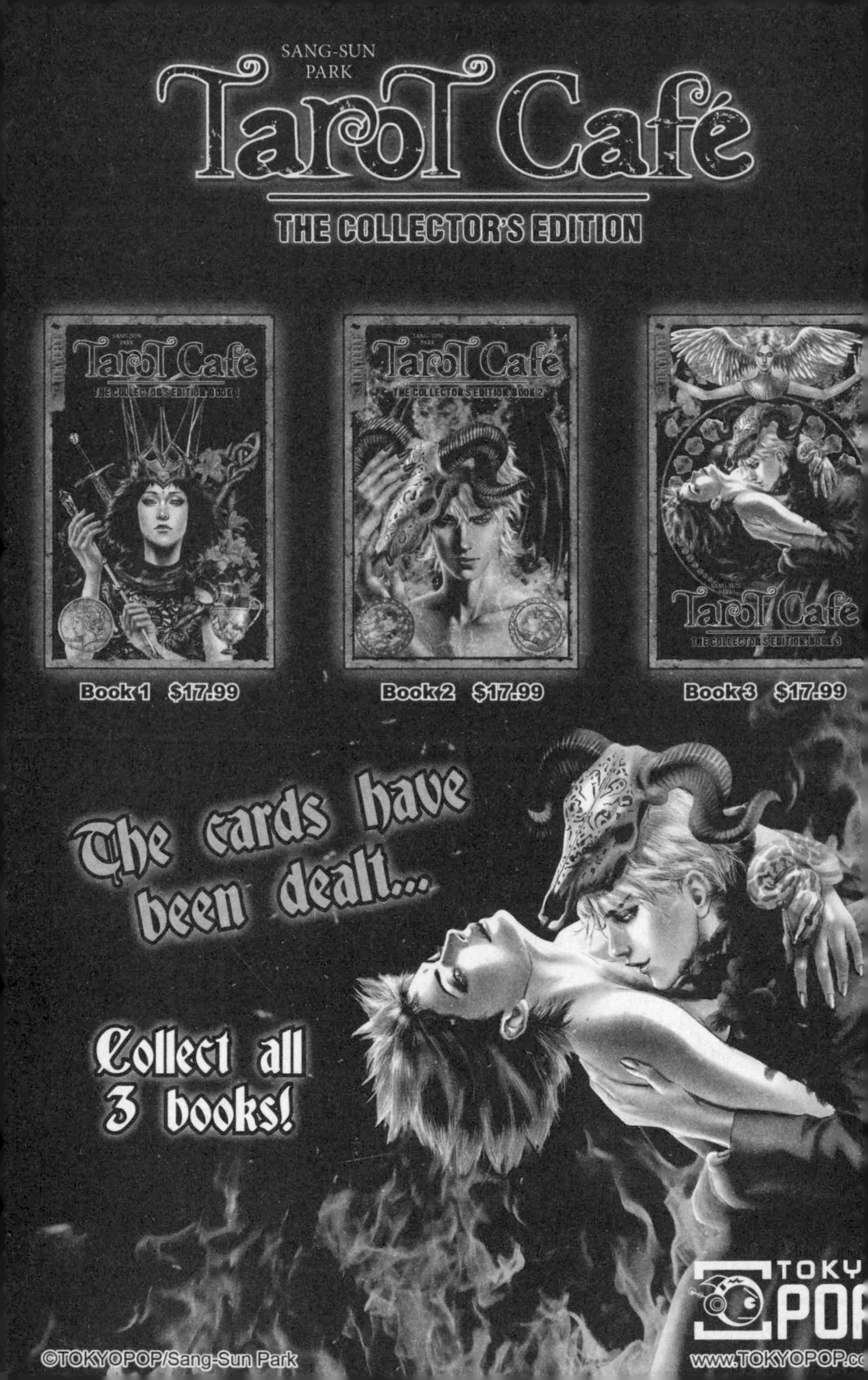
SANG-SUN PARK
Tarot Café
THE COLLECTOR'S EDITION
Book 1 $17.99
Book 2 $17.99
Book 3 $17.99
The cards have been dealt...
Collect all 3 books!
©TOKYOPOP/Sang-Sun Park
www.TOKYOPOP.co

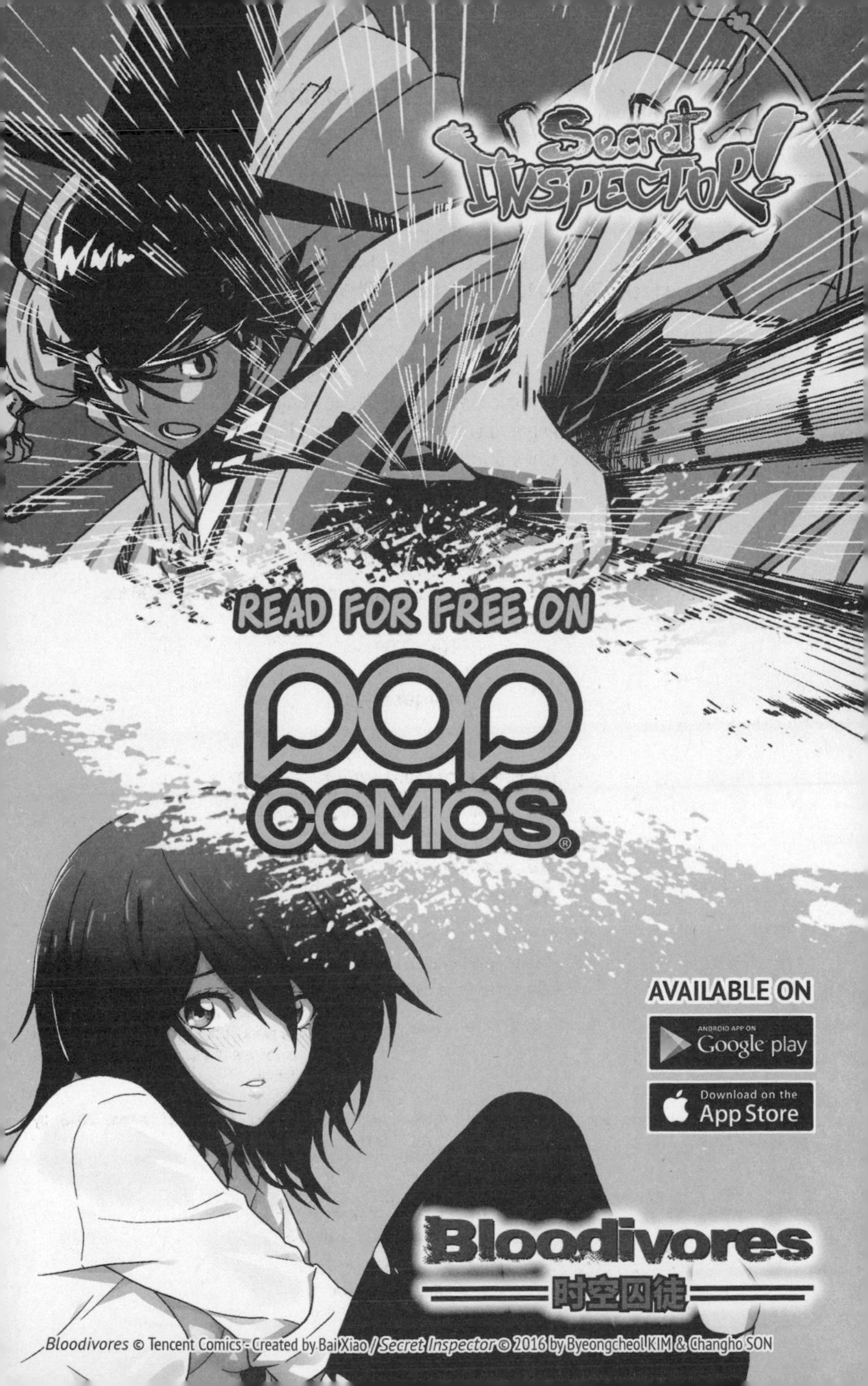
Secret INSPECTOR!
READ FOR FREE ON
pop COMICS®
AVAILABLE ON
ANDROID APP ON Google play
Download on the App Store
Bloodivores
时空囚徒
Bloodivores © Tencent Comics - Created by Bai Xiao / Secret Inspector © 2016 by Byeongcheol KIM & Changho SON